Maureen Keane, M.S., and Daniella Cl
Foreword by John A. Lung, M

WHAT TO EAT IF YOU HAVE DIABETES

UPDATED SECOND EDITION

HEALING FOODS THAT HELP CONTROL YOUR BLOOD SUGAR

New York Chicago San Francisco Lisbon London Madrid Mexico City
Milan New Delhi San Juan Seoul Singapore Sydney Toronto

The *McGraw·Hill* Companies

Library of Congress Cataloging-in-Publication Data

Keane, Maureen, 1950-
    What to eat if you have diabetes : healing foods that help control your blood
   sugar / Maureen Keane and Daniella Chace. — 2nd ed.
       p.   cm.
   Includes bibliographical references and index.
   ISBN 0-07-147397-1
   1. Diabetes—Diet therapy.   I. Chace, Daniella.   II. Title.

   RC662.K43   2007
   616.4'620654—dc22   2006022561

1 2 3 4 5 6 7 8 9 10 11 12 13 14 15 16 17 18 19 20   FGR/FGR   0 9 8 7 6

ISBN-13: 978-0-07-147397-2
ISBN-10:   0-07-147397-1

McGraw-Hill books are available at special quantity discounts to use as premiums
and sales promotions, or for use in corporate training programs. For more information,
please write to the Director of Special Sales, Professional Publishing, McGraw-Hill, Two
Penn Plaza, New York, NY 10121-2298. Or contact your local bookstore.

This book is printed on acid-free paper.

*This book is dedicated to Daniella's sister, Darcie,
in gratitude for helping us better understand the realities
of living with diabetes and eating well.*

CONTENTS

FOREWORD

Diabetes is a disorder of sugar metabolism that affects millions of Americans. Although the cause of diabetes is not completely understood, it usually involves either a deficiency of insulin (a blood sugar–lowering hormone from the pancreas) or a failure of insulin to do its job properly in the body (insulin resistance). Individuals with diabetes are at high risk of developing serious complications, including heart and blood vessel disease; damage to the eyes, kidneys, and nervous system; and reduced ability to fight infections.

There is considerable scientific evidence that dietary modification can reduce and sometimes completely normalize elevated blood sugar levels in diabetics. That is important, because maintaining blood sugar close to or within the normal range may reduce the risk of developing complications. In addition, specific nutritional supplements have been shown to improve blood sugar control and may also help prevent some of the organ damage that results from diabetes.

In this book, Daniella Chace and Maureen Keane present an easy-to-understand overview of this common medical condition. They also describe the dietary changes and individual nutrients that may be beneficial for diabetics. Of particular importance is their discussion about foods that are high in fiber and complex carbohydrates. Diabetics who incorporate these types of foods into their diet often experience a reduction in blood sugar and may be able to reduce the dosage of their diabetes medication.

The information in this book is important for most people who struggle with diabetes. Please note, however, that diabetes should be treated only under medical supervision. While dietary changes and nutritional supplements may be helpful in the long run, they can also influence medication requirements. People who fail to lower their medication dosages appropriately could develop a potentially dangerous fall in blood sugar levels. In addition, some individuals with long-standing diabetes have already developed kidney damage; in such cases, a high-fiber diet could actually result in a dangerous buildup of potassium in the body. On the other hand, if a doctor monitors a diabetic's nutritional program, the potential benefits are enormous.

—ALAN R. GABY, M.D.
PAST PRESIDENT,
AMERICAN HOLISTIC MEDICAL ASSOCIATION
PROFESSOR OF NUTRITION, BASTYR UNIVERSITY

ACKNOWLEDGMENTS

For this second edition, Maureen wishes to thank her agent, Sydney Harriet, for his guidance; her husband, John, for his patience; and her Maine coon, Maeve, for her constant companionship.

Daniella wishes to thank the following friends, family, and colleagues for their input, research, computer help, advice, and support: Linda Kay Landkamer, LaMar Harrington, Merrilee Gomez, Manuel Gomez, Nuria Gomez, Tom Gomez, Marcus Wojcik, Sally Rockwell, Suzanne Myer, David Butler, Julie Mermelstein, Michelle LaRock, Tara Hubbard, Jennifer James, Gary Boyer, Dave Stevenson, and Heidi Bresnahan.

Both Maureen and Dani want to thank our editor, Natasha Graf, for adopting our books.

INTRODUCTION

When she was still young, my sister was diagnosed with diabetes mellitus. Our family doctor wanted her to start taking insulin injections immediately. Darcie's blood sugar levels were sporadic. Our mother, Linda, who is constantly at work to make our lives just a little easier, would not accept this without a fight. She knew the dangers and complications of taking insulin and began reading all the studies she could find regarding treating diabetes naturally. She set to work interviewing doctors in hopes of finding alternatives.

She spoke with naturopathic doctors, nutritionists, and dietitians. She read case studies of patients whose diabetes was halted or reversed with a complex, high-carbohydrate, leguminous diet. These led her to the research of Dr. James Anderson, who had developed a diabetic diet based on plant protein from beans. Many of his patients were able to stabilize their blood sugar with this one simple change in their diets—eating more beans. These patients could reduce the amount of insulin they needed to take.

Beans were not a part of our meals, so Mom found legume recipes and began testing and tailoring them to meet my sister's tastes. Darcie, you see, lived for apple pie and deep-fried chicken. She craved the fast food that was promoted on TV and that everyone else was eating. I remember her scrunching up her nose in rejection at bean soups and lentil burgers and crying when she was told she could not have a piece of her own birthday cake.

Somehow, through unrelenting persistence and a whole lot of love, our mother made beans acceptable. Darcie finally started eating some beans each day. We were delighted to find that her blood sugar levels remained within normal range. After several months, Darcie thought maybe she was out of the woods and began to slip on her diet. She started eating fast food and cut back on her consumption of beans. Soon her blood sugar began to crawl back up. This culminated in an emergency visit to the hospital, where her doctor started insulin shots and told her she would have to take them the rest of her life.

Darcie needed insulin at that point, and I am thankful that we have this miracle of medicine. But I was left to ponder whether she would have ever had to start taking insulin if she had continued to eat beans each day. My mind was opened to the possibilities of nutrition as an adjunct to treatment for diabetes.

Over the next few years, I watched her blood sugar stabilize when she ate beans and included supplements such as magnesium, chromium, and vitamin C. We learned so much in those experimental years, with Darcie as our begrudging subject to lead us on our path of discovery. We saw how the wrong foods made her ill. When her blood sugar level went up, she became more dehydrated, which raised her readings even higher. We also noticed her sugar level drop dramatically when she simply rehydrated with water. We saw her blood sugar levels jump past 300 milligrams per deciliter on several occasions after she drank diet sodas alone. And we learned that a can of olives does not count as a vegetable serving. That can of "vegetables" sent her to the hospital with a sugar level of 700.

But we also learned that beans are stabilizing and that taking a chromium supplement assuaged Darcie's headaches immediately. We learned that you can take a whole lot less insulin if you are exercising regularly and that stress alone can throw your blood sugar out of balance.

Diabetes mellitus (DM) directly affects about sixteen million Americans and affects eighty million indirectly, and these numbers are growing at an alarming rate. As a society, we pay a high price for this largely avoidable epidemic in medical costs, lost wages, energy, and time. Since this book was first published, a great deal about diabetes treatments has changed, and with this updated edition, we present the most current theories, research, and nutritional treatment of diabetes and hypoglycemia. We will introduce you to the tools for developing an individually tailored program that includes a diet of nutritionally rich and satisfying meals.

The first part of the book takes an in-depth look at the amazing machines in which we live—our bodies. We will take you on a tour of your body, introducing you to the microscopic world inside you, to your cells, tissues, organs, and organ systems, all the way through to the transportation of nutrients through your bloodstream. Understanding your own anatomy and physiology will help you see the profound difference that food choices make in fueling your body so that it will run well for you.

In Part II you will learn to develop a nutritional therapy regimen just for you. Choosing the best foods for blood sugar regulation can help those who have a predisposition to diabetes and/or hypoglycemia avoid developing the disease. Those with type 2 diabetes may even be able to reverse their metabolic disorder. Those with type 1 diabetes who are already taking insulin will find they have better control and fewer complications with this individualized program. Regulating blood sugar with diet greatly reduces the need for corrective medical procedures, such as retinal surgery, amputations, neural therapy, organ transplants, and dialysis. Proper supplementation may help prevent such complications of diabetes as neuropathy, retinopathy, nephropathy, micro- and macroangiopathy, and cataracts. (*Alternative Medicine Review* 1997).

Part III contains two diet plans with different menus designed to provide a high level of nutrition at various calorie levels. To develop your own personalized nutrition program, choose a diet and then add the recommendations for any side effects you may be experiencing. In the back of the book you will find references to help you participate in your treatment plan. These include a list of resources for information, support, and products.

If diabetes is a fact of life for you or a loved one, then you are very lucky if you have an angel like our mother to watch out for you. But if you don't, you can be your own angel. Diabetes is your cue to get healthy and do whatever it takes to avoid developing complications. The really good news is that although diabetes is a complicated physiological disease, it can be controlled so that you will feel well again. The primary therapy for blood sugar disorders is diet. Whether you are taking insulin or just experiencing hypoglycemia, you will benefit from eating fresh whole plant foods, getting some exercise, and taking the appropriate supplements.

With this solid education in the care and maintenance of DM, you have the knowledge to reduce the ravages of disordered blood sugar and begin the journey to wellness. I wish I could be there to be the angel for you on your journey. Enjoy your "therapy"—and watch out for those olives.

—DANIELLA CHACE, M.S., C.N.

. . . .

PART I

THE BODY, DIABETES, AND NUTRITION

Getting diagnosed with diabetes is somewhat similar to taking a crash course in medical school. Within a few months of your diagnosis, you will know more about the research being conducted than your family doctor does. This self-education is vitally important because knowledge is power—power over your disease and power over your treatment. Start with your local library and work up to the medical library at the nearest medical school. Get on the Internet and search for the most up-to-date treatment options. Many diabetes and nutrition research journals are now online, and often there is no cost to read or download studies (for links to these journals and instructions on how to use them, go to Maureen's website: keanenutrition.

. . . . .

com). Join online patient discussion groups and subscribe to newsletters to discover what other diabetes patients are doing. The more you know, the more options you will have. Join a local support group and call knowledgeable friends for information, advice, and support. The more friends who know you have diabetes, the more support you will have. Don't keep your diabetes a secret, and you will have fewer people trying to force sweets, alcohol and extra calories on you.

Part I of this book will help you understand the concepts behind the words and terminology you will soon be learning. If you have just been diagnosed and know little, this is the best place to start your education. These chapters simplify the anatomy of the body and the chemistry of nutrition and explain how and why nutrition therapy works. It is also a good introduction to nutrition and diabetes treatment for spouses, family members, caregivers, and health care professionals, as it will help them to understand what you are trying to accomplish.

1

The Microscopic World Inside You

What Is Diabetes?

Imagine for a minute that your body is a country and your cells are its citizens. You, the president, live in the capitol building, the head. For a nation to be strong and healthy, its citizens must have honest work, proper tools to perform that work, a communication system, a transportation system, food and water, and a method to remove waste and trash. They must be sheltered from the environment and protected from attack by terrorists from within and enemies from without. But, most of all, they must be provided with the energy to accomplish these things.

The food you eat supplies your nation of 75 trillion cell-citizens with fuel in the form of glucose and fatty acids. When you have diabetes, fuel distribution is interrupted and cells cannot get access to the energy they need to perform their jobs.

With type 1 diabetes immune-system terrorists kill off the cells that produce insulin, the hormone responsible for glucose absorption. Without insulin there is no way for glucose to get inside muscle, fat, and liver cells. The end result is a famine in those tissues even though the cells are literally surrounded by food. Without imported insulin to restore energy production the nation afflicted with type 1 diabetes dies.

With type 2 diabetes there are two problems: a decreased number of insulin-producing cells and a condition called insulin resistance, in which the cells of the muscle, fat, and liver cells do not respond to insulin the way they should. The end result is less insulin, less energy production, more fat deposited in the fat bank, more fat in the blood, and an overabundance of unused sugar. The latter two act like a poison affecting the cells responsible for sight, sensation, and circulation. In order to restore energy production and help prevent complications from diabetes you must become familiar with the cells that populate your body.

Maturity-onset diabetes of the young (MODY) is a group of rare genetic disorders that cause diabetes. Six types have been identified, but more are likely. Although it most often manifests itself in early adulthood (before age twenty-five), it is not type 1 diabetes in an adult, and it is not type 2 diabetes in a young person. The genetic defect causes a decrease in insulin secretion, but patients remain insulin-sensitive. Symptoms are similar to a mild to moderate case of type 1 diabetes.

Basic Structure of the Cell

All cells share some common features, although they may not look alike. Just as our larger selves do, your "mini me" has internal organs, a skeleton, and a skin cover. These miniature organs, or organelles, each perform a unique and specialized function related to growth, repair, maintenance, or control. Different cells contain different amounts and types of **organelles** according to the cell's function. For example, muscle fibers need large amounts of energy to contract, so they contain large numbers of the organelles that produce energy. Most cells contain hundreds of organelles, and some even have a thousand. The largest and most recognizable organelle is the nucleus, which is located more or less in the center of the cell.

Back in the sixties, we were taught that a cell was little more than a bag of water with the organelles and nucleus floating freely in the cytoplasm. Today we know that cells are highly structured and organized. The entire cell is filled with a scaffolding in which the nucleus and organelles are embedded.

Nucleus: The Cell Brain

The nucleus, the largest structure in the cell, serves as your cell's head. Like the rest of the cell, it is covered with a skin, called the **nuclear membrane**. It contains the cell's equivalent to a brain—the **chromosomes**. These coiled bodies contain the DNA instruction manual for everything that goes on inside the cell. The actual encoded information is in units called **genes**. Before you were born, your genes determined everything from the color of your eyes to the shape of your little toe. They gave you your father's artistic ability and your Aunt Ethel's predisposition to diabetes. When the cell is not dividing, DNA is found as dark threads called **chromatin**. The compact form of chromatin contains the regions of DNA that are not used or that are used infrequently, and the less compact form contains frequently used DNA.

Each cell contains the instructions for every job available in your country. But since each cell can have only one job, not all of the DNA instructions are needed. The unneeded parts of DNA are turned off. For example, the pancreatic islands contain two kinds of hormone-exporting cells: the alpha cells that make glucagon and the beta cells that make insulin. Both types of cells contain the DNA to make both hormones, but only in the beta cells are the DNA instructions to make insulin turned on (expressed). Those instructions would be found in the less dense chromatin, where they could be easily reached. Unfortunately, once a cell becomes specialized, it stays that way. So, a pancreatic cell that produces digestive enzymes cannot start producing insulin, even though it contains the encoded insulin-producing information. Those genes are turned off and cannot be turned on.

All cells in the body, with the exception of the red blood cells, have a nucleus. A few types even have more than one.

Cell Fibers: Cellular Muscles

Extending from the membrane of the nucleus to the outer membrane of the cell are the **cell fibers**, which form a three-dimensional scaffolding throughout the cell. All the organelles are embedded in this scaffolding. The cell fibers also serve as your cell-citizen's muscles, producing movement within the cell by contracting and expanding the scaffolding, allowing the cell to change shape.

Ribosomes: Protein Factories

The membrane that surrounds the nucleus is connected to the membrane that surrounds the cell via the **endoplasmic reticulum** (**ER**), a network of membrane-lined canals and flat, curving sacks. The ER twists and turns its way through the cytoplasm, serving as a transportation tunnel and manufacturing site for proteins, lipids (fats), and other molecules.

Dotting the outer surface of the "rough" ER are small, round structures called **ribosomes**. These round molecular machines are the cell's protein factories. Instructions for a protein are carried from the nucleus to the surface of a ribosome, where the protein is assembled from the amino acid building blocks floating free in the cytoplasm. The kind of proteins made here depend on your cell-citizen's job. It is in the ER of the pancreatic beta cells that insulin is made.

Strings of ribosomes are also found in the cytoplasm. This is where the cell makes the structural proteins and enzymes it needs for its own use. The functions of the smooth ER, that part without ribosomes, are less known. It is believed that lipids needed to form the cell membrane, steroid hormones, and carbohydrates are made there.

Some researchers have proposed that the ER may in some way be involved with beta cell damage. An increased demand for insulin because of obesity, insulin resistance, or the use of drugs that stimulate insulin production (sulfonylureas) may cause an overload on the ER as beta cells struggle to keep up with insulin production. This organelle is sensitive to stress and might trigger apoptosis—cellular suicide—in affected cells.

Golgi Apparatus: Packaging Plants

The protein molecules made in the endoplasmic reticulum are funneled into the **Golgi apparatus**, an organelle that manufactures and packages products for export. The Golgi apparatus manufactures large carbohydrate molecules, which combine with the protein manufactured in the ER to form glycoproteins. It resembles a series of flat, stacked sacs. As the sacs fill up with the glycoproteins, they become more globular until they pinch off as perfect little spheres. The neatly packaged glycoproteins then migrate toward the cell surface and pass through the cell membrane. Outside the cell, the sacs break open and their contents are released. These contents can range from mother's milk to antibodies, digestive juices, and sweat.

Mitochondria: Energy Factories

The energy for these activities and others is manufactured in the cell's energy factories, the **mitochondria**. These sausage-shaped organelles are made up of two membranes forming a sac within a sac. The outer membrane gives each mitochondrion a smooth appearance, while the inner membrane has many folds. On top of this folded inner membrane lie as many as five hundred enzymes used to produce energy.

The energy produced is in the form of several molecules—one of the most common is ATP, or adenosine triphosphate—and the energy is carried within a chemical bond to phosphate. When energy is needed for a chemical reaction, the cell uses its ATP like an energy credit card. The phosphate molecule is removed and the energy it contains is freed to fuel the reaction. The result is the low-energy ADP (adenosine diphosphate). It works the other way too. When energy is produced by a reaction, the cell pulls out the used ADP card and uses the reaction to recharge it back to ATP. It is the ATP molecule that carries the energy from the mitochondria to where the reaction is taking place. An enzyme holds the raw materials in place while ATP wanders over and adds the energy for the two molecules to form a new molecule.

You can imagine that the more active cells such as those found in the liver, kidney, and muscle tissue have large numbers of mitochondria to keep up with the energy needed to function. If you are a diabetic, the mitochondria in your muscle cells do not produce as much energy as those of healthy people. Some studies have found them to be smaller.

In a recent study reported in the journal *Nature*, scientists investigated the effects of high blood glucose on the endothelial cells that line the arteries. They found that high blood sugar increases the production of free radicals in the mitochondria and that this single mechanism initiates all three of the biochemical pathways (the polyol pathway, PKC, and AGEs) responsible for damaging endothelial cells.

Mitochondria have their own DNA and their own protein-producing ribosomes, which allows them to reproduce themselves as needed. This has led many researchers to speculate they are the descendants of bacteria that were swallowed but never digested by larger cells billions of years ago.

The digestive system of the cell is a collection of **lysosomes**. These are sacs that contain enzymes for digesting all of the major components of a cell. When an object—for example, a bacterium—gets inside of a cell, it is surrounded by a lysosome, which digests the intruder. Lysosomes can also burst and digest the cell in which they live. Thus, they are sometimes called "suicide bags."

Membrane: Cellular Skin

Finally we reach what is perhaps the most important structure for the person with diabetes to understand, the outer skin of the cell. The scientific name for this layer is **plasma membrane**. Both the inner and outer membrane are made the same way. Each sheet of cells is made of molecules that resemble balloons on strings. The balloon side is a water-loving side, and the string side is a fat-loving side. Since both the inside and outside of the cell are made of water, the two fat-loving sides face each other, leaving the water-loving sides facing inward toward the cytoplasm and outward toward the watery environment outside. The attraction between the sheets of fat-loving "strings" keeps the two membranes together. Scientists believe the cell membrane is fluid, which allows parts of the membrane to flow to other parts. In this way, molecules embedded in the membrane distribute themselves evenly over the whole cell surface. Cholesterol molecules embedded in the membrane help to stabilize it.

Just as your skin keeps water from penetrating your body, the cell membrane repels water and prevents the cell from filling up like a water balloon. The same goes for water-soluble substances such as ions and glucose. However, fat-soluble substances such as oxygen, carbon dioxide, and alcohol easily pass through.

A variety of protein molecules are attached to the cell membrane. Some of these molecules pierce through both layers of membrane. They can occur in groups of two or four to form pores, or channels. These protein channels act as a guarded door, allowing only certain small molecules to enter the cell. Other surface molecules act as transport molecules or protein carriers for molecules that cannot pass through the membrane on their own.

Other proteins embedded in the surface allow the cell to communicate with other cells. As noted earlier, some act as molecular ID tags so that other cells can tell what the cell is and what it does. Some molecules, called **receptor sites**, act like little mailboxes, receiving packages such as hormones or nutrients. For example, nerve cells receive packages of neurotransmitters from other nerve cells. The neurotransmitter binds to its receptor site and allows it to communicate with other nerve cells. Other receptor sites act as keyholes. The key molecule then unlocks a membrane door, which allows a certain molecule to enter. A good example of this is **insulin**. The average cell has tens of thousands of receptor sites on and in its cellular skin.

Glucose is the fuel used by most cells, but most cell types cannot absorb glucose directly through the cell membrane. For this, they need a hormone with which you are probably familiar called insulin. Insulin acts like a key. When blood sugar levels rise after a meal, the pancreas releases insulin keys into the bloodstream. When an insulin key comes close to a hungry cell, the key fits into one of the locks and activates it. Within thirty seconds, the glucose door on the membrane unlocks, and transport molecules called glucose transport units (GLUT family transporters) then carry the glucose through the membrane.

When a person has type 1 diabetes, the pancreas no longer makes insulin keys. Blood sugar levels rise, and the cell starves while it is virtually surrounded by food. In such cases, insulin from an outside source is absolutely necessary for survival.

In other cases, the pancreas is able to secrete insulin, but it just does not secrete enough of it. Often this reduced number of keys is accompanied by cells with not enough receptor locks. For example, the average overweight person has only five thousand glucose receptors per cell (down from the 20,000 in healthy people). Sometimes the locks are there, but some of them don't work to unlock the membrane's glucose doors. Sometimes the glucose doors open, but there are not enough glucose transporters available to carry the glucose over the threshold. If any one or a combination of these scenarios should occur, blood sugar levels rise and cells do not get enough energy. This is type 2 diabetes.

How Cells Are Born

Different types of cells have different life spans, depending on their location and function. Some cells, such as **neurons** (the cells of nerves), are made to last a human lifetime. Others, such as white blood cells, live for only two days. The cells that line the gastrointestinal tract live for only thirty-six hours before they are sloughed off. And just as with people, cells can get sick and injured, causing death. For a tissue to function properly, damaged or dead cells must be replaced.

New cells are produced by the process of cell division, or **mitosis**, during which one parent cell divides into two identical daughter cells. A cell knows when to grow, or divide, by talking to its neighbors. A cell in a new neighborhood of rapidly growing tissue will get the go-ahead to propagate, while a cell in a crowded healthy tissue will be told that more citizens are not welcome. Since a good cell-citizen is a team player, it divides or travels only when the community deems it proper and necessary.

How Cells Die

There are two ways a cell can die: programmed cell death and necrosis. **Necrosis** is cell death from tissue trauma. It can be caused by injuries, infections, cancer, heart attacks, or inflammation. It happens when the lysosomes are broken and the cell digests itself. When the cell dies, it releases a number of chemicals that can damage other cells too. Necrosis is common in diabetic foot disease.

In **programmed cell death**—and a particular type of programmed death called **apoptosis**—an unwanted cell commits suicide. The decision to die may be independent, or it may be an order from neighboring cells. If the presence of a virus initiates apoptosis and that virus also prevents the cell from killing itself, the cell can continue to live and divide, causing a cancer. Fifty million to seventy million cells die from apoptosis each day. There are several theories as to what causes beta cell death in type 2 diabetes. Some scientists suggest it is increased frequency of apoptosis in the beta cells.

Tissues

A cell-citizen can do little on its own. In order to get its job accomplished, it must group together with other like minds. Each of your cell-citizens belongs to a **tissue**, a community of physically similar cells. Cell-citizens of the same tissue type belong to a sort of union. Members of the same union may not live in the same neighborhood or town, but they look alike and perform the same job. There are four main types of tissue unions: epithelial tissue, connective tissue, muscle tissue, and nervous tissue.

Epithelial Tissue

Most of the cells you can see on your body are epithelial cells. Cells in this union earn their living by covering, lining, secreting, and absorbing. Wherever your body comes into contact with the outside environment, **epithelial tissue** can be found. It covers all of the external parts of your body from hair to toenails, lines the cavities of hollow body organs, and forms the inner lining of the body cavities. The gastrointestinal tract from mouth to anus is lined with epithelial tissue. So is the respiratory system. The inside of the uterus, bladder, and all blood vessels are lined with epithelial tissue as well.

Epithelial cells come in two types: glandular and membranous. **Glandular epithelial tissue** contains small **exocrine glands** (glands that secrete their products into ducts). These glands secrete various substances into the environment, organ cavity, or body cavity. In the gastrointestinal tract, for instance, glandular epithelial cells make the passage of food and waste products easier by secreting a lubricating mucus. In the stomach they secrete hydrochloric acid and the intrinsic factor necessary for vitamin B_{12} absorption.

Membranous epithelial tissues serve as coverings or linings. These cells are classified according to their shape and type of cell layer. For example, simple squamous epithelium is composed of flat cells one layer deep. Substances easily cross this kind of tissue. Stratified transitional epithelium, on the other hand, has the ability to stretch and so lines the bladder.

Epithelial cells are **avascular**, meaning they do not have a blood supply. When they die, they slough off. Examples are the gradual shedding of skin cells and the not-so-gradual shedding of dandruff. Epithelial cells must divide quickly to replace cells lost to wear and tear.

Endothelial Tissue

Every complex system needs intelligent leaders who make decisions, give directions, and coordinate actions. In the circulatory system this role is filled by the **endothelial cells**, which are a very special type of epithelial cell. Endothelial cells when taken together weigh 1.5 kilograms, a mass equal to the size of five hearts. This tissue has so much control over other cells that some researchers consider it an organ.

Structurally, the **endothelium** forms the lining of the cardiovascular system, is the sole component of the capillaries, and forms the blood-brain barrier. Until 1980 it was considered to be simply a passive barrier, keeping the blood in the blood vessels and tissue fluids in the tissues. Now we know that the endothelial organ regulates permeability and nutrient exchange. These cells tell the muscle cells when to perform the following actions:

- Tighten, decreasing the size of the space inside the vessel and raising blood pressure
- Relax, increasing the size of space inside the vessel and decreasing blood pressure
- Divide, increasing the exterior width of the vessel

They also tell the platelets when to clump and clots when to form. All of these instructions are given in the form of chemical messages.

When endothelial cells are damaged, these messenger substances are not released, and nearby cells are at a loss to know what to do. The result is abnormal blood clotting and atherosclerosis, which leads to angina, heart attack, hypertensive heart disease, thrombosis, and stroke. Endothelial cells can be damaged by elevated levels of glucose (glucotoxicity) and insulin, which is one reason atherosclerosis is so common in diabetics.

Connective Tissue

Connective tissue cells are the jacks-of-all-trades. They form delicate webs, fluid blood, and hard bones. Cells in this union make their living by connecting, supporting, transporting, and defending the body. Connective tissue is a complex of live cells separated by various types of fibers embedded in a nonliving material called the matrix or ground substance. The type of matrix material and fiber determines what kind of characteristic the connective tissue exhibits. For example, cartilage tissue has a gel-like matrix, bone tissue has a hard mineral matrix, and blood tissue has a liquid matrix.

Adipose Tissue. Adipose, or fatty, tissue is a type of connective tissue that specializes in the making and storing of fat (triglycerides). The **adipocyte**, or **adipose cell**, appears to be bloated with so much fat that the nucleus is pushed over to one side and the cytoplasm is pushed up against the cell membrane to make room for the fat storage droplets. There are two types of fat deposits: subcutaneous fat, which is just under the skin, and visceral fat, which lies among the organs. Visceral fat is associated with insulin resistance and heart disease.

It is believed that the number of adipose cells remains constant after infancy and that the cells increase only in size thereafter. This may be what predisposes large infants and overweight children to obesity in adulthood; they have more cells to fill with fat than a slim person, who has only a limited amount.

Scientists used to think that adipocytes were simply a storage depot for fat—chubby little cells that did little but sit on their chubby little bums. Now we know that fat cells are very busy despite their size, and they are finally getting the respect they deserve. Secretly they have been controlling a number of body functions that are only now being discovered. Adipocytes secrete a number of chemicals that are known collectively as **adipokines**. They include adipokine, leptin, angiotensinogen, resistin, vesfatin, tumor necrosis factor (TNF), and plasminogen-activator inhibitor type 1 (PAI-1). Some researchers think the metabolic syndrome is the result of an imbalance in adipokines.

Your gut is home to the killer adipocytes. Researchers have known for years that people with central obesity (also called male, android, or apple shape) are much more likely to be insulin resistant and to develop heart disease and hypertension. Women past menopause can have an android, or "male," shape too, so it is not limited to men, and neither is the risk. Central obesity is a marker for visceral fat, fat that is around the visceral organs in the gut. (This type of fat can also surround the heart.) It secretes the wrong kind of adipokines and is the most dangerous. Fat that lies on the surface of the waist is less so. No matter what you call it, your beer belly, love handles, or spare tire are not good for you.

One of the adipokines, **adiponectin**, may increase both insulin sensitivity and the burning of fat. It is secreted by the "good" fat that lies beneath the skin and enhances glucose uptake by muscle cells and has an anti-inflammatory effect on endothelial cells. Inflammation is associated in some way with the plaque lesions on endothelial cells that cause atherosclerosis. Adiponectin acts on the endothelial wall to prevent all the actions that lead to plaque deposition in arteries. Low levels of adiponectin are associated with insulin resistance and even colon cancer. Exercise has been shown to elevate adiponectin levels. A low level of adiponectin is so dangerous that it even has a name: **hypo-adiponectinemia**. Waist circumference is a more reliable marker than body mass index in predicting adiponectin levels; as circumference increases, the levels diminish.

Leptin is another adipokine: the higher the level of leptin, the higher the level of fat. Leptin levels are how your adipocytes tell the brain how much fat they currently have stockpiled. What the brain does with this information is not well understood. Subcutaneous fat secretes more leptin than visceral fat, and women make more than men. Its role in appetite regulation is controversial.

Muscle Tissue

Muscle tissues are the brawn of your cell population. They function as the expert movers of the body and are highly specialized for contraction. This means movement as well as the production of heat and the maintenance of posture. There are three types of muscle tissue, classified by their functions and structures.

- **Skeletal muscle tissue** attaches to bone and moves the skeleton. This tissue is called voluntary, because you can tell it to contract or relax.
- **Smooth muscle tissue** is found in the soft internal organs of the body (the viscera) such as the stomach and intestines. This tissue is called involuntary, because you cannot control its movement.
- **Cardiac muscle tissue** is a cross between the two. The cells resemble skeletal muscle, but the tissue is involuntary, like smooth muscle.

Nervous Tissue

Finally, nervous tissue specializes in sensitivity; it forms the organs of the brain, spinal cord, and nerves. Nerve cells are the telephone and data communication workers of the body. They are the "hard" wires that make fast electronic communications possible, and in the brain they form the network that holds our memories. Although it is hard to believe, our consciousness exists in the delicate webs of nervous tissue that form our brain. All that we are is stored inside of them.

The structural and functional cells are called neurons. They conduct nerve impulses (electrical communications) to neighboring cells, tissues, organs, and organ systems. Neuroglia cells connect and support the neurons.

The next chapter will help you understand the basic anatomy of the body and how diabetes affects almost every organ and organ system. Only by understanding how your organs respond to diabetes can you prevent the devastating side effects of the condition.

2

Organs and Organ Systems

This chapter will explain which organ systems are affected by diabetes so that you will better understand your doctor's concerns. Your doctor can't be with you all the time, so you need to learn how to monitor your own body for damage. Ultimately, all of the damage done to the body is a result of high blood glucose. By getting and keeping your blood sugar levels in normal range, you can help to prevent the damage described in the following pages.

Each of your cell-citizens lives in a town. Some of the towns, such as the brain, heart, liver, and skin, are more like large cities and perform an indispensable service. The great city of your heart, for example, is where large numbers of the muscle family live and work. These cells enjoy the harried existence of life in an essential organ. Other cells fancy the simple life of the heart's suburbs, in the arteries and veins of the limbs. They prefer the reduced-stress lifestyle of a nonessential organ. Each organ-town is a composite of several types of tissues. And, even though the cells look different and come from different tissues, they all work together toward a common goal.

Each town or city also belongs to a larger organization with the same mission. These are the organ systems, and they are composed of varying numbers and types of organs acting together to perform a necessary job for the body. Each organ in the organ system depends on the others, and each organ system is closely related to the other organ systems. An example is the musculoskeletal system: the skeleton is responsible for body movement, but it cannot provide the movement itself; for that function, it must rely on the muscles. With its components working together, the musculoskeletal system gets the body from here to there.

There is one final level of organization, a United Nations. This is where your nation of seventy-five trillion cells interacts with other nations. You are not an island, and you need the support of others like yourself to stay physically strong and mentally happy. When nations war against each other, it disrupts harmony and puts a great deal of stress on all the organs and organ systems. When they work together, all the organ systems seem able to accomplish much more.

Medical science has sorted organs into systems, with related organs being grouped together and specialists then assigned to each. The problem is what you consider to be related organs. For example, are the muscle and skeletal systems one organ system or two? Is the lymphatic system part of the cardiovascular system, or is it better grouped with the immune system? In the end it is just a matter of preference. For the purposes of this book, we will divide the organs into ten organ systems: musculoskeletal system, nervous system, endocrine system, immune and lymphatic systems, circulatory system, respiratory system, digestive system, urinary system, integumentary system, and the reproductive system.

The Musculoskeletal System

The musculoskeletal system is made up of two organs—the skeleton and the many muscles attached to it. Without the musculoskeletal system, you would resemble a jellyfish on land, having no form and incapable of moving from one place to another.

Bones give your body shape and give the muscles somewhere to hang. The ribs form a cage to protect your lungs and heart. The skull acts as a helmet to protect the brain and sensory organs. Bone tissue serves as a kind of mineral bank. Bone cells secrete substances including protein fibers into their surroundings. Minerals are then deposited into this soft matrix to harden, or calcify, it into bone. These calcium, magnesium, and phosphate molecules can be withdrawn later when they are needed. For example, muscle fibers need calcium to contract and magnesium to relax, and they get these minerals from the blood, which ultimately gets them from your diet. When your diet is low in minerals, the blood automatically takes the calcium and magnesium meant for bone formation. The result is a loss of bone mass.

The Skeletal System and Diabetes

When compared with the ever moving muscle tissue, bone appears to be positively immobile; it doesn't pulse with life as many other organs do. However, if you were to view bone tissue under a microscope, you would see that it is active; bone cells and the hard matrix that surrounds them are constantly being destroyed (resorption) and created (formation). When we are children, formation is greater than resorption, and the bone grows. When we enter adulthood, there is a delicate balance between the two opposing forces; one equals the other, and the bone remains strong. But as we continue to grow older, bone resorption slowly starts to outpace bone formation, gradually causing bone tissue to become porous and weak. **Bone mineral density** (**BMD**) is said to be low. This loss of bone mass is called **osteoporosis**. This is the disorder that causes the stooped posture of old age and the fragile bones that are vulnerable to breaks. It has no symptoms, and the disease can be advanced by the time it is discovered. Osteoporosis is associated with a lack of minerals in the diet and a host of other causes, including diabetes.

Women with type 1 diabetes generally have decreased bone mass, a greater risk of breaking a bone, and a longer healing time for breaks than women without diabetes. Both type 1 and type 2 diabetes put women at increased risk for developing a broken bone related to osteoporosis. One recent study found that women with type 1 diabetes had a greater than twelve-fold higher risk for hip fractures compared with women in the general population, while women with type 2 diabetes had a 1.7-fold increase. Hip fractures are a particularly dangerous type of break: one year after suffering a hip fracture, half of patients cannot walk without help.

Bone loss has been observed to be greater in patients with poorly controlled diabetes than in those whose diabetes is in good control. Other factors, such as neuropathy and impaired vision, may contribute to the increased fracture risk.

To maintain healthy bones, you must get enough exercise. When your leg strikes the ground, it causes new bone growth to be laid down along the lines of stress. The result is a denser bone. This is why only exercises in which a bone strikes the ground can prevent osteoporosis. When you walk, your feet strike the ground more often than when you run, which is why walking is a better exercise than running for the prevention of osteoporosis.

The Muscular System and Diabetes

The muscle tissue attached to your skeletal bones is made up of striated muscle bound to the bones by fibrous connective tissue. The cell-citizens in this muscle have two major duties: movement and heat production. Although the joints of the skeletal system allow movement, they cannot make movement. For this, they require the contraction of striated muscle. The muscular system also serves as the major heat generator for the body, keeping organs warm.

When your muscles get hungry, that is a lot of mouths to feed, so a good portion of the calories you eat each day goes toward fueling them. To assure that your cell-citizens get the food they need, cell membranes are very sensitive to insulin. As soon as insulin is secreted by the pancreas, almost all of the glucose and amino acids are cleared from the blood, most going to muscles. When muscle fibers become insensitive to insulin, as happens in type 2 diabetes, more insulin is required to allow glucose to enter the cells. In between meals, when glucose is not available, muscle cells are able to burn the fatty acids stored in fat cells.

Just as bone serves as a reservoir of minerals, muscle can serve as a reservoir of protein. When you do not get enough protein from your diet, your body must get it from some other source. That source is your muscles. They can provide protein to make the enzymes needed to run the body. Muscle can even be burned to provide energy when glucose is not available. When muscle tissue decreases, the individual muscle is less able to perform its job, causing weakness.

The Nervous System

The brain, spinal cord, and nerves are the organs of the nervous system (Figure 2.1). This system consists primarily of nervous tissue supported and protected by connective tissue. The cell-citizens of your nervous system are the nerve cells, or **neurons**, and they work in several critical jobs. They are responsible for rapid cell-to-cell and organ-to-organ communication. Cells in these organs produce **neurotransmitters**, which initiate and sustain

Figure 2.1 The brain

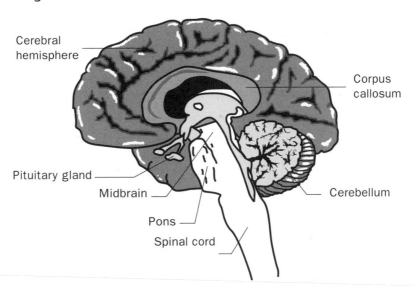

Cerebral hemisphere

Corpus callosum

Pituitary gland

Midbrain

Pons

Spinal cord

Cerebellum

electric impulses. This allows your brain to talk to organs far and near—controlling, coordinating, and integrating their work. Neurons are vulnerable to damage from diabetes. The damage suffered by many other organs is a direct result of the damage done to the nerves that serve them.

The only fuel that nerves can use is glucose. Other tissues can burn fatty acids for fuel when glucose is not available, but nerve cells are totally dependent on glucose for energy. Therefore, when the brain senses that blood glucose levels are dropping, a condition called **hypoglycemia**, it gets concerned. Both the autonomic nervous system (ANS) and the endocrine system respond, and it is through their combined efforts that glucose levels return to normal. Nerves in the ANS "call" the adrenal glands that lie on top of your kidneys and tell them to release a hormone called epinephrine (adrenalin). The epinephrine in turn travels in the blood to the liver and tells it to produce more glucose, causing glucose levels to return to normal. It is the epinephrine that gives rise to the familiar symptoms of hypoglycemia: your heart races and pounds, your hands tingle, your body trembles and shakes, and you sweat.

While nerve cells are concerned with not getting enough glucose, a greater threat to them is getting too much. Neurons do not need insulin to absorb glucose; it easily crosses the membrane into the cells.

Diabetic Nerve Disease (Neuropathy)

Diabetes is associated with some slowing of the electrical impulses that travel along nerves, but more severe problems can develop too. Diabetic nerve disease, or neuropathy, is a group of disorders that alone or in combination affect the nervous system. It occurs when nerves are damaged from high levels of glucose or when their blood supply (nerves have blood vessels too) is interrupted by damage to the blood vessels. Neuropathy is the most common complication of both type 1 and type 2 diabetes, occurring in 60 percent to 70 percent of all patients.

Neuropathic pain is usually described as burning, shooting, or like an electric shock. For others it can be felt as tingling or itching. Some patients may have extremely painful symptoms, while others with more nerve damage may have no symptoms. Symptoms can be intermittent and can manifest in any part of the body, although the feet and legs are the most common sites. Neuropathy increases with age, length of diabetes, and worsening of glucose tolerance. The American Diabetes Association recommends that type 2 diabetic patients be screened for neuropathy when diagnosed and that type 1 diabetes patients be screened five years after diagnosis, and both should be screened at least once a year thereafter.

Until recently, diabetic neuropathy was believed to be irreversible. Damaged nerve cells usually do not grow back, or they grow back at such a slow pace that damage from high blood glucose overcomes the repair. Good blood sugar control should accelerate this repair process.

The Somatic Nervous System and Sensorimotor Neuropathy

The cells of the somatic, or sensorimotor, nervous system include the **sensory nerves** that monitor our environment and carry messages to the brain, as well as the **motor neurons** that make movement possible and that carry messages from the brain. The sensory nerves function as sensors in the skin, reporting to the brain on any pain, pressure, touch, heat, cold, light, or sound they experience in their surroundings. Most activities of the nervous system start with a report from one of these sensors on the body surface. When your brain wants the body, an organ, or a muscle inside an organ to move in any way, it sends a message via the motor nerves.

Sensorimotor (or peripheral) neuropathy affects the sensory and motor nerves. Symptoms can range from numbness to burning, tingling, pain from normal touch, and constant pain in the feet, toes, and/or hands. Up to 50 percent of people with this kind of neuropathy have no symptoms at the start. This type of neuropathy is common in the feet.

The Autonomic Nervous System and Diabetic Autonomic Neuropathy

The autonomic nervous system, or ANS, is made up of nerves that connect the brain to the visceral organs. The nerves of the ANS do not require conscious thought to fire. They control the heartbeat; the smooth-muscle contraction of organs such as the lungs, bladder, gallbladder, reproductive organs, arteries, eyes, and GI tract; and even the release of hormones by some glands, such as the digestive, adrenal, tear, and sweat glands. The vagal nerve is part of the ANS.

The autonomic nervous system can also be affected by neuropathy, and because this system sends impulses to the internal organs, virtually every system in the body can be affected. Most of the digestive problems associated with diabetes—including loss of appetite, nausea, vomiting, constipation, diarrhea, and decreased gastric emptying (gastroparesis)—occur because of **diabetic autonomic neuropathy**, or **DAN**, and not some problem native to a digestive organ. This condition can affect the cardiovascular system, causing sudden death, silent heart attacks, and decreased ability to exercise. In women it can affect the bladder, causing the sensation of always having to urinate or of not being able to fully empty the bladder. In men it can cause erectile dysfunction.

Diabetic Eye Diseases and the Nervous System

The eye is a specialized sense organ that works closely with the brain and the nervous system. It is connected to the front of the brain via the optic nerve. The eye translates light waves into electrical impulses, which the brain decodes into an image. Cells that live in the eye are the monitors of the body. They help the body to navigate its environment and to screen it for dangers that can be avoided by nervous system action. Eye problems are often the first symptom of diabetes.

When light first enters the eye, it passes through the **cornea**, the clear and curved area in the front of the eyeball. The cornea protects the eye while focusing light, which then passes through the **lens** for more focusing.

Cataracts. Rapid changes in blood sugar levels can cause blurry vision. The cause is **osmosis**, a process in which water molecules are drawn to areas where there is less of a concentration of water. Sugar enters the cells of the lens, and then water follows to dilute it. This causes water to enter the lens, which swells, changing the focal parts of the eye. Over time, this is thought to result in a **cataract**. Age is one cause of cataracts, but diabetics are twice as likely to develop them and at an earlier age.

Retinopathy. Light passes through a fluid-filled chamber in the center of the eye (the vitreous) and strikes the back of the eye, the **retina**. If the eye is a camera, then the retina is the film. It records the images focused on it and relays them to the brain via the **optic nerve**. High glucose, high insulin, and low oxygen levels team up to damage the capillaries that supply oxygen and other nutrients to the retina. The blood vessel wall becomes leaky, and fluid and blood seep into the retina, causing it to swell. This condition is called **nonproliferative diabetic retinopathy**. If this swelling affects the center of the retina, the problem is called **macular edema**, and vision loss can result. If you also have high blood pressure, the problem is exacerbated.

Over time, nonproliferative retinopathy can progress to a more serious form called **proliferative retinopathy**. The damage to the small blood vessels leads to a decrease in blood flow, which triggers new blood vessel growth in the retina. These new vessels are weak and can leak blood, blocking vision, which is a condition called vitreous hemorrhage. The new blood vessels can also cause scar tissue to grow. After the scar tissue shrinks, it can distort the retina or pull it out of place. This is called **retinal detachment**.

Diabetic retinopathy is the most frequent cause of new cases of blindness among adults under age seventy-four. Almost all type 1 diabetics and more than 60 percent of type 2 diabetics will develop retinopathy in the first two decades of disease. People who keep their blood sugar levels closer to normal are less likely to have retinopathy or to have severe forms.

Glaucoma. The eyeball is not solid; it contains two cavities, and the posterior cavity is filled with a fluid having a soft, gel-like consistency. This semisolid fluid provides enough pressure to keep the eyeball from collapsing. But when the pressure in the eyeball rises so high that it starts to damage the optic nerve, the result is **glaucoma**. Diabetes can cause elevated pressure. This condition can be controlled with eyedrops that decrease pressure.

The Endocrine System

If the nervous system is like the telephone company, then the endocrine system (Figure 2.2) is like the postal system.

Figure 2.2 Endocrine system

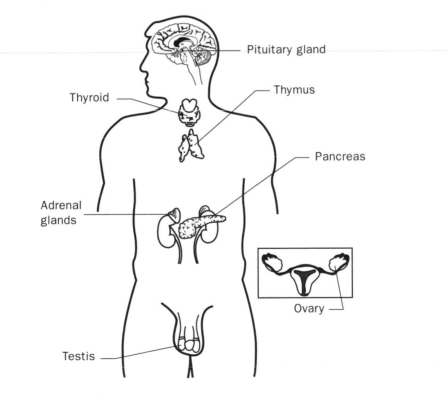

It allows the individual cells of a gland to send instructions next door or to the other end of the body with messages called hormones. Our glandular postal service delivers these messages via the circulatory system. The nervous system specializes in fast messages that produce rapid, short-acting responses. Hormones specialize in messages that produce slower but usually longer-acting responses. The two communication systems complement one another, forming a single **neuroendocrine system** that allows all the organ systems to coordinate their activities and work together in harmony. In many ways, they are the glue that holds the individual body parts together so that they work as a single organism.

Hormones are the main regulators of metabolism, growth and development, and reproduction. The endocrine system includes the pancreas and liver, pituitary, hypothalamus, thyroid, adrenal glands, ovaries, placenta, and testes. The glands in the endocrine system are different from other kinds of glands. **Exocrine glands** have a more practical purpose: they secrete their products into ducts that lead to where the product is used. For example, the salivary glands produce saliva, and their ducts deliver it to the mouth. Likewise, sweat glands produce sweat, which is delivered to the skin. In contrast, **endocrine glands** have no ducts, and their products are hormones, which they release into the blood. Some glands, such as the pancreas, are both endocrine and exocrine.

Hormone Receptors

Each hormone message is addressed to one type of cell, called the **target cell**. As explained in the first chapter, each cell has molecules embedded on its surface that act as identification tags. Some announce what kind of cell it is, while others have more practical uses. Each cell can have thousands of ID tags on its surface. Many hormones, such as insulin, act like keys. When a key message from a gland comes into contact with a target cell, the key fits into one of the receptor locks and activates it.

The hormone is able to change how chemicals act on the inside of the cell by binding with the receptor. However, hormones can increase or decrease normal cell activity. Hormones can't make a cell do something it doesn't normally do. What happens when the key turns the receptor lock depends on the type of receptor.

Hormone Regulation

The rate at which a gland secretes its hormones is tightly regulated by some kind of internal control system. Insulin is controlled by the simplest control system—**humoral stimuli**. This means that the product of the hormone's action builds up to the point where it prevents the gland from secreting any more hormone. When the amount of product falls, the hormone's control over the gland stops. The low level of hormone again stimulates the release of product, and the cycle begins once more. For example, high glucose levels in the blood stimulate the beta cells in the islets of Langerhans (see below) to release insulin. Insulin causes glucose to leave the blood and go into cells, and the level of glucose drops. The beta cells sense that glucose levels have fallen, and they stop releasing their insulin. In an emergency situation, the nervous system can override the normal hormonal control. For example, when the brain perceives an emergency, it can override hormones and elevate blood sugar.

Sometimes the target cell responds poorly to the hormone, and the product does not get the chance to build up or fall low enough to turn off the gland. In other words, the receptor on a cell is resistant to the actions of its corresponding hormone. This is what happens when a person is insulin resistant, a condition that often occurs before diabetes.

Low glucose levels in the blood are sensed by the cells in the pancreas. The beta cells respond by stopping their production of insulin, and the alpha cells respond by releasing glucagon. As insulin levels decrease, glucagon levels increase. Glucagon and insulin oppose each other and keep blood sugar in balance.

The Pancreas and Diabetes

The pancreas is a pink, fish-shaped organ about six inches long. Most of this gland is exocrine, with 98 percent of its cells producing the digestive juice necessary for digestion. But 2 percent of the cells in the pancreas are endocrine. These are the islets of Langerhans, cells that live in groups, or islands, tucked in among the cells that produce digestive enzymes. The hormones they produce are insulin, made by the beta cells, and glucagon, made by the alpha cells. As will be shown in the next chapter, insulin controls carbohydrate metabolism—it decreases blood glucose, while glucagon opposes insulin and increases blood glucose.

The pancreas is the gland most directly affected by diabetes. Although how this occurs is not well understood, we know that something triggers an autoimmune reaction in people with the genetic tendency for it. The immune army that is normally there to protect cells now attacks and kills the beta cells. It's as if someone has framed these healthy cells and accused them of being a danger. The alpha cells that lie mixed in with the beta on their little islands are not touched and will continue to make their hormone, glucagon. This is called **type 1 diabetes**, and it usually happens in children.

It also is not known how the beta cells are killed in **type 2 diabetes**. It is known that insulin resistance happens before diabetes. One theory is that high glucose levels caused by insulin resistance are **glucotoxic** to the beta cells and kills them. This theory explains why patients with type 2 diabetes always have insulin resistance and a loss of beta cells.

The Immune and Lymphatic Systems

The lymphatic system (Figures 2.3 and 2.4) is made up of the lymphatic vessels, lymph nodes, lymph, thymus, and spleen. It acts as a second transportation system, carrying the fat-soluble nutrients and triglycerides absorbed from meals away from the digestive tract in its lymph fluid to a blood vessel outside of the portal system. The **lymph nodes** are a combination police station and barracks. These round or kidney-shaped structures are usually found in groups around the body. You have between 500 and 1,500 lymph nodes that range in size from tiny to about one inch in diameter. When nodes in the neck, armpits, or groin

Figure 2.3 Lymphatic system

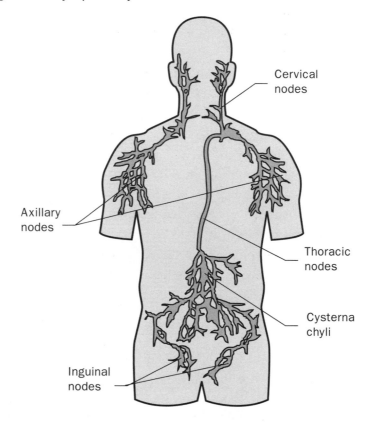

are enlarged, they can be felt. This is why your doctor feels around your neck and probes around your abdomen.

The immune system is often compared to an army because of its role in defending the body. It is composed only of cells but often uses parts of the lymphatic system. When an attacker such as a bacterium or virus is picked up by one of the white blood cells, it is brought to the lymph node to be imprisoned and studied. When large numbers of these troublemakers are incarcerated, or when

Figure 2.4 Location of lymph nodes in the head

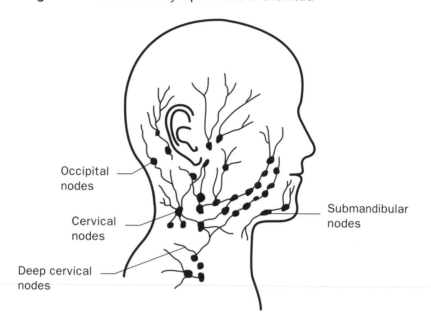

Occipital nodes

Cervical nodes

Deep cervical nodes

Submandibular nodes

the immune army beefs up its security due to a threat, the bulging barracks can be felt by the doctor.

The white blood cells are the army of the body. **Neutrophils** are a type of white blood cell that are responsible for defending your body from infections. **B cells** are portable antibody factories. They patrol the circulatory and lymphatic systems. When they are exposed to antigens, they transform into antibody-producing plasma cells. Antibody meets antigen: if the antigen is on a cell, the cell is killed. **T cells** are responsible for cell–mediated immunity. They also protect against infection by parasites, fungi, and protozoans and can kill cancerous cells. They circulate in the blood and become associated with lymph nodes and the spleen.

The Immune System and Diabetes

Sugar is the favorite food of invading bacteria and yeast. When you feed a germ that has wandered into a cut, you don't get one sated bacterium; you get ten hungry ones. Feed them, and soon you have a hungry horde and a serious infection. This is one reason why people with diabetes are so prone to infections. To bacteria, high blood sugar levels are like an invitation to a free dinner. The bladder, kidneys, vagina, gums, skin, and feet are common areas of infections. Early treatment of infections can prevent more serious complications.

Signs of Infection

Cut or wound that does not heal

Red, warm, or draining sore

White patches in the mouth or on the tongue

Pink color on toothbrush after brushing

Bad breath and red, swollen, and sore gums

Vaginal itching

Pain or burning during urination, frequent urination, or a constant urge to urinate

Bad odor to urine, or bloody or cloudy urine

Skin rash

Fever over 101 degrees Fahrenheit

Sore throat or pain on swallowing

Nausea, vomiting, or diarrhea

Flu- or coldlike symptoms: sweats, chills, headache, fatigue, achiness

The Circulatory System

For our purposes, the circulatory system is made up of four organs: blood vessels, blood, the heart, and the endothelium. It is the transportation system of the body, a living river flowing through a vast series of intelligent, interconnected canals. These canals pulse with the rhythm of the heart, contracting and dilating to direct blood flow and regulate blood pressure. Your organs are stitched together with thousands and thousands of miles of blood vessels. They penetrate deep into every organ of your body to touch each and every cell. Your survival depends on how well your cardiovascular system is able to nourish the cells it reaches. Cardiovascular disease will kill up to 75 percent of patients with type 2 diabetes, and it occurs at a younger age among people with diabetes versus others.

The liquid part of blood is a straw-colored fluid called **plasma**. It contains a vast and varied number of substances, including water, various nutrients, waste products, blood glucose, and insulin, along with other hormones used for communication. The heart is at once the beginning and the end of the cardiovascular system. It produces the force needed to propel the blood on its never-ending journey around the body. The heart has to pump nine to ten tons of blood each day, a cupful at a time with each beat.

The **endothelial organ** is the most deceptive-looking organ. It may look to be a simple lining, but in reality it is the brain of the cardiovascular system, so complex that not all of its functions are yet understood. It regulates, controls, releases, converts, activates, and inactivates. The endothelium also manufactures a great number of messenger substances that "talk" to the circulating blood cells and the underlying smooth-muscle cells of the artery walls. Atherosclerosis is a disease of the endothelium.

The Circulatory System and Diabetes

Because it is just a single layer of cells, the endothelium is extremely delicate. When blood flows too fast or with too much force, endothelial cells can peel away from the artery, leaving the space underneath raw and open to invaders. Chemicals, bacteria, and free radicals are other sources of injury. Its fragility could be called the Achilles' heel of the cardiovascular system. When your endothelium is not healthy, the rest of your body suffers.

The elevated levels of insulin and glucose found in the diabetes are extremely toxic to the endothelial cells. This is **glucotoxicity**.

Getting Your Blood Pressure and Cholesterol Levels Under Control

Blood pressure control can reduce cardiovascular disease (heart disease and stroke) by approximately 33 percent to 50 percent and can reduce microvascular disease (eye, kidney, and nerve disease) by approximately 33 percent.

In general, for every 10 millimeters of mercury (mmHg) reduction in systolic blood pressure, the risk for any complication related to diabetes is reduced by 12 percent. Improved control of cholesterol or blood lipids (for example, HDL, LDL, and triglycerides) can reduce cardiovascular complications by 20 percent to 50 percent.

The Respiratory System

The respiratory system and the digestive system were built to the same model. Both are technically on the outside of the body. Both bring external substances into themselves, process them in some way to remove toxins, and then expose them to a single layer of absorptive cells. The cells take what they need, waste products are added, and the product is expelled. Both work closely with the circulatory system, relying on it to pick up the nutrient(s) passing through the absorptive cells. Both can forcefully eject their contents when a toxin is detected, although a sneeze represents a much tidier process than its digestive-tract counterpart.

Air moves through the lungs by way of the **diaphragm**, a thin structure made of muscle that lies at the bottom end of your lungs. When you breathe in, you are pulling your diaphragm upward. To breathe out, your body simply lets go of the diaphragm, and it falls back into place. Blood glucose levels are associated with the amount of air your lungs can hold: the higher the blood sugar, the lower the lung capacity. High blood glucose levels are also associated with a decrease in the lung's ability to move air effectively.

The Respiratory System and Diabetes

The lungs are another target organ for diabetic damage. They are responsible for bringing a single nutrient into your body—oxygen. The body cannot store oxygen because it is a gas, so you must have a continuous supply. The lungs also act as filters, removing carbon dioxide as the blood passes through them. Carbon dioxide and water are all that is left of the sugar that has passed through the digestive tract. Along the way to the gas transport area, cells filter impurities from the air. Each day, the brave cells that live along the respiratory tract are exposed to more than ten thousand liters of air containing toxins, dust, microorganisms, and other hazardous airborne particles. This is an important function for people with diabetes because they are vulnerable to the health effects of airborne particles, including tobacco smoke, which paralyzes the minute hairs that are part of the air-cleaning system of the lung. The incoming air is also warmed and saturated with water.

The transfer of oxygen and carbon dioxide takes place in the paper-thin **alveoli**. These balloonlike structures are composed of one layer of flat cells on the lung's side and one layer on the vascular system's side. Just as the digestive tract depends on the vascular system to distribute its absorbed nutrients, so does the lung. Anything that affects the vascular system is therefore going to affect lung function. Autopsies on patients who had diabetes have shown that the walls of the capillaries in their alveoli were thickened, a situation that could decrease oxygen and carbon dioxide transfer. Scientists have found that CO_2 transfer is lower in patients with diabetes.

The Digestive System

The digestive tract is a long, open-ended muscular tube. As with the respiratory tract, the inside of the digestive tube is technically outside of the body. Food passes through it and is processed into glucose, amino acids, and fatty acids, which are then exposed to an absorptive surface. The absorptive cells take what they need, add waste products, and expel the result. The circulatory system takes over from there. Food moves through the tube via a series of wavelike muscle contractions called **peristalsis**.

The digestive tube depends on the nervous and circulatory systems. Anything that damages them will indirectly damage the cells that live in the digestive tract and prevent them from performing their jobs. This makes the digestive system (Figure 2.5) a target for diabetes complications.

The digestive tube is divided into regions based on the type of jobs they do. The major divisions are the mouth, esophagus, stomach, duodenum/small intestine, large intestine (or colon), rectum, and anus. But the digestive

Figure 2.5 Digestive system

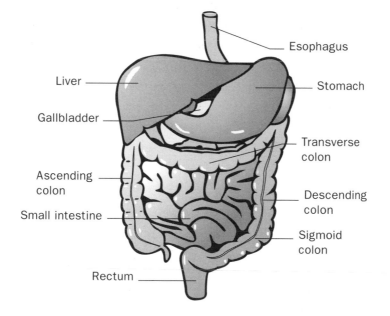

tract cannot do the job alone. Helping the digestive tube achieve its goal are the teeth, tongue, salivary glands, liver, gallbladder, and pancreas. The nerve that serves all of the digestive organs is the **vagus nerve**. It originates on the underside of the brain, runs down the neck, and wanders through the trunk. When it is damaged by high blood sugar or poor circulation, the result is felt all through the digestive tract.

The veins coming from the stomach, small intestine, colon, gallbladder, pancreas, and spleen have their own blood system—the **portal system**. The blood that comes from all of the other abdominal organs is sent to the **inferior vena cava**, a large blood vessel that goes to the lungs, but the blood from the digestive organs feeds into the portal vein, which goes directly to the liver. This means the liver gets first access to glucose, the water-soluble vitamins, and all the other nutrients coming from the digestive tract. Toxins from the digestive tract also go first to the liver, for detoxification, before they have a chance to damage other organs. Fat and the fat-soluble nutrients bypass the portal system. Instead, they are absorbed into the lymph vessels and carried up the body in the thoracic duct to where the lymphatic system joins with the cardiovascular system in the left shoulder. This gives the cells of the muscles and other organs first access to the fats and fat-soluble nutrients.

The Mouth and Diabetes

The mouth is the start of the digestive tract. Here food is chewed by the teeth, mixed with saliva secreted by the salivary glands, and prepared for its long journey down the gut. Anything that prevents the teeth from chewing—such as pain or ill-fitting dentures—will interfere with the body's getting the nourishment it needs. A dry mouth from salivary glands that produce insufficient saliva can make swallowing difficult. Both can contribute to bacterial and fungal infections that can thrive in the mouth's moist, warm environment. Cavities are caused by a bacterium. Diabetes weakens the white blood cells of the immune system, which defend the tissues of the mouth from infections. It also decreases healing time of any sore or dental surgery. **Periodontal disease** (gum disease) is common in people with diabetes.

Your mouth and heart are related in some way that is not yet clear. Many people with aggressive gum disease also have high cholesterol levels. Some researchers have theorized that the inflammation caused by the bacteria in the mouth in some way leads to the inflammation that may cause atherosclerosis.

The Stomach and Diabetes

The stomach is the first out-pouching of our tube. It's a comma-shaped organ that, when empty, is the size of a large sausage. When filled, it can distend to an indeterminate volume. The stomach lies just below the diaphragm and moves up and down with the movements of that organ. When a large meal is eaten, the distended stomach can limit this movement of the diaphragm, making breathing difficult. It can also push upward against the heart, giving the sensation in the chest that the heart is crowded.

As the term *heartburn* implies, pain in the stomach can be mistaken for pain in the heart. Food is kept in the stomach during its vigorous actions by the valve at the top—**the lower esophageal sphincter** (LES)—and at its bottom with the **pyloric sphincter**. When the LES is weak, it cannot completely close, and stomach acid can splash out of the stomach and onto the sensitive lining of the esophagus, causing a severe burning and/or a pain that runs up the jaw and into the ear. This condition is called **gastroesophageal reflux**.

Cells that live in the stomach can specialize in a number of jobs, but they all serve to liquefy your meal, sterilize it, and start its absorption. The vast majority of cells live in one of the three muscular layers. A smaller number make up the folded stomach lining; they secrete hydrochloric acid, which aids in digestion and helps to sterilize food, and a layer of mucus to protect themselves from the acid. An even smaller number live in the glands tucked in among the gastric folds; some cells secrete acid, some secrete digestive enzymes, and some secrete the intrinsic factor necessary for vitamin B_{12} absorption.

How fast the stomach empties can determine how fast sugars from carbohydrate digestion are absorbed. Foods that are high in volume and high in fat can empty at a slower speed, thereby keeping glucose levels more even, and those that are highly refined and lower in volume can exit faster, causing higher glucose levels. When the branch of the vagus nerve that serves the stomach is damaged from diabetes, the result can be a type of neuropathy called **gastroparesis**. Peristalsis slows, so that food stays too long in the stomach. This can cause pain, loss of appetite, and nausea and vomiting and can make glucose control more difficult. Some of the drugs used to treat type 2 diabetes can also induce nausea and loss of appetite.

The Intestines and Diabetes

The small intestine is a coiled, twenty-foot tube that fills most of your abdomen. The cells that earn their living here specialize in absorption. The first ten inches of the small intestine is the **duodenum**. This is where the acidic juices of the stomach are neutralized by pancreatic juice so that the enzymes that work in an alkaline environment can get to work. The rest of the small intestine—the **jejunum** and the **ileum**—is devoted to absorption.

The main function of the epithelium of the small intestine is to absorb nutrients. The lining of the small intestine is wrinkled with velvety folds called **rugae**. The rugae are covered with millions of small, fingerlike projections called **villi**. Each villus is one millimeter in height and has a small artery, a vein, and a lymph vessel running through its center. It is covered with a single layer of cells that have even finer projections on their top exposed surfaces, called microvilli. Each cell on the villus has about 1,700 of them. Under the microscope, the microvilli projecting out from the end of each cell give the appearance of a paintbrush and are referred to as the "brush border." Enzymes necessary to digest foods are produced in the brush border near the top of each villus. The digested nutrients then pass through the villi walls and into the blood or lymph vessels. This arrangement of villi and microvilli increases the absorptive area of the small intestine to about 250 square meters, the size of a small tennis court.

The **large intestine**, or **colon**, has a wider diameter than the small intestine. It ends in the rectum, which holds fecal matter until it is excreted. The anus is the opening at the end of the digestive tract.

The nerves that serve the intestines may be affected by diabetes, causing **enteric neuropathy**. The nerve damage decreases peristalsis, so that food moves through the intestine at a slower speed. Delayed emptying and the stagnation of fluid in the small intestine can cause bacterial overgrowth syndromes. The result is abdominal pain, bloating, and diarrhea. Antibiotics can help reduce the bacterial growth, and your doctor can prescribe drugs to help increase the speed of fluids though your small intestine.

Enteric neuropathy can affect the motility of the colon: decreasing passage time causes constipation, and increasing passage time causes diarrhea. Just as sensorimotor neuropathy of the feet causes pain, enteric neuropathy can cause a chronic abdominal pain syndrome.

The Biliary System

The biliary system includes the liver, which makes bile; the gallbladder, which stores the bile; and the pancreas. A common duct delivers both bile and pancreatic enzymes to the duodenum.

The digestive tube processes and absorbs nutrients, but the liver decides what to do with them. This underappreciated organ is involved in the metabolism of all three macronutrients. It soaks up glucose and then doles it out later when needed. This keeps a minimum level of glucose always available for the brain and nerves, which are totally dependent on it.

Because its job is so important, the liver has a tremendous ability to regenerate. If large areas of cells are killed or removed, the liver will regrow them and resume most of its functions. The liver is responsible for more than two hundred jobs, but these are the major tasks that concern us now:

- The liver is the major organ of detoxification. The blood picks up poisonous substances in the digestive system and carries them to the liver, where, through a series of chemical reactions, they are changed into nontoxic compounds. Alcohol absorbed through the stomach wall is detoxified here.
- Liver cells (**hepatocytes**) secrete bile, a cholesterol-containing substance that acts like soap and breaks fats into more accessible droplets.
- Liver function is the only way the body has of getting rid of cholesterol (excreted in its one pint of bile per day). The cholesterol will be reabsorbed unless there is soluble fiber in the intestine to bind to it and carry it out of the body.
- The liver is a storage depot for vitamins A, B_{12}, and D and iron.

Liver function enzymes are often elevated in people with diabetes, perhaps caused by fatty infiltration of the liver, which is common in patients with type 2 diabetes. A fatty liver can cause an enlarged liver and abdominal pain.

The Exocrine Pancreas

The pancreas is a fish-shaped organ that contains both endocrine tissue (which secretes hormones into the blood) and exocrine tissue (which secretes its products into ducts). In its role as an exocrine gland, the pancreas is part of the digestive system.

The "head" of the pancreas lies within the C-shaped curve of the duodenum, or, as some books say, "in the arms of the duodenum." The pancreas produces pancreatic juice, which is a cocktail of three enzymes, one for each macronutrient. After the enzymes are secreted, they empty into small ducts that eventually merge with the large duct that runs the length of the pancreas. This pancreatic duct enters the duodenum shortly after it leaves the pancreas.

When cells in the duodenum sense acid from the stomach (as the acidic chyme enters), they make a hormone called **secretin** and release it into the blood. Secretin travels through the circulation until it reaches the pancreas, lying next to the duodenum. It tells the pancreas to release a fluid high in bicarbonate but low in enzymes. The bicarbonate neutralizes the acid and leaves the chyme slightly alkaline, just how the pancreatic enzymes like it. Secretin is also released when the intestinal cells sense fat. It causes the liver to increase its output of bile. A second intestinal hormone, **cholecystokinin**, causes the pancreas to secrete a digestive juice rich in enzymes.

The Urinary System

The job of cleaning up the bloodstream falls to the cells of the urinary system (Figure 2.6). They are the renal "sanitation engineers" who are experts in waste removal. The urinary system includes a pair of kidneys and ureters, the bladder, and the urethra. The cells that live in the kidneys filter more than 1,700 liters of blood each day through a vast network of capillaries to produce about one liter of highly concentrated urine. The kidneys are like fine sieves—straining out waste products, detoxified substances, excess vitamins, and water.

Urine drips from the kidney down through a long tube called the **ureter** until it reaches the bladder. The bladder is a hollow muscular organ that expands as it fills with urine. Urine is temporarily stored here. When the bladder reaches a certain level of fullness, it sends the brain a signal to empty, and urine exits through the urethra.

The kidney knows the upper limit for a vast number of chemicals, and when it detects any level over that limit for

Figure 2.6 Urinary system

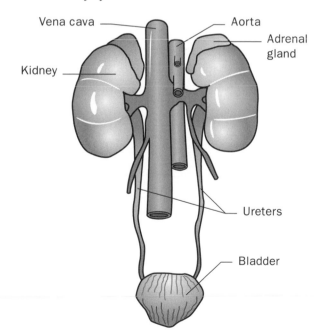

a particular chemical, the excess goes into the urine. When conditions change in the body, the kidney can respond by removing more or less of a substance. In maintaining and storing fluids, the kidneys are essential to controlling the balance of water, electrolytes, and acid in the body. They also play a role in making red blood cells, regulating blood pressure, and activating vitamin D.

The Kidneys and Diabetes

Kidney cells are vulnerable to glucotoxic effects. In long-term diabetes, the walls that form the capillaries in the kidneys tend to thicken and become more porous. The proteins they are supposed to concentrate and store spill into the urine instead. This can produce **uremia** as toxic levels of nitrogen waste products from the urine accumulate in the blood. The extreme level of toxicity leads to kidney failure and can be treated only by dialysis or a kidney transplant. Diabetes patients are prone to bladder infections and high blood pressure, both of which can lead to kidney complications. Proper maintenance and strict control of blood sugar can prevent and sometimes reverse certain kidney damage.

Diabetes is the leading cause of end-stage renal disease, accounting for 44 percent of new cases. In 2002, according to the American Diabetes Association, 44,000 people with diabetes began treatment for end-stage renal disease. A total of 153,730 people with end-stage renal disease due to diabetes were living on chronic dialysis or with a kidney transplant. Detecting and treating early diabetic kidney disease by lowering blood pressure can reduce the decline in kidney function by 30 percent to 70 percent.

The Integumentary System

The integumentary system is the medical term for "skin"; it is made up of the skin and its various attachments, including hair, lips, fingernails, and toenails. The workers in this organ serve as the defenders and regulators of the body and belong to three major unions: surface epithelial tissue, which lies atop a base of connective tissue, with nervous tissue penetrating both layers. The epithelial tissue contains cells that make pigments. The number of pigment-making cells determines your skin color. The skin also contains cholesterol. Research has shown that a high level of cholesterol in outer skin cells is a sign of atherosclerosis.

The skin also contains parts of other organ systems—blood vessels and endothelial tissue from the cardiovascular system, and glands from the endocrine system. All of these tissues and organs work together to fulfill the skin's responsibilities. The skin cells return the favor by helping other organ systems with their jobs. They help the kidney and digestive system get rid of waste materials, and they help the immune system to defend the body.

The skin's most obvious responsibility is to keep your insides in and your outsides out. It also helps to keep you watertight. It is your skin that prevents your bathwater from swelling you up like a sponge and prevents your sunlamp from shriveling you into a raisin.

The skin cells help to regulate the weather system in your body by altering blood flow. When the temperature inside gets too high, the sweat glands are turned on, to bring it back to the comfort zone. When it gets too cold, fat pads beneath the skin act as insulation to keep your internal organs warm. The skin also helps the brain sense the outside environment so that it can recognize danger.

Nerve endings communicate information to the brain about touch, pressure, and pain. When the skin sweats, it not only regulates your body temperature but also rids the body of waste materials. Your sweat tastes salty because two of those waste materials are sodium and chloride.

A major duty of skin cells is defense. They act as border guards, preventing the illegal immigration of the vast majority of bacteria, viruses, and fungi that try to sneak into your body. They work with the immune system as the body's first line of defense against the hostile forces of disease-bearing microorganisms.

Not all invaders are alive. Because it is waterproof, the skin also helps to block the entry of water-soluble toxic chemicals. It also protects the body from radiation such as the sun's ultraviolet rays. However, small amounts of radiation are bound to sneak through. The skin cells use these rays to make vitamin D from a precursor molecule. This vitamin is important for the absorption of calcium and phosphorus from foods.

The nails on the ends of your fingers and toes are also part of the skin. The live cells are hidden under the cuticle and are pushed up as they die. The dead translucent nail cells lie on a bed of epithelial tissue, which gets its color from the numerous blood vessels in the nail bed. Because of this, your nails reflect what is happening to your circulation. For example, they can take on a yellow cast and thicken. This is especially evident on your toenails.

The Integumentary System and Diabetes

All of these responsibilities of the cell-citizen can be affected by diabetes. Nearly one-third of diabetics have a skin condition related to diabetes, and with time, the skin of all people with diabetes will be affected in some form. Sometimes a skin disorder is the first sign that a person has diabetes.

Doctors have noticed that patients with diabetes have thicker skin than people without diabetes, and their nails, palms, and soles can be yellow. You should also be aware of the following disorders:

- **Acanthosis nigricans:** A velvety, light brown to black thickening of the skin, usually on the back, the side of the neck, under the arms, and in skin folds of the groin. It is usually found on obese patients and is a sign of insulin resistance.
- **Diabetic dermopathy:** The most common skin problem in diabetes. Also called shin spots, it appears on both shins as oval pigmented lesions; the lesions will disappear on their own, leaving scars behind.
- **Diabetic bullae:** Large blisters that are usually confined to the hands and feet. They are associated with nerve damage.
- **Eruptive xanthomas:** Fatty skin deposits on the knees, backs of the arms, and front of the legs. This condition is associated with high fat levels in the blood.

Narrowed arteries from atherosclerosis and damaged blood vessels cause poor circulation in the legs and feet. This means your cell-citizens do not get all the oxygen and nutrients they need to repair and replace damaged cells.

High levels of sugar can also feed bacteria so that they reproduce faster than immune cells can kill them. Moist, warm areas of the body such as folds of skin become an inviting home to fungal and yeast infections such as candida. The high blood sugar provides them with food, and obesity provides them with skin folds. Candida infections can be an early sign of diabetes. High blood glucose also increases the loss of water from the body. This results in dry, shiny skin that can crack and become infected. It is important to keep your skin moisturized.

The nerve cells in the skin can be damaged too, causing diabetic neuropathy. Symptoms include a sensation of pins and needles, inability to sense temperature, and loss of sensation. The ability to sense pain is vital. For instance, without discomfort to tell us to move a limb because it has been in the same position too long, circulation is cut off and pressure ulcers eventually develop. Loss of sensation also makes it easy to ignore infections and sores. Untreated, the wounds get larger, and poor circulation makes them slow to heal. Sometimes an infection never heals. For most diabetics it was a skin ulcer that eventually led to an amputation.

The most effective solution is gaining control of your blood sugar. Once that is achieved, the symptoms appearing on the skin will likely subside. You should also examine your skin closely every day for any blister, sore, or ulcer you may not feel. This is especially important for the skin on your feet. Treat any skin break promptly. If it doesn't heal, see your doctor. Be aware of any loss of sensation in the skin.

As discussed earlier in the chapter, all patients with diabetes should also be screened for diabetic peripheral neuropathy within five years of diagnosis for type 1 diabetes and at the time of diagnosis for type 2 diabetes, since the disease has been active for at least five years at that time.

Why It's Important to Get Your Blood Sugar Under Control

The federal government conducted a landmark study from 1983 to 1993 that profoundly changed the management of diabetes. The study involved 1,441 volunteers with type 1 diabetes at twenty-nine medical centers in the United States and Canada. The United Kingdom Prospective Diabetes Study in 1998 produced similar results for people with type 2 diabetes.

The results from both studies proved that the level of blood sugar control predicts the onset and severity of diabetes-related complications for both types of diabetes. This means that if people with diabetes can keep their blood sugar levels as close as possible to normal, they can live a normal life span, with few complications or even no complications at all.

The Reproductive System

The organs of the reproductive system specialize in colonization. However, despite investing billions of sperm and hundreds of eggs, whether by choice or by chance, the reproductive department succeeds in birthing only an average of 2.1 colonies in its lifetime. Luckily, this department has another purpose. This purpose is not well known or appreciated, but it is vitally important.

Some countries have close bonds, sharing borders and standing together as allies. The intercourse between them is a demonstration of the commitment they have made to each other. The reproductive department strengthens that commitment and facilitates communication between them. This serves to nourish the independence of the colonies they have formed between them.

The Reproductive System and Diabetes

Erectile dysfunction, or **ED**, is the inability to achieve or sustain an erection rigid enough for sexual intercourse more than 75 percent of the time. It is common, affecting up to 80 percent of men with diabetes, compared with 22 percent to 25 percent of men without diabetes, and it tends to occur ten years earlier in the former group. Sexual activity requires the interaction of nerves and blood vessels. Both can be damaged in men with diabetes. Therefore, even men who have normal amounts of male hormones and who desire to have sex may not be able to achieve or sustain a firm erection.

Erectile dysfunction can be an early warning of coronary artery disease. The blood vessels that serve the penis are vulnerable to the same sort of damage that can cause heart disease. ED is often one of the first symptoms of damaged cardiac blood vessels.

ED can more than just damage a sex life. Sexual activity is a kind of communication. For many men who cannot verbally express affection, making love is how they express their love and commitment to their partner. When lovemaking is no longer possible, that communication suffers.

Now that we understand the anatomy involved in diabetes, we will turn our attention to the biochemistry of the condition.

3

Carbohydrates, Carbohydrate Metabolism, and Diabetes

In the human diet, carbohydrates provide most of the energy for your cell–citizens and are the nutrients that most directly affect blood sugar (glucose) levels. However, as we learned in the last chapter, your cells can get too much of a good thing. Too much glucose damages cells and causes complications that can threaten your life, limbs, and sight. In this chapter we explore how the diet can be manipulated to keep glucose levels low. We begin with a "Who's Who" of carbohydrates that will give you the vocabulary to understand your doctor's and nutritionist's instructions regarding your diet and carbohydrate intake. Then we explore carbohydrate metabolism and what goes wrong to produce diabetes.

Carbohydrate Classification

There are many ways to classify carbohydrates—so many ways that it becomes very confusing to the consumer to sort out what is and isn't useful to know. When used properly, these classifications can help you to manage your carbohydrate intake. Today, carbohydrates can be categorized according to their structure, their complexity, their effect on blood sugar (the glycemic index and the glycemic load), and their effect on satiety.

The oldest method of classifying carbohydrates is according to their chemical composition.

All carbohydrates are made up of chains of glucose rings. Sugars are simple carbohydrates with one or two rings; starches are complex carbohydrates with chains of many rings. The American Diabetes Association (ADA) now discourages the use of terms such as "simple sugars," "complex carbohydrates," and "fast-acting carbohydrates"; it prefers that carbohydrates be classified as sugars, starch, and fiber. Sugars are easily recognized in foods because of their sweet taste, starches are polysaccharides, and fiber is the carbohydrate roughage that resists digestion.

Starches

Half of the carbohydrates we eat are in the form of starches. They have been the main energy source for mankind since the agricultural revolution ten thousand years ago. In some cultures starch was eaten in the form of rice; in others it was in the form of wheat, potatoes, or corn. These staples contained not only starch but also protein, so they could sustain a population for long periods without any additional source of protein or calories.

Chemically, a starch is a **polysaccharide**, or chain of sugar molecules. In foods polysaccharides come in two types: **amylose** and **amylopectin**. Amylose is made of several hundred glucose units arranged in a straight unbranched chain. Amylopectin is made of several thousand glucose units arranged in highly branched chains. Starch molecules are too large to be absorbed through the intestinal lining. It is the job of enzymes called amylases to break them into smaller units.

The shape of each starch molecule gives you a clue as to how they affect the body. Amylose, being a chain, has only two ends for enzymes to attack. Digestion of this starch is going to be slow—the end products will enter the blood slowly and raise blood glucose levels slowly. Amylose can be considered a time-release form of energy. The many chains of amylopectin, in contrast, offer the enzymes more places to snap off glucose and maltose molecules. Digestion will be quicker, and glucose will enter the bloodstream and raise glucose levels quickly.

Disaccharides

Amylases produce two sugar molecules called disaccharides. Three disaccharides are found in the food you eat:

- **Sucrose** is the disaccharide with which you are probably most familiar, since it is the sole component of refined white sugar. It is made up of one molecule of glucose joined to one molecule of fructose.

- **Lactose** is milk sugar. It is composed of one glucose molecule and one galactose molecule.
- **Maltose** is composed of two glucose molecules. Besides being a product of starch digestion, maltose is found in germinating cereals and is used to make malt beverages.

Although disaccharides are small, they are still not small enough to be absorbed through the intestinal wall. **Sucrase**, **lactase**, and **maltase**, the enzymes needed to snap these molecules apart, lie on top of the microvilli of the small intestine. As the bond between the sugars is broken, the cell membrane waits below, ready to absorb them.

Simple Sugars

Sugar is the favorite carbohydrate and the one with the worst reputation. Something that tastes so good has got to be bad. Inside our bodies, though, it is another story: Glucose, or blood sugar, is the good guy. It is the only fuel the cells in your central nervous system (brain and spinal cord) can burn for energy, and they polish off nine tablespoons of glucose each day. Your red blood cells use three tablespoons. It is the preferred fuel of your muscle, liver, and fat cells, although they can happily burn fatty acids too if they can't get any sugar.

Chemically speaking, the basic unit of the carbohydrate is the **monosaccharide**. Other monosaccharides you may be familiar with are **fructose** (the main sugar in fruit) and **galactose** (the sugar that, together with glucose, forms lactose, or milk sugar). Fructose, glucose, and galactose all are made of six carbons in a ring. In fact, these simple sugars are all composed of the same elements: six carbon, twelve oxygen, and twelve hydrogen atoms arranged in a ring. The atoms are simply arranged differently in the different sugars. The molecular formula is written as: $C_6H_{12}O_6$. A six-sided ring gives you a rough idea of what a glucose molecule looks like.

The sugars are still too large to cross cell membranes by themselves. They need transport proteins or sugar carriers. Glucose enters cells with the help of the glucose transport proteins (GLUT) that were described in Chapter 1. Immediately after glucose enters a muscle cell it is changed into glucose-6-phosphate which locks it into the cell.

Fructose absorbed from a meal goes to the liver, where it is changed into glucose in a complicated process. No other organ can change fructose into glucose, so no other organ can use fructose. Fructose also does not stimulate insulin release and so does not directly raise blood sugar. As a result, fructose escapes the tight control that the body has on glucose metabolism. The end result is that fructose does not dampen the appetite and it can lead to overeating. It also raises plasma triglycerides.

Our bodies were never designed for the fructose-heavy foods we eat. Statistics show that the consumption of sucrose has decreased, but the use of fructose has soared. Most of the sweetener used in food today is in the form of high fructose corn syrup. Soft drinks are one of the main sources of fructose in the American diet.

Fiber

We're told these days that we need fiber (also called rough-age or bulk) for a well-functioning digestive tract. Fiber-rich foods can lower your risk of developing heart disease and hypertension, although it is not understood what component of these foods is responsible. For the purposes of this book, we will define fiber as a group of carbohydrates or other substances that show three properties:

- They resist digestion by human enzymes.
- They are able to reach the colon in much the same form in which they were eaten.
- They have some effect on gastrointestinal function.

Fiber includes cellulose, lignin, hemicelluloses, gums, and pectin, among other substances. Crude fiber is a scientific measurement of the cellulose and lignin in a food that is treated with acid and alkali. Estimates of crude fiber are often found in food tables. Dietary fiber includes two to five times more substances than crude fiber.

Fiber can be divided into two main subclasses, commonly called soluble and insoluble.

Soluble fiber. As its name suggests, soluble fiber is able to dissolve in the watery contents of the digestive tract, where it is thickened into a gel-like consistency. Soluble fiber resists digestion, which is not the same thing as not being digested. But all or almost all soluble fiber reaches the colon without being broken down. It is easily fermented by the friendly bacteria that grow in the colon to produce gases (carbon dioxide, hydrogen, and methane), lactic acid, and short-chain fatty acids, mainly acetate, propionate, and butyrate. These fermentation products then interact with the cells of the digestive tract or are absorbed into the bloodstream. Short-chain fatty acids can travel to the liver, where they reduce cholesterol production and influence the metabolism of glucose and fats.

This is the kind of fiber associated with lower blood glucose levels. Soluble fiber such as the beta-glucan in oatmeal can reduce the speed with which food leaves the stomach by increasing the viscosity of the food mass. This leads to the delayed digestion of starch and therefore to the delayed absorption of glucose. A diet high in soluble fiber is also associated with lower serum cholesterol levels and an increased feeling of fullness.

Pectin, gums, mucilages, and algeal substances are examples of soluble fiber. Most fiber laxatives are made almost entirely of soluble fiber. Metamucil is one such product; it is made from ground psyllium seed. Soluble fiber can trap some medications in its matrix, so take them at different times.

Insoluble fiber. The insoluble fibers are cellulose, hemicellulose, and lignin. They are not appetizing to the bacteria in the colon and leave the body in much the same form as they enter. Insoluble fiber has a local effect on the digestive tract: it absorbs and holds water, thereby increasing the size and weight of the feces. This increases the frequency of bowel movements, stimulates peristalsis (muscle movement), and reduces the time it takes for food to travel through the digestive system. A diet rich in insoluble fiber is associated with a decreased risk of colon and rectal cancer, decreased constipation, and a reduction in blood pressure. Researchers do not know if it is the fiber itself that is affecting cancer and blood pressure risk or if fiber foods contain some other component. This should not matter to you; you don't need to know how high-fiber foods protect you—just that they do.

Cellulose is the most abundant organic (carbon-containing) substance on earth. It forms the structural framework of almost all plants, giving them shape. The glucose units that compose cellulose have a type of bond that resists breakdown by human enzymes. This means that the cellulose from fruits, vegetables, legumes, and grains enters the colon without being digested. Cellulose is the component of fiber that absorbs and holds water, increasing the bulk and softness of the feces.

Hemicellulose is a polysaccharide found along with cellulose. **Lignin** is a fiber that is not a carbohydrate, although it is found in the cell walls of plants. Sources include wheat bran and woody portions of fruits and vegetables. Lignin is associated with a lower incidence of some cancers.

Alcohol

When yeast ferments the glucose in sugar, fruits, or cereal grains, **ethanol** (a type of alcohol) is produced. Chemically, ethanol is a small, water-soluble molecule that is very easily absorbed. It is metabolized and detoxified in the liver.

Alcohol is a double-edged sword: in some people it causes addiction, and in others it has health-promoting effects. Alcohol can interact with other drugs and alter their effectiveness, so it is very important to tell your doctor how much alcohol you consume each day. Alcohol also puts additional stress on the liver at a time when this important organ needs support. When you have consumed too much, your liver is not able to release glucose into your bloodstream when levels fall.

Oligosaccharides

In between disaccharides with two glucose units and poly-saccharides with ten or more, there is a group called the oligosaccharides. The beneficial oligosaccharides are the **a-galactosides** and **fructo-oligosaccharides**. The a-galactosides family contains carbohydrates with names such as raffinose, stachyose, and verbascose. Enzymes in the gastrointestinal tract cannot digest these sugars, so they reach the large intestine unscathed. However, the bacteria in the colon do contain the enzymes to digest them, and gas is produced as a by-product.

Vegetables that contain a-galactosides include peas, beans, and lentils, which owe their notorious production of flatulence to this component. Luckily, there is now an enzyme product, Beano, that will help digest these oli-gosaccharides and greatly reduce the amount of gas they form. You can find it at health food stores, pharmacies, and supermarkets. Swallow the enzyme with the first bite of food, and the gas disappears. You can find information on how to order Beano in the Resources section in the back of the book.

The other oligosaccharide group is the fructo-oligosaccharides. The Jerusalem artichoke is the richest source, but they can also be found in wheat, rye, triticale, asparagus, and onion. Syrup from the yacon root contains fructo-oligosaccharides and is used as a natural low-calorie sweetener.

Polyols

Polyols are sugar alcohols You will see them listed as ingredients in sugar-free, reduced-sugar, and low-glycemic foods and products. They vary in their sweetness, ranging from about half as sweet as sugar to about as sweet. **Sorbitol**, **mannitol**, and **xylitol** are polyols that are often used as sugar substitutes. Sorbitol-sweetened candies used to be creatively marketed as sugar-free candy or diabetic candy. However, they are neither sugar or calorie free. Xylitol is used as a sweetener in toothpaste and other oral care products. It does not promote tooth decay, tastes better than artificial sweeteners, and has some health benefits of its own.

Polyols, like fiber, provide fewer calories per gram than other carbohydrates because they are slowly and incompletely absorbed. What is absorbed requires less insulin than an equal amount of another carbohydrate. What is not absorbed reaches the large intestine. However, when eaten in too large a quantity these short-chain carbohydrates have a laxative effect: they pull water into the colon, causing cramps and diarrhea.

Carbohydrate Complexity

Like lots of things in the 1950s and '60s, carbohydrates were considered to be either simple or complex. Simple carbohydrates were the mono- and disaccharides. They were sweet and were quickly digested because of their simplicity. Complex carbohydrates were the polysaccharides. They were starchy and slowly digested because of their complexity. The rate of digestion was based on the theory that the longer the carbohydrate chain, the longer it would take to digest. Therefore, the very short single and double sugar mono- and disaccharides would raise blood sugar, and the very long chain starches would not. Even today you will sometimes hear starch described as time-release carbohydrate.

People didn't question this theory because it was based on so much common sense. And it made no sense wasting money to prove the obvious.

Understanding the Glycemic Index

Then in the 1980s, along came Dr. David Jenkins, of the University of Toronto, who changed forever how we think about carbohydrates. In his patients with diabetes, he observed that some complex carbohydrates actually increased blood sugar levels more than some simple sugars. Instead of assuming the answers to his questions, he tested them scientifically. His groundbreaking paper, "Glycemic Index of Foods: A Physiological Basis for Carbohydrate Exchange," appeared in March 1981. It was the first time researchers had measured how different carbohydrates affect blood sugar levels.

In Jenkins's study, healthy volunteers were given fifty grams of carbohydrate from a variety of carbohydrate-rich foods, and their blood sugar levels were measured two hours later. Foods were assigned a number, with 100 being white bread; today pure glucose is used. A few foods are higher than 100, but most rank below. A carbohydrate with a high **glycemic index (GI)** causes a spike in blood glucose levels. The carbohydrate in a low-GI food does not cause a large spike. There is evidence that healthy people can benefit from eating low on the GI scale.

Low GI = 55 and below
Medium GI = 56 to 69
High GI = 70 and above

Problems with the GI. A common misunderstanding is that the GI of a food ranks the food. For example, the early GI charts listed the GI of carrots as 92. A health professional most likely would understand the meaning of this number, but a layperson would simply assume that the GI of a raw carrot was indeed 92. But GI does not refer to the food but the carbohydrate in the food. Carrots do not have a GI of 92; the carbohydrate in carrots has a GI of 92. However, a single serving of carrots contains so little carbohydrate that its GI, no matter how high, is insignificant. When evaluating the GI of a food you must always keep in mind the amount of carbohydrate in question.

Since those early charts were first published, many of the measurements have been corrected, including the GI of carrots, which was found to be 41 and not 92. This puts carrots firmly in the low-GI category (55 or less) instead of the high (70 or more). However, you can still find those incorrect GIs quoted in articles and listed on websites.

This brings us to another problem consumers have with understanding the GI: not all samples of a given food are the same, even though they may look the same. The amount of carbohydrate in a fruit or vegetable differs by country, by variety, and by growing conditions. For example, raw carrots from Romania have a GI of only 16. The GI is not written in stone. There is no single value for a particular food—there can't be when you are referring to live food. Nature varies too much.

Consumers need to learn how to put information from the GI into perspective. The glycemic index cannot tell you if a food is good or bad for you. It is just one tool you need to make good food choices. There are other ways to evaluate the healthfulness of a food.

Research versus real world. The GI has not been enthusiastically embraced by the nutrition community. While researchers have found that it can help control blood sugar levels, nutritionists and dieticians who work with patients are less enthused. The problem with the glycemic ratings is that they can be difficult to use in the real world. Here are some examples:

- The GI measures each food separately, but we rarely eat foods this way—we eat them as mixtures, as parts of meals.
- The GI of a carbohydrate does not take other components of the food and meal, such as fiber and fat, into consideration. Both can decrease the speed with which food leaves the stomach, so that it is absorbed slowly and the glucose released from it increases in the blood slowly.
- The extent of processing influences a food's ranking in the GI, including how long a food is cooked and the size of the food particle or piece.
- Produce might look alike but have very different GIs. How long produce is stored and storage conditions, produce ripeness, and even a produce's species and variety affect the GI.

• Blood glucose response to a particular food is not
uniform. In populations it can vary from person to
person, and in individuals it can vary from day to
day and even hour to hour.

Understanding the Glycemic Load

A better indicator of the effect of a particular food on blood
sugar levels is the **glycemic load (GL)**—the amount of
carbohydrate multiplied by its GI. This measure was developed to make the results of the GI much more consumer
friendly. As with the new DRIs, the results are for a single-
serving size, so the GL is a much more accurate measure of
how blood sugar levels are affected by a specific food.

Low GL = 10 and below
Medium GL = 11 to 19
High GL = 20 and above

This fixes one problem, but there are others with both of
the glycemic rankings.

Factors affecting the glycemic measures. The GI/GL
appears to be determined by how fast the carbohydrates in
a food are broken down. The speed at which this happens
can be affected by many factors.

In order for digestion to occur, the digestive enzyme,
pancreatic amylase, must be able to touch the molecules.
Anything that delays enzyme and starch from interacting
decreases the GI/GL. Cooking changes starches so they
are easier for pancreatic amylase to reach. This increases

the rate of digestion and raises the GI/GL when compared with the raw form of the food.

A dense food matrix such as spaghetti makes it difficult for amylase to get at the carbohydrate molecules. This is why spaghetti has a low GL. However, when the matrix is softened by overcooking, amylase can get through the matrix to reach the starch, and the GL rises. This is why canned spaghetti has such a high GI when compared with spaghetti cooked al dente.

The type of starch affects GI/GL. Of the two forms of starch molecules, amylopectin is digested faster than amylose because it is branched, with more "ends" for amylase to reach. Foods with a high percentage of amylose starch, such as long-grained rice, are digested at a slower rate than foods with a high percentage of amylopectin starch.

Other components in a meal can affect the GI/GL of a starch. Both fat and fiber can affect how fast a starch is digested. For example, beta glucan is a type of fiber found in oatmeal. It reduces GI when added to a portion of carbohydrate.

It seems logical that sucrose, a disaccharide, and fructose would elevate blood glucose, since they require so little digestion. But fructose is taken up by the liver as it comes through the portal blood system, and sucrose is half fructose. Very little fructose enters the bloodstream. This is why many high-sugar foods have a lower GI/GL than long-chain starches.

Not only does the type of starch affect how fast a carbohydrate is digested, but other components in the meal affect it as well. For example, when a meal contains both fat and a starch such as potatoes, the fat substantially reduces how fast the meal is digested.

Diabetes and the Glycemic Measures. Information from the Nurse's Health Study II indicated that a high–GI diet was associated with an increased risk for developing diabetes. But once a person develops diabetes, is a low–GI diet still beneficial? Many researchers believe it is the amount of carbohydrate that is important when you have diabetes and not the kind. This is the theory behind carbohydrate counting.

People with diabetes do not handle carbohydrates the same way as healthy people. Under normal circumstances, when a carbohydrate is eaten, insulin is secreted, which stops glucose production. This is because with glucose coming in, the body does not need the extra sugar being made by the liver; it is best to save that sugar for when the body is hungry. But when a person with diabetes eats a carbohydrate, glucose production does not stop. Now the blood has two sources of sugar: sugar from the carbohydrate and sugar made by the liver. This is one reason why blood sugar levels are so high in people with diabetes. When you add in the effects of insulin resistance, which prevents glucose removal from the blood, any benefit from a low–GI/GL diet may be lost in the metabolic abnormalities.

The benefit of the glycemic ratings is that they can help a person predict the body's response to a food. Want to know how much your blood sugar is likely to rise when you eat a slice of whole wheat bread? Look it up in the index. Table 3.1 shows values of the glycemic index (GI) and glycemic load (GL) for a few common foods. Remember that GIs of 55 or below are considered low, and 70 or above are considered high. GLs of 10 or below are considered low, and 20 or above are considered high.

However, when you have diabetes and are testing your blood sugar frequently, you already know your body's

Table 3.1 Glycemic load and glycemic index
for common foods

FOOD	SERVING SIZE	GL	GI	NET CARBS
Peanuts	4 ounces	2	14	15
Bean sprouts	1 cup	1	25	4
Grapefruit	½ large	3	25	11
Pizza	2 slices	13	30	42
Low-fat yogurt	1 cup	16	33	47
Apples	1 medium	6	38	16
Spaghetti	1 cup	16	42	38
Carrots	1 large	2	47	5
Oranges	1 medium	6	48	12
Bananas	1 large	14	52	27
Potato chips	4 ounces	30	54	55
Snickers bar	1 bar	35	55	64
Brown rice	1 cup	23	55	42
Honey	1 tablespoon	9	55	17
Oatmeal	1 cup	12	58	21
Ice cream	1 cup	10	61	16
Macaroni & cheese	1 serving	30	64	
Raisins	1 small box	20	64	
White rice	1 cup	33	64	52
Sugar (sucrose)	1 tablespoon	8	68	12
White bread	1 slice	10	70	14
Watermelon	1 cup	8	72	11
Popcorn	2 cups	7	72	10
Baked potato	1 medium	28	85	33
Glucose	(50 grams)	50	100	50

response to a slice of whole wheat bread. You eat the bread, and after one hour and two hours you measure your blood sugar. Frequent blood sugar testing allows you to know how your individual biochemistry reacts to a particular food. No need to rely on charts and the effect of a food on someone else's body. You can construct your own glycemic index. That is why it is so important to keep a record of what you eat, along with your glucose levels. Learn which foods help to keep your blood sugar levels under control and which foods fuel your hunger. Then avoid the foods that cause your glucose and hunger levels to rise.

The low-GL diet is going to be rich in whole grains, fruits, and vegetables. A whole-foods diet rich in unrefined whole grains and minimally processed produce is going to be a low-GI/GL diet too. The end result is the same with both diets, so it is just a matter of how you want to approach it. We think the whole-foods diet is easier and in the end healthier. There are no charts to figure out, and if you were to limit yourself to foods that are low-GI/GL, you would miss a wide variety of foods that are rich in vitamins, minerals, phytochemicals, and dietary fiber, all of which protect health. Both the GI and the GL are tools to help users choose a healthy diet. The glycemic measures are a way to supplement the information available, not to replace it. You should not choose a diet based solely on its effect on blood sugar.

Caloric Intake

The purpose of the glycemic measures is to help you choose one food over another. When low-glycemic foods make up the largest part of the diet, glucose levels are easier for you to control. There is an easier way to manipulate carbohydrates that we have not yet explored: eat fewer of them. The fewer carbs you eat, the less sugar there is in the body. This is the purpose of the low-calorie diet. The chief problem with eating less is the hunger that accompanies it. Hunger can be easier to control when most of your food choices are high in volume.

Net Carbs

Net carbs is a concept created by the Dr. Atkins of low-carb fame in response to complaints from dieters who were suffering from the gastrointestinal side effects of not having enough fiber. Since fiber did not affect blood sugar, it could be subtracted from the total carbs. Now high-fiber foods could meet the definition of low-carb.

Total Carbohydrates − Dietary Fiber = Net Carb Count

Then manufacturers found that other ingredients also had a negligible or minimal impact on blood sugar levels, and these could also be subtracted from the total carb count. Now we had a new equation:

Total Carbohydrates − Dietary Fiber − Glycerin − Sugar Alcohols = Net Carb Count

Unfortunately, this equation does not quite add up. Soluble fiber is digested in the colon and the calories absorbed. Sugar alcohols are partly absorbed too. We think it is a marketing attempt to make a packaged food seem lower in carbs than it really is.

Satiety Index

You ate lunch just an hour ago, and already you want a snack. Why didn't lunch satisfy your hunger more, and what foods won't have you rummaging around in your fridge looking for more? From the same group of researchers who gave us the glycemic index comes the satiety index. The satiety index is a measure of how well a given food satisfies your hunger. There are many factors involved in satiety, appetite, and hunger regulation: adipokines, hormones, and neurotransmitters are just a few. Now we know that food selection also plays a role.

The satiety index is the baby of Susanna Holt, of the University of Sydney. She wanted to construct an index that would measure the ability of different foods to produce satiety and relieve hunger. The result was Holt's satiety index (Table 3.2). The satiety value of a food is rated relative to a slice of white bread, which again was given a value of 100. The higher the number, the greater the food's ability to satisfy. The experiment ran for only two hours, so it measured only short-term satiety, but the index is an important first step.

For this study, student volunteers were given 240 calories worth of various foods, including doughnuts, peanuts, jelly beans, and apples. They rated their hunger every fifteen minutes and were allowed to continue eating that same food but nothing else. Of course, 240 calories of a high-fat food is going to be a smaller mass than 240 calories of a high-carbohydrate or high-fiber food. Thus, students who ate the fruit were originally more satisfied because of the amount of food; but because fruit quickly leaves the stomach, they were hungry again by the end of the second hour.

Table 3.2 The satiety index*

BAKERY PRODUCTS	CARBOHYDRATE-RICH FOODS	SNACKS & CONFECTIONARY
Croissants: 47	French fries: 116	Peanuts: 84
Cake: 65	White pasta: 119	Yogurt: 88
Doughnuts: 68	Brown rice: 132	Crisps: 91
Cookies: 120	White rice: 138	Ice cream: 96
Crackers: 127	Grain bread: 154	Jelly beans: 118
	Brown pasta: 188	Popcorn: 154
	Potatoes: 323	

PROTEIN-RICH FOODS	BREAKFAST CEREALS W/MILK	FRUITS
Lentils: 133	Muesli: 100	Bananas: 118
Cheese: 146	Special K: 116	Grapes: 162
Eggs: 150	Cornflakes: 118	Apples: 197
Baked beans: 168	HoneySmacks: 132	Oranges: 202
Beef: 176	All-Bran: 151	
Ling fish: 225	Porridge/oatmeal: 209	

* All are compared with white bread, ranked as 100.

The results of the study included a few surprises. Foods high in fat made the volunteers hungrier, which was unexpected, since fat is usually thought to relieve hunger. Also, a food's GI did not predict the ability of the food to reduce hunger—a claim made by several authors of low-carbohydrate diet books. According to them, high-carbohydrate foods are supposed to stimulate the appetite, and low-GI foods are supposed to satisfy. This is why a low-GI diet is supposed to be best for weight loss. The fiber content of food did not predict satiety either, contrary to a claim made by another diet book. The large-volume characteristic of high-fiber foods was said to promote satiety and encourage weight loss.

Satiety is too complex a concept to be reduced to a single factor such as macronutrient content. It is affected by chemicals secreted by various glands and brain cells as well as food aroma, taste, texture, and appearance. All the senses are involved in satisfaction. No doubt our genes are mixed in there too: a diet that controls one person's appetite may have no effect on another's. You are unique, and your body's reactions to food are unique too.

The Well-Oiled Machine of Carbohydrate Metabolism

Your cellular machinery works in harmony in part because of the glands that direct and coordinate the daily activity of your seventy-five trillion cell-citizens. Your glands do this by sending chemical messages known as hormones. The activities these messages cause must be kept in balance so that there is not too much of this or too much of that. The glands handle this job by sending hormone messages that oppose one another. When an activity swings too much one way, an opposing message is sent to make it swing back the other way until the activity is balanced.

The hormone messages that control how energy is used are insulin and glucagon. Insulin is the hormone message that tells your cells to *use* glucose and *store* fat. Glucagon is the hormone message that tells your cells to *make* glucose and *burn* fat. The liver is the organ that manages changes in blood glucose; when levels are too high, it absorbs glucose, and when levels are too low, it releases glucose. Together the liver, insulin, and glucagon regulate how and when your body uses carbohydrates and fats.

When one of these glands or its hormones is damaged or becomes ineffective, the harmony of the body is disrupted, and the effect is felt in all the organs and systems in the body. The result is a group of diseases we call diabetes. Many other hormones are involved in the complex topic of carbohydrate metabolism, but these are the major ones you need to know so that you'll be better able to understand diabetes and your treatment plan.

To accomplish that goal, you must be armed with sufficient knowledge of normal carbohydrate metabolism and how it is possible to both decrease insulin demand and improve how your cells respond to insulin by controlling the kinds of foods you eat. This can help your body use the insulin it does produce more effectively.

Glucose: The Sun Trap

Just like you, your cells need to eat. They need fuel to burn for energy so that they can perform their jobs. You supply this energy to them in the food you eat, but ultimately all energy comes from the sun.

As you may remember from high school chemistry, plants can directly absorb energy from the sun's rays through their leaves. This is why plants have leaves—they are nature's solar panels. In a process called photosynthesis, the green pigment (chlorophyll) in plant cells uses the energy from the sunlight to make glucose ($C_6H_{12}O_6$) and oxygen (O_2) out of the carbon dioxide and water molecules. Through the magic of chemistry, the sunlight is now trapped inside the bonds of the glucose molecule. With the addition of nitrogen molecules from the soil, the plant can make protein molecules too. Fats are made and packed inside seeds to feed the seedling when it reaches new ground.

People and animals are different from plants; we aren't green and we don't have leaves. We could sit under the sun all day, and the ultraviolet radiation shining on our skin would at best make lots of vitamin D and at worst give us a bad sunburn. So, our cells must get their energy secondhand; we steal it from those clever plants. By eating their green leaves and roots, we can absorb the energy they have stored. Or we can get the energy thirdhand and eat animals that have eaten the green plants. In order for this to work, our meal must first be digested, absorbed, and metabolized.

Your Food-Processing Center

The purpose of your entire digestive system is to reverse the process of photosynthesis and liberate the energy locked within the glucose molecules. First, though, it must digest, or break down, the plant's components into small enough pieces to be absorbed.

Digestion begins in the mouth with the carbohydrate-digesting enzymes in your saliva. As you chew a piece of bread, you will notice that it starts out savory, but the longer you chew, the sweeter it becomes. The sugar molecules are being snapped off of the larger starch molecule by enzymes—hence the sweet taste. Enzymes are like pairs of disembodied hands, each pair designed to work with only one specific type of molecule or groups of molecules that complement that enzyme hand's unique shape. When a pair of enzyme hands finds its molecular match, it holds onto the molecule firmly and snaps it apart. Different digestive enzymes—all of which have names that end with "ase"—catalyze different types of macronutrients: proteases digest protein, lipases digest lipid or fat, and amylases digest carbohydrate.

Recall from Chapter 2 that your digestive system is basically a long tube with muscular walls. From the perspective of your cells, it functions like an assembly line. The cells remain stationary while the meal moves slowly through the tube in front of them. Some of the cells work in another department—in the pancreas, for example—and send the products they make down a chute (the common bile duct) that pours the product onto the assembly line as it moves by. Each type of cell does the same job over and over. The food is propelled along our assembly line by a series of wavelike muscle contractions called peristalsis. At each stop along the line, the chewed meal is subjected to some process until it reaches the end and exits, looking nothing like when it entered.

Metabolism After Meals

The glucose absorbed through the intestine immediately goes into the portal system, the blood vessels that connect the intestinal blood supply directly to the liver. The liver then has first crack at the glucose, absorbing up to two-thirds of it. After the liver filters out what it wants, the rest eventually enters circulation. As a meal is digested, the amount of blood glucose rises.

The purpose of glucose is to supply energy for your cells. However, glucose cannot pass through the membranes of all cells to provide that energy. It easily enters nerve and brain cells but not the cells of the muscles, fatty tissue, and liver. These tissues represent most of the mass of the body. When glucose reaches the membrane of one of these cells, it finds itself locked out.

In the meantime, glucose has also reached the islets of Langerhans in the pancreas. The surfaces of its beta cells are dotted with glucose transport molecules called **GLUT-2 (glucose transport) proteins**. Glucose latches onto the GLUT-2 transporters and is carried across the cell membrane. This triggers the beta cells to release their insulin. In a way, the GLUT-2 transporters act like a glucose meter.

Within seconds, insulin is in the blood, flooding muscle, fat, and liver cells with the keys that glucose needs to open the cell membrane. As explained in the first chapter, an insulin key will fit into one of the twenty thousand cell receptor locks that dot the cell surface, activating it and opening its doors. Transport molecules then escort the glucose into the cell. (For a more detailed explanation, refer to Chapter 1's description of the cell membrane.) Half of the insulin in the blood is gone in six minutes. All of it is cleared from the blood within fifteen minutes after release, with most of it going to muscle cells. Before breakfast, blood sugar levels are normally 80–90 mg/dl (milligrams per deciliter). During the first hour after the meal, that number rises to 120–140 mg/dl. Blood sugar is back to normal within two hours after the body last absorbed the carbohydrates in the meal.

Your Cellular Energy Banks

When the cells in your liver and muscles have more energy than they can use, they save it in a granule that is made of a many-branched molecule called glycogen. These glycogen granules are a sort of cellular piggy bank. The liver soaks up much of what comes to it through the portal system and stores it as glycogen. About three-quarters of a pound of glycogen is stored in the cells of your liver and muscles, enough to fuel your body for about fifteen hours.

But glycogen granules can hold only so much glucose. When you eat a high-carb meal that is easily and quickly digested, glucose floods through the bloodstream. An equally large surge of insulin quickly removes this glucose from the blood. It is far more than your cells can use or store as glycogen, and that excess must go somewhere. That somewhere is the fatty tissue that serves as the U.S. Bank of Jane or John Doe. When times are good and energy plenty, the banks will be overflowing with glucose stored as fat. This is not good for you, the bank owner. When the banks bulge with stored energy, so will you.

These banks were founded in long-ago times when the food supply swung from feast to famine. During famine times, the cells would withdraw all the fat to burn for energy. Today, with a high-calorie food supply available year-round and with no times of famine, the banks just keep on filling with fat. Your cellular banks were first filled before you were born. The last few weeks inside Mom, you grew fat cells and filled them.

To retrieve the saved glucose, the cell need only use an enzyme, which it thoughtfully stored with the glycogen, to snap off as many glucose molecules as it needs. Then, when insulin levels fall and no glucose is available from the blood, the cell turns to its glycogen piggy bank and snaps away on all the ends of the branched molecule. If you are walking, there is only enough glucose in your blood to keep your cells supplied with energy for fifteen minutes, so your cells need these banks. Muscle cells cannot share the glucose they have stored with other cells. Once glucose enters a muscle cell, it is chemically changed, so it cannot leave. At some point it must be burned as fuel.

The liver is different. It soaks up glucose and then doles it out later when needed. This helps to keep the body provided with fuel between meals. It also keeps a base level of glucose always available for the brain and nerves, which are totally dependent on glucose.

After a meal has been digested and all the glucose has been removed, the low blood sugar levels cause the alpha cells in the pancreas to release its hormone—glucagon. Because glucagon is like the anti-insulin, it wants to get blood glucose levels up. It tells cells to use the glucose they had just saved as glycogen and tells the liver to release some of its sugar. Fat cells get the message to release some of their fatty acids too. When you go to bed at the end of the day, your body continues to burn glycogen and then fat all night. If you skip breakfast the following morning, your cells consider becoming cannibals and eating protein tissue.

This is why women who are pregnant must eat a good breakfast. Baby has not been fed all night either and needs the calories for a busy day of growing.

To summarize the role of insulin in carbohydrate metabolism:

- It lets your liver cells know that since glucose is plentiful, no extra is needed: *please stop making more, and don't release what you have stored.* It does this by stopping glucagon release.

- It lowers blood glucose levels. It tells your muscle, liver, and fat cells (which make up the bulk of your body) that glucose is plentiful and enables them to absorb it.
- It tells the muscle, liver, and fat cells to burn all the glucose they can and store what they can't. Muscle will store the extra as glycogen, fat cells will store the excess as fat, and liver cells will store the extra as glycogen and make fatty acids.
- It tells the liver to convert excess glucose into amino acids and tells the muscle cells to make more protein.
- It prevents the muscle and liver cells from partaking when the particle that distributes triglycerides (fats) to cells comes around. This leaves more triglycerides for when the particle reaches the ever-hungry fat cells, and they get fatter.

The Diabetic Wrench in Carbohydrate Metabolism

As you can see, the body works like a well-oiled machine with regard to energy production. Each organ knows its role, and each cell in each organ likewise knows its role. However, sometimes a wrench gets stuck in the works. For one reason or another, the beta cells in the pancreas do not make enough insulin, and the result is diabetes. With type 1 diabetes, the beta cells are destroyed and thus secrete no insulin. With type 2 diabetes, there are two problems: the pancreas secretes progressively less insulin, and the insulin produced does not work as well as it should, a condition called insulin resistance.

Insulin Resistance

Sometimes there is a small glitch in the system, a warning of things to come. The beta cells secrete insulin, but many of the twenty thousand or so insulin receptors on muscle, fat, and liver cells resist insulin's action. Either the insulin keys cannot activate these receptor locks or the insulin works and the doors open but there are no transporter proteins (GLUT-2) to bring it in. As a result, glucose levels remain high and the beta cells secrete still more insulin, thinking that more glucose has arrived from the gut. Now both insulin and glucose levels are high, conditions called **hyperinsulinemia** and **hyperglycemia**.

However, not all the receptors are broken, and when insulin levels are high enough for the keys to find working receptor locks among the thousands that dot the membrane, glucose goes into the cells, and the level of glucose finally falls, followed by the level of insulin. The poor beta cells in the pancreas can take a break until the next meal arrives. In the liver the results are a bit different. You will remember that the liver absorbs and stores glucose after a meal so that it can release it as needed between meals. This keeps blood glucose levels even. Normally, the falling insulin level tells the liver cells to stop releasing glucose they have made into the blood. When insulin levels remain high, liver cells release glucose; the result is that less glucose is stored and more remains in the blood, contributing to the high glucose levels too. Insulin resistance is sometimes called prediabetes because it can progress on to diabetes.

Researchers believe that the high levels of glucose produced by insulin resistance are glucotoxic—high enough to kill some of the beta cells. Or the pancreas "wears out" in some manner from producing so much insulin.

Causes of Insulin Resistance

What causes insulin resistance? This is an exciting area of research with a number of theories, but no one knows the cause just yet. One theory involves glycogen. Normally, after glucose is absorbed cells turn it into glycogen for storage. The first step is to change glucose into glucose 6 phosphate (G6P), a molecule that cannot leave the cell. This step serves to lock the glucose molecules inside so they cannot leave and be used elsewhere and requires an enzyme called hexokinase The next step is to change G6P into glycogen. The reaction looks like this:

Glucose + Hexokinase → G6P → Glycogen

Studies have found high glucose levels inside fat and muscle cells in insulin-resistant patients, and researchers believe these cells are not able to convert glucose into glycogen. The reaction is blocked before it can reach that point. As a result, glucose builds up inside the cell, causing it to resist allowing any more to enter.

There are other defects in the liver. Researchers recently discovered that knocking out a single gene in mice can disrupt insulin production. The gene contains instructions for an enzyme called GnT-4a, which, among other things, keeps the glucose transporters on the surface of beta cells. When the body lacks enough GnT-4a, the GLUT-2 transporter misses a part needed to keep it on the cell surface. As a result, the GLUT-2 transporters sink into the cell, where the glucose molecules cannot reach them, and the beta cells are not triggered to produce insulin. In addition, inherited differences in the gene for GnT-4a may affect variations in susceptibility to type 2 diabetes.

Obesity and Insulin Resistance

Obesity—particularly abdominal obesity—is closely related to insulin resistance. Overweight people have fewer glucose receptors on their muscle, fat, and liver cells—five thousand versus twenty thousand in the healthy person. Weight loss and exercise are known to increase the number of glucose receptors. But which comes first? Does gaining weight cause insulin resistance, or does insulin resistance cause gaining weight?

A recent study found that insulin resistance first appears ten to twenty years before the diagnosis of diabetes. These researchers studied the children of diabetics and how their muscles responded to insulin. Some of the children were still young and lean. In the control subjects insulin increased the amount of energy produced by the muscles (as they burned glucose for fuel) by 90 percent. But the insulin had very little effect on energy production of the insulin-resistant children.

Researchers also examined how insulin affected the amount of phosphate in both groups. Phosphate is a mineral involved in energy production. In the control subjects insulin caused an increase of phosphate in the muscle cells, and this was reduced in the insulin-resistant subjects too. These results have significance for the insulin-resistant individuals. Starting at an early age they appear to require fewer calories for basic body functions. It is important that any children who are at risk for having diabetes get involved in an exercise program they like and will follow. It should include both resistance training (such as lifting weights), aerobic exercise, and an active lifestyle. They must also follow a low-saturated-fat diet that is also low in calories to prevent weight gain. Unless they eat less and exercise more they will become overweight, insulin resistant, and then diabetic.

Gestational Diabetes

Insulin resistance is normal during the last few months of pregnancy. The extra glucose produced is then used by the baby for the growth spurt it has at this time. Seventy percent of the baby's eventual weight is gained during the final two months of gestation. However, too much of a good thing can be a problem. If the mother is also producing low levels of insulin, glucose levels can become too high. Insulin resistance that happens during pregnancy is called gestational diabetes. If the mother is not treated and her glucose levels remain high, the baby grows fat on the sugar. The result is an infant who might be too large to deliver normally. After delivery the mother's glucose level returns to normal but her low insulin levels put her at risk for developing type 2 diabetes. For more information, see Chapter 10, "Gestational Diabetes."

Type 2 Diabetes

All types of diabetes have one thing in common: all cause elevated glucose levels. In type 2 diabetes there are two major defects: insulin resistance and the progressive decrease of insulin production. By the time most patients are diagnosed with type 2 diabetes, they have already lost 50 percent of their beta cells.

Initially, the pancreas is able to keep up with the elevated glucose levels by secreting more insulin. But the pancreas can't keep up with this, and eventually not all of the glucose can be removed from the blood, causing hyperglycemia. At first the hyperglycemia shows up after a meal (postprandial) because that is when the greatest concentration of glucose enters the blood. As insulin production falls, it can no longer prevent the liver from making glucose, something that the liver is only supposed to do between meals. This adds to the glucose already in the blood. Now hyperglycemia shows up on fasting blood-glucose tests done the morning after fasting all night.

The kidneys normally filter the blood, removing glucose so the energy is not lost in the urine. However, when glucose rises to the levels found in diabetes, the kidneys cannot keep up, and some of the glucose is lost to the urine, where it can be detected by a urine test. This gives the urine a sweet taste. In fact, ancients diagnosed diabetes by tasting the urine from prospective diabetics. The classic symptoms of diabetes include increased thirst, increased urination, and increased fatigue. Type 2 diabetes is more common in several minority groups; its highest rates are among Native Americans, and higher-than-normal rates also are found among African Americans and Hispanics. It occurs more frequently in women than in men.

Type 1 Diabetes

Type 1 diabetes, which typically occurs during childhood, is an autoimmune disease that attacks the beta cells of the pancreas. Even though the alpha cells coexist side by side with the beta cells in the pancreas, only the beta cells are killed by the immune system; the glucagon-producing alpha cells are left untouched. Beta-cell death is quick in type 1 diabetes compared with the gradual loss of beta cells in type 2 diabetes.

Once the beta cells are dead, muscle, liver, and fat cells find themselves surrounded by glucose but are unable to absorb any of it. Glucose levels remain high, causing some to spill out into the urine. With no glucose for food, the body quickly goes into a catabolic state, in which tissue is broken down for energy. It starts to make glucose and burn fatty acids for fuel. The fatty acids are mobilized from the fat banks, and cells can feed upon them for as long as they last, which is not long since most new diabetes cases are children.

When fatty acids are burned they produce waste products called **ketone** bodies. Burning too many fats and not enough carbs causes these ketones to build up in the blood. They are excreted from the body through the urine and also by way of the lungs, which produces the trademark fruity or acetone odor in the breath of people on low-carbohydrate diets. When ketone levels get too high they can throw off the acid/base balance of the blood, making it more acidic producing—a dangerous condition called **ketoacidosis**.

Before the discovery of insulin in 1921, everyone with type 1 diabetes died within a few years of diagnosis. Today a person with type 1 diabetes needs insulin injections to survive. With today's immediate-acting insulins and accurate glucose detectors, people can act as their own surrogate pancreas, sensing how much glucose is in the blood by testing their blood sugar often. When glucose levels are high after a meal, diabetics can inject themselves with as much insulin as the cells need to open the membrane doors and allow glucose to enter.

Tests for Diabetes

The fasting blood-glucose test is now the preferred way to diagnose diabetes. After the person has fasted overnight (at least eight hours), a sample of blood is drawn and sent to the lab.

- Normal fasting plasma glucose levels are less than 100 milligrams per deciliter (mg/dl).
- Fasting plasma glucose levels of more than 126 mg/dl on two or more tests on different days indicate diabetes.
- When fasting, a blood glucose stays above 100 mg/dl but in the range of 100–126 mg/dl—this is known as impaired fasting glucose (IFG).

Long-term blood-sugar control can be measured by the **glycosylated hemoglobin Alc**, or **HbAlc**, test. Its results are not affected by short-term changes. The HbAlc test measures the amount of sugar stuck to hemoglobin molecules in red blood cells. Because red blood cells normally live for 120 days, this test gives your doctor the overall condition of your glucose control. The American Diabetes Association recommends levels below 7 percent. The International Diabetes Federation and American College of Endocrinology recommends values below 6.5 percent. There is research that suggests that macrovascular disease risk decreases by about 24 percent that every 1 percent reduction in HbAlc values. The HbAlc test should be done every three to six months, depending on your treatment plan.

The gold standard for making the diagnosis of type 2 diabetes is the **oral glucose tolerance test** (OGTT); however, it is now only used to diagnose gestational diabetes. After a person fasts overnight (eight to sixteen hours), blood is drawn to determine the fasting plasma glucose level. Then the patient is given a drink containing seventy five grams of glucose (one hundred grams for pregnant women), and blood samples are drawn at specific intervals to measure blood glucose. The OGTT may lead to one of the following diagnoses:

- Normal response—the 2-hour glucose level is less than 140 mg/dl, and all values between 0 and 2 hours are less than 200 mg/dl
- Impaired glucose tolerance—the fasting plasma glucose is less than 126 mg/dl, and the 2-hour glucose level is between 140 and 199 mg/dl
- Diabetes—two diagnostic tests done on different days show that the blood glucose level is high
- Gestational diabetes—any two of the following on a 100 g OGTT: a fasting plasma glucose of more than 95 mg/dl, a one-hour glucose level of more than 180 mg/dl, a two-hour glucose level of more than 155 mg/dl, or a three-hour glucose level of more than 140 mg/dl.

4

Fats, Fatty Acids, and Diabetes

This is an especially important chapter—75 percent of people with diabetes die of cardiovascular disease. It starts with just enough biochemistry to help you understand the language of fat and protein digestion and metabolism. This is the terminology that is used by your doctor, listed on blood test results, and thrown around by the media. You also need to understand these terms in order to follow your nutritionist's diet prescription.

Heart disease is the leading cause of diabetes-related deaths and hospitalizations. Adults with diabetes have heart disease death rates that are two to four times higher than those without diabetes, and the risk of stroke is four times higher. If you have diabetes, you are at high risk for blockages in the arteries that feed the heart (coronary heart disease), hemorrhages in the brain (stroke), disease in the arteries of the arms and legs (peripheral arterial disease), and an enlarged heart (cardiomyopathy). Men are also at risk for erectile dysfunction.

Thus, it is imperative for people with diabetes to reduce their chances of getting heart disease. By changing your diet as needed and frequently monitoring your glucose level, you can be among the 25 percent who live a longer life. But first you must understand the enemy, and how your diet and the balance of fats and proteins can affect it.

What Is a Fat?

The words *fats*, *oils*, and *lipids* are used interchangeably for the same nutrient. Technically, fats and oils (which are liquid fats) are part of a group of substances called **lipids**. In a general sense, lipids are organic (carbon-containing) substances that will not dissolve in water. This diverse class of nutrients includes **fatty acids** (the building blocks of fats); **triglycerides** (the form that fat takes in food and in your body); **phospholipids** (phosphate-containing lipids); **lipoproteins** (protein-containing lipids); **glycolipids** (carbohydrate-containing lipids); **sulpholipids** (sulfur-containing lipids); fat-related compounds such as the fat-soluble vitamins A, D, E, and K; coenzyme Q10; sterols such as cholesterol; and certain phytonutrients found in foods, such as the orange and red carotene pigments.

All fats contain the same number of calories, but not all fats are created equal. Some fats are health promoting, some are neutral, and some are damaging. Sometimes it is not the type of fats eaten that causes a problem, but the amount. To help you to distinguish between healthful fats and those that may promote cardiovascular blockages and other diabetic complications, a bit of biochemistry is in order.

The Function of Lipids

Although people have a tendency to consider lipids bad, these nutrients are necessary for human life. They perform several vital functions:

- Fats are the most concentrated form of energy. They provide nine calories for every gram burned, which is more than twice the amount of energy per gram of carbohydrate.
- Adipose (fat) tissue holds organs in place, and the subcutaneous (below the skin) layer of fat provides insulation from the cold and helps maintain body temperature.
- Fat spares the B vitamin thiamine. Thiamine is required when carbohydrates are used for energy.
- Fat spares protein. When fat is present, the body does not have to burn protein for fuel.
- Fat helps in the absorption and transport of the fat-soluble vitamins A, D, E, and K.
- Lipids slow the rate at which foods leave the stomach. This means that the carbohydrate that is also present is not released all at once, keeping insulin and blood sugar levels even.

- Lipids provide the building blocks from which sterols, prostaglandins, thromboxanes, prostacyclins, and cell membranes are made.
- Fat makes foods more palatable.

Fatty Acids

The basic building block of lipids is the fatty acid (Figure 4.1), much as the basic building block of the carbohydrate is glucose. The foundation of the fatty acid is a simple chain of carbon atoms. Each carbon atom has four arms with which to "hold hands," or bond. Carbon atoms are very friendly and need to have some other molecule to hold on to all the time.

When carbon atoms form chains as they do in fatty acids, the carbon atom in a chain can hold either hand of the carbon next to it (single bond) if it is on the end, two hands (double bond), or three hands (triple bond). If a carbon atom finds itself with a free hand, it quickly grabs on to one of the plentiful hydrogen atoms that are always available. In the last chapter, simple carbohydrates were described as one or two rings of carbon atoms, while

Figure 4.1 Composition of a fatty acid

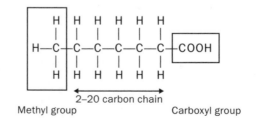

digestible and nondigestible starches are chains of sugar rings. Fats are less complicated; they are simple chains.

There are three types of fatty acids in foods: saturated, polyunsaturated, and monounsaturated. No food is made up of a single fatty acid; all foods contain different combinations of two or three. For example, you may think butter contains only saturated fat, but the reality is that almost a third (32 percent) of its fatty acids are monounsaturated. The remaining fatty acids are saturated (65 percent) and polyunsaturated fatty acid (3 percent). In food and in the body, fat exists in the form of triglycerides, a molecule with one fatty acid hanging on each of the three rungs of a glycerol molecule. In addition to burning fatty acids for energy when glucose levels are low, the body uses the fatty acids you eat to make the membranes that form the skin of your cell-citizens and the lipoproteins that travel through your body, delivering fat molecules to cells. These membranes take on the properties of the fatty acids used to make them. If you want healthy membranes, you must furnish your body with healthful fats. Fatty acids can also travel through the blood as free fatty acids as long as they are attached to a protein molecule.

The fatty acids that are the building blocks of lipids can be classified according to how many hydrogen (H) atoms they hold (called the degree of saturation), the location of the first carbon atoms that hold two hands (a double bond), and the length of the carbon chain.

Saturated and Unsaturated Fatty Acids

When the carbon atoms in a fatty-acid chain all hold single hands, it is called a saturated fatty acid (SFA) (Figure 4.2).

Figure 4.2 Saturated fatty-acid chain

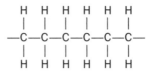

The term derives from the fact that all the free hands are saturated, or taken up with hydrogens. This is the "bad" fat you have been warned so much about. As you can see in the illustration, the chain of a saturated fatty acid is straight, making it easy for the molecules to be packed tightly together like stacks of folded chairs. This results in a solid fat at room temperature. A high level of SFAs in your diet means a high level of SFAs in the membrane skin of your cells too. A high percentage of SFAs makes your membranes rigid and less pliable.

Whereas the double bonds between carbon atoms found in polyunsaturated fats are vulnerable to attack from the oxygen in the air, SFAs have no double bonds that can be oxidized (made rancid), so fats that contain high percentages of them are very stable and resistant to oxidation. When heated, they do not form dangerous trans fats or free radicals. For deep-frying, SFA-rich fats are a safer choice than polyunsaturated-rich vegetable oils.

If saturated fats don't form oxidized fatty acids, then why do they have such a bad reputation? Beyond their effects on cell membranes, eating too many saturated fats can cause your liver to make cholesterol and increase your levels of serum cholesterol (**low-density lipoprotein, or LDL**). This will increase your chances of developing heart disease. It's also a matter of the company they keep: foods rich in saturated fats are also usually rich in cholesterol, and cholesterol is vulnerable to oxidation too. Moreover, saturated fats, for all their stability, are still fats and as such are concentrated sources of energy. In other words, too much fat will make you fat, and obesity is yet another risk factor for insulin sensitivity, diabetes, and heart disease.

Polyunsaturated Fats and Diabetes

When two carbon atoms next to each other hold two hands instead of one, it is said to be a double bond. *Poly* means "many," so a polyunsaturated fatty acid (PUFA) (Figure 4.3) is a fatty acid with many (two or more) double bonds. As you can see in the illustration, these double bonds make kinks in the otherwise straight carbon chain. This makes it difficult to stack the chains, just as it is difficult to stack folded chairs on top of a partially opened chair. The chains, like the folded chairs, fall around each other. As a result, fats that contain a high percentage of PUFAs are liquid at room temperature. They do not stack easily like the straight, saturated fats. The PUFAs you eat are also incorporated into the membranes of your cell-citizens, which keeps them fluid and pliable. They are usually found in plant foods.

Figure 4.3 Polyunsaturated fatty acid

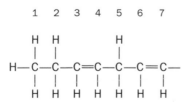

The double bonds in PUFAs are particularly attractive to oxygen molecules, so they are very vulnerable to attack from oxygen in the air. Reactive oxygen molecules attack the double bonds, changing them into single bonds by attaching one of themselves to the carbon chain. The addition of an oxygen molecule in this way is called **oxidation**, and the result is an oxidized PUFA, one of the types of fat most strongly implicated in atherosclerosis. Other types of free radicals can also break the double bonds. The PUFAs can become oxidized either outside of your body as the result of high-temperature food preparation, inside your body as the result of free radicals, or inside the arterial wall where a plaque lesion is developing.

In several experiments, researchers working with rabbits showed that the oxidized fat in the diet increased the amount of oxidized fat in the blood and increased how fast atherosclerosis developed. Researchers then tagged the oxidized fat before feeding it to the rabbits so that they could track where it went in the animal's body. After a year, the rabbits were sacrificed and researchers examined the fat that had accumulated in the animals' arterial walls. The very same oxidized fat fed to the rabbits had ended up in their arterial walls. This means that you could decrease your chances of getting heart disease by decreasing your intake of oxidized fats. To do this, avoid PUFAs that have been exposed to high levels of heat such as cooking oil and the foods cooked in the oil. Antioxidant nutrients— nutrients that help prevent oxidation—can protect PUFAs. Vitamin E is an antioxidant that helps prevent oxidation, and vitamin C works with vitamin E by recharging it so that the same vitamin E molecule can be used over and over.

Monounsaturated Fats and Diabetes

A fatty acid with one double bond is said to be a monoun-saturated fatty acid (MUFA) (Figure 4.4). Fats with a high percentage of MUFAs are the best oils to use to reduce heart disease. The main fatty acid in this group is **oleic acid**, an omega-9 fatty acid. The 9 refers to the double bond found at the ninth carbon atom (as explained under "Omega Number of Fatty Acids" in this section). Olive oil is the richest source of oleic acid, although almond and canola oil are also good choices.

Researchers believe that the low incidence of heart disease in the Mediterranean may be due to the population's high consumption of MUFAs. Some studies have found that oleic acid increases levels of **HDL (high-density lipoprotein)**, the good cholesterol. The jury is still out on their effectiveness in preventing heart disease, but since virgin olive oil is also rich in antioxidants, you should substitute some of these oils for PUFAs in your diet. MUFAs have been shown to lower cholesterol in general and decrease the production of all lipoproteins.

When PUFA-rich oils become oxidized, the addition of the oxygen atom causes changes in flavor and odor, and the oil is said to be rancid. In addition to their off flavors, rancid oils can be toxic in large doses. To prevent oxidation, the food industry developed a process called hydrogena-

Figure 4.4 Monounsaturated fatty acid

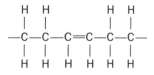

tion, in which all the double bonds in a PUFA are broken and the fatty-acid chain is saturated with hydrogens. Now there are no double bonds to be oxidized, and the product is more stable (Figure 4.5).

Hydrogenation and Trans-Fatty Acids

While stabilizing a fat may sound like a good idea, hydrogenation changes a healthful vegetable PUFA into a dangerous saturated fat. This process also destroys the essential fatty acids present in these oils (the essential fatty acids contain double bonds). Worse, hydrogenation also causes the formation of **trans–fatty acids**—a molecular configuration that does not occur in nature. Trans-fatty acids are notorious for increasing blood cholesterol levels. Hydrogenated oils are solid at room temperature. The greater the degree of saturation, the more solid a fat becomes. The hydrogenated fats that are most familiar to Americans are margarines and shortening. Tub margarines have a lower degree of saturation than those that come in sticks.

Omega Number of Fatty Acids

Another way of classifying fatty acids is by the location of the first double bond. This location is found by counting from the methyl end of the molecule. For example, in a polyunsaturated fatty acid, the first double bond is found on the third carbon (see Figure 4.3). Therefore, its omega number is 3. Oils rich in omega-3 fatty acids (in particular, fish oil) are often in the news these days.

The body can make all the fats it needs except for two—linolenic acid and linoleic acid, which the body must get from the diet. These are called the essential fatty acids, or EFAs. Linolenic acid is an omega-6 fatty acid (first bond at carbon 6), while linoleic acid is an omega-3 fatty acid. Each of these EFAs has a different pathway, producing chemicals that oppose one another. For health, you need to balance your EFAs.

The three important omega-3 fatty acids are **eicosapentaenoic acid (EPA)**, **docosahexaenoic acid (DHA)**, and **linolenic acid**. Both EPA and DHA can be manufactured by the body, but sometimes it may not produce all that it needs. EPA and DHA are the two oils that give fish their atherosclerosis-fighting power. The omega-3 fatty acids are also precursors for (i.e., used to make) **prostaglandins**, which are messenger molecules that enable the endothelial cells to "talk" to local tissues. The omega-3 fatty acids produce series 1 and 3 prostaglandins, which send "good" messages that tell your arteries to relax, reduce inflammation, and prevent blood clotting. Although the omega-3 fats are polyunsaturated and prone to oxidation, they provide other benefits that make them an important part of a heart-healthy diet.

The omega-6 fatty acids also have unique properties. They include linoleic acid, the other essential fatty acid;

Figure 4.5 Hydrogenation

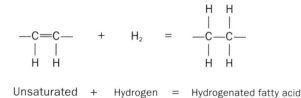

arachidonic acid, which is manufactured from linoleic acid; and gamma linolenic acid (GLA). **Arachidonic acid** opposes the effects of EPA and DHA: it promotes inflammation and encourages blood clotting and cellular growth. Inflammation is involved in obesity and both types of diabetes, as well as heart disease. It makes sense to reduce inflammation in your body as much as possible. Unfortunately, the typical Western diet that is high in meat and animal products is high in omega-6 fatty acid and low in omega-3 fatty acid. There needs to be a balance between the two. You can help by reducing your intake of animal products and increasing fish oil and vegetable oils.

Gamma linoleic acid is the good omega-6. It is not turned into arachidonic acid as linoleic acid is. GLA is manufactured as a result of the first step toward the production of another series of helpful prostaglandins. Not everyone manufactures enough GLA; those who don't can benefit from supplements.

Chain Length of Fatty Acids

Let's see how we would classify the molecule in Figure 4.6. It has three double bonds, so it is a polyunsaturated fatty acid. With eighteen carbon atoms, it is a long-chain fatty acid. Double bonds are at carbon numbers 3, 6, and 9, so its omega number is 3.

This fatty acid has a **cis** configuration—both the hydrogens on the double-bonded carbons are on the same side of the molecule. Cis and **trans** are descriptions of the arrangement of hydrogen atoms around the double bonds. The cis configuration is the one that occurs in nature.

Figure 4.6 Linolenic acid

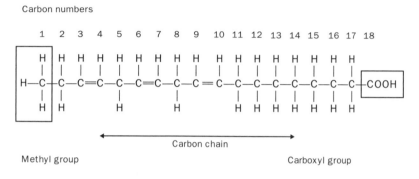

The shape of a molecule determines its function. Alter the shape, alter the function. Molecules that are trans versions do not have the same effect in the body as the natural, cis version. This has been demonstrated with trans-fatty acids found in margarines and spreads. They elevate cholesterol just as much as, if not more than, saturated fats. Now that manufacturers are required to put the amount of trans-fatty acids on their labels, many have reformulated their products to remove them.

Triglycerides

So far we have been talking about the building blocks of fats—fatty acids. Now it's time to assemble them into a fat. Triglyceride (Figure 4.7) is the chemical form in which most fat exists in food and in the body. You will notice that your blood test contains a value for triglyceride along with your cholesterol (LDL and HDL) levels. Its structure is simple: a glycerol molecule with three fatty acids hang-

Figure 4.7 Formation of a triglyceride

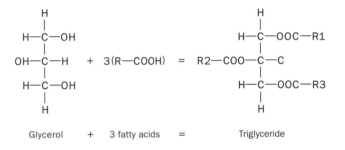

ing from it. The glycerol molecule has three rungs that act as hangers. One fatty acid hangs from each rung.

The body can do one of two things with triglycerides. If the body does not need energy, the triglycerides will be stored in white fat (adipose) cells as liquid. Between meals, when glucose levels are normally low, the body will burn the fatty acids they contain for energy. Burning this alternative fuel creates by-products called ketones or keto-acids. The healthy body is able to neutralize the acidity in the blood and excrete the ketone bodies. After meals, when glucose is available again, the body switches to burning glucose and making fat, and the production of ketones stops. Some types of cells can burn the ketones themselves to make energy.

Ketoacidosis and Diabetes

When fat is burned for too long, ketones are produced faster than they can be removed, and at a certain level, they spill out into the urine just like glucose. This is called **ketonuria**, and it can be detected with a simple home urine test. Diabetes can cause ketonuria, but it also occurs with diets that are very low in carbohydrates. This, of course, is the point of such a diet: to force the body to burn only fat. The ketones produced in this manner are acetone, beta hydroxybutyrate, and acetoacetate. Ketones can be excreted from the lungs; it is the acetone that gives breath in ketosis its characteristic fruity aroma. If you have been around anyone on a low-carbohydrate diet, you are probably familiar with the odor.

The situation is different in people with diabetes. **Ketosis** is a sign of uncontrolled high blood sugar and an indication that the person's diet and/or drug plan is no longer working. If not treated right away, ketosis can progress to a state of **ketoacidosis**. The body is already dehydrated from the high blood sugar—loss of sugar in the urine creates a loss of water too—and nausea and vomiting from the ketones makes the dehydration and loss of electrolytes worse. The water loss in patients with ketoacidosis totals about six liters. For more information on ketones and the danger of ketoacidosis, see Chapter 8.

Triglyceride Digestion

Triglyceride molecules are too large to pass through the intestinal wall without being digested. They are digested by enzymes called **lipases** (*lipo* = "fat"; *ase* = "enzyme"). Gastric lipase breaks apart triglycerides, and many of the freed short-and medium–chain fatty acids are absorbed before they have a chance to reach the small intestine. Unlike the long chains, these short and medium chains do not need to be reassembled into triglycerides after absorption. They easily dissolve into the blood and are carried via the portal vein to the liver. Because they bypass the slow-moving lymph system, they are absorbed as fast as glucose, making them an excellent source of energy for people who have damage to their intestinal villi due to malnutrition or who lack sufficient pancreatic enzymes. Much of the fat in milk is short-chain fatty acids; they are easy for immature digestive systems to absorb. Short-chain fatty acids are also produced in the colon by the friendly bacteria that live there.

The rest of the disassembled triglycerides are absorbed into the small intestinal wall and then reassembled on the other side into triglycerides. However, being fats, triglycerides and other fat-soluble substances cannot enter the portal system, because they cannot dissolve in the blood. Instead, intestinal cells package them into droplets called **chylomicrons** for shipment via the lymphatic system up the body, where they enter the bloodstream near the left shoulder blade. After a fat-rich meal, the chylomicrons are large enough to make plasma look "milky." They circulate in the blood and become a sort of "meals on wheels" particle, quickly seeking out the capillary beds with their millions and millions of hungry cells.

The cells use an enzyme, **lipoprotein lipase**, to unlock and distribute the triglycerides, phospholipids, and fat-soluble nutrients and antioxidants packaged in the chylomicrons. Cholesterol is unable to leave the particle, since none of the cells has the key to release it. Most cells don't need it anyway, because they can manufacture their own.

When insulin levels rise after a meal, it prevents most cells from being able to access triglycerides. The only cells allowed to remove triglycerides are the fat-storage cells.

This is how insulin encourages fat deposition. If insulin levels are high all the time, less fat reaches muscle and other tissue cells to be burned for energy. Much of it is stored in fat cells, making them even fatter.

This journey is complete within an hour, when most of the chylomicrons finally find their way to the liver, where your hepatic cell-citizens fish them out of the bloodstream. They are much smaller but still full of all the cholesterol packed into them by the enterocyte. The sacs are digested, and the cholesterol is finally freed. For now the liver puts it into storage.

LDL lipoproteins. Between meals, cells also get hungry, so the body has a mechanism for keeping food constantly available to them. It sends out another "meals on wheels" particle, the very low-density lipoprotein, or VLDL. From its name you can deduce that this particle must have more lipids in it than protein. The VLDL particle resembles a chylomicron in organization but is much smaller. Its protein identification tag is apo B-100, which is a single very large protein molecule.

The liver is able to manufacture a variety of VLDL particles in which density and size vary purely as a result of their triglyceride content. In healthy individuals with normal triglyceride levels, the liver produces a small VLDL particle. But as triglyceride levels increase, so does the VLDL size. Large VLDL particles are usually overproduced in people who are resistant to the hormone insulin. This includes those who are overweight or who have non-insulin-dependent diabetes. These same groups also have a large amount of small, dense LDL. The liver packs cholesterol into the sac along with the triglycerides and then releases them into the bloodstream. The VLDL is carried to the capillary beds, where it distributes triglycerides to hungry cells. As before, the cholesterol remains. Little by little, the triglyceride is drained from the sac, causing it to get smaller and denser.

Some of the VLDL particles eventually return to the liver, where hepatic cells check their identification tags and pull them out. About half continue to circulate through the bloodstream, and these are now called intermediate-density lipoproteins (IDL) or VLDL remnants. It is only twenty minutes from the time the VLDL particle was released from the liver to its return to the liver or transformation into IDL. Ultimately, no triglycerides are left in the IDL particles; only the cholesterol, phospholipid sac, and single large molecule of apo B-100 remain. This dense, small sac is now called a low-density lipoprotein (LDL) particle. This is the so-called bad cholesterol that is checked by your doctor.

An excess amount of triglycerides in the plasma has a tongue-twisting name, **hypertriglyceridemia**, a condition linked to atherosclerosis. Elevated triglycerides are often seen in people who have diabetes or who are insulin resistant. Like cholesterol, increases in triglyceride levels can be detected by plasma measurements. These measurements should be made after an overnight fast. For now, just remember that your triglycerides are composed of the fatty acids you eat. If your diet is full of oxidized fat, saturated fats, and cholesterol, then the triglycerides in your body are going to be full of oxidized fat, saturated fats, and cholesterol.

The same can be said of your LDL particles: if your antioxidant levels are low, so will be the levels in your

LDL particles. Then they will be vulnerable to attack from oxygen-free radicals and oxidized. This is important because before an LDL particle can penetrate the arterial wall and cause damage, it must be oxidized.

Now the particle is empty of triglycerides, and it is time to start distributing its cholesterol. The LDL particles continue to circulate in the capillaries until they come into contact with a cell bearing an apo B-100 receptor. The receptor recognizes the LDL's apo B-100 protein and latches on to it so that the cell can pull the entire LDL sac inside for dinner. It is digested and used to make new cell components. When one of your cell-citizens does not want cholesterol, it reduces its production of LDL receptors so that fewer LDL particles are absorbed. The LDL that is not removed by cell receptors circulates in the bloodstream until it again reaches the liver. Receptors on the hepatic cells recognize the LDL and fish it out. In the average person, 70 percent to 85 percent of the LDL is removed by the liver, with only 15 percent to 30 percent being removed by cells in the body. When many of the LDL particles return to the liver, the liver recognizes that less cholesterol is needed, and it decreases its manufacture. In this manner, the cells of the body are able to tell the liver how much cholesterol is needed.

There are several variants of the LDL particle. The particles can become oxidized, producing a type called **minimally modified LDL (mmLDL)**. The second type is small, dense LDL. This smaller version is associated with high levels of triglycerides and an inability of the body to use the hormone insulin. Treatments that reduce triglyceride levels also increase LDL size. Small dense LDL is more easily oxidized than normal LDL and binds less easily

Storage of Lipids

If you eat an extra 500 calories a day, it will add up to 3,500 extra calories a week. Your body will change that extra glucose into one pound of fat and deposit it in an adipose tissue bank for a rainy day.

Where your fat is stored is important. Years ago, researchers came to the understanding that it was the fat around the waist that was dangerous and not the fat on the buttocks, arms, and thighs. Fat around the waist corresponded to the bad, apple shape, while fat around the hips related to the good, pear shape. But now scientists have refined their recommendations. While the fat on the abdomen of all those apples is risky, it is not as risky as the fat deep in the gut, called visceral fat. Even a little extra fat in the wrong place increases your risk for developing a number of diseases.

One way to get rid of that visceral fat is through exercise. Researchers have shown that obese members of both sexes benefit from exercise. So, if you are an apple, get moving!

to the LDL receptors responsible for removing LDL particles from the bloodstream. This increases the time that small dense LDL remains in circulation, perhaps giving it more of an opportunity to interact with and infiltrate the endothelial cells. The rate at which LDL particles cross the endothelium and enter the subendothelial space is related to their size. Small dense LDL will cross at a faster rate than either large LDL, IDL, or VLDL.

HDL lipoproteins. High-density lipoprotein is commonly referred to as the "good" or "happy" cholesterol, since it is responsible for transporting excess cholesterol back to the liver for storage or elimination. About one-third to one-fourth of blood cholesterol is carried by HDL.

HDL is the recycling truck of the lipoprotein world. It goes from cell to cell looking for excess cholesterol that can be returned to the liver so that more will not have to be manufactured. The transfer of cholesterol is accomplished through cell receptors. Cells display a receptor that HDL particles recognize and can latch on to. The contact between receptor and particle sends a chemical messenger to the interior of the cell, which returns with excess cholesterol. This is then fed into the flat HDL sac. As the sac distends, it breaks contact with the receptor, and the particle is free to leave. We talk more about HDL and LDL in Chapter 11.

5

Vitamins and Diabetes

Vitamins, minerals, and trace minerals are called micro-nutrients because they are required only in small amounts compared with the macronutrients (carbohydrates, proteins, fat, and water). They are essential components in enzymes and coenzymes. This chapter spotlights vitamins, their relationship to blood sugar metabolism and control, and ways they can affect treatment and prevention of diabetic complications.

This chapter is not about treatments or cures. It is about education. Currently, very few micronutrients can be recommended as treatments for diabetes. While many small and/or short-duration studies have investigated the effects of various micronutrients, often the results have been contradictory. Thus, these studies do not suggest a treatment; they suggest the need for larger studies.

However, most of us don't want to wait for the larger studies to be done. A few positive studies are all we need to want to do a study of one on ourselves. You should already be taking all the nutrients presented in this chapter, either through food or through supplements. Unfortunately, you probably are not. If a result for a particular nutrient sounds interesting to you but is based on megadoses, check with your doctor before taking it. Consult your pharmacist too regarding possible drug interactions.

As you read, keep in mind that the suggestions offered are just that. You may come across a study tomorrow that contradicts something mentioned here—and then another study contradicting that one the following month. Before larger studies are undertaken, completed, and published, this process will have repeated itself many times. This back-and-forth motion is the nature of scientific inquiry—but it drives some people crazy.

Dietary Reference Intake

In 1994 the Food and Nutrition Board of the Institute of Medicine replaced the old recommended dietary allowance, or RDA, with the new DRI, which stands for dietary reference intake. The levels of some nutrients in the DRI are higher than in the RDA. This represents a shift from recommendations based on preventing deficiency diseases to recommendations based on preventing chronic diseases.

DRIs are composed of four values: the RDA, the Adequate Intake (AI), the Estimated Average Requirement (EAR), and the Tolerable Upper Intake Level (UL). The RDA is the nutrient level thought to meet the needs of most healthy individuals. When there is not enough scientific evidence to establish an RDA, the AI is used. The EAR is the level of nutrient intake believed to meet the requirements of half the healthy individuals in a given age group, and sex and is used to determine the chance of a deficiency in that nutrient. The UL is the greatest level of nutrient intake for which no adverse side effects have been noted. You can read the full text of all the DRI documents without charge from the National Academy Press Website, www.nap.edu.

When considering the DRI, remember the following parameters:

- The *D* in DRI stands for "dietary"—not "daily." You do not need to eat the DRI for each nutrient each day.
- The *R* stands for "reference"—not "recommended." The values are meant as guidelines, not requirements.
- The DRIs are guidelines for populations, not individuals.
- The DRIs are also guidelines for healthy populations and not those with a chronic disease such as diabetes, who may need additional amounts.

For example, the DRI for niacin is 16 mg (milligrams), but that does not mean that your body needs 16 mg of niacin every day; even the water-soluble vitamins have short-term stores. It also does not mean that the government is recommending that you, a person with high cholesterol, get 16 mg of niacin. It does means that a healthy *population* should be getting 16 mg of niacin a day. The DRIs, just like the RDAs, were designed to be used by nutrition professionals, not laypersons, but you can expect to read and hear about them as they become more commonly used. Understand what they are so you will recognize when they are abused.

Vitamins

When nutrition was a young science, researchers found that a synthetic diet of carbohydrate, lipids, proteins, water, and minerals was not enough to allow animals to grow and thrive. This led to the discovery of a group of unrelated carbon-containing compounds called vitamins. Human growth and development requires thirteen vitamins.

In 1994, the FDA replaced the old US RDAs (Recommended *Daily* Allowance) that were used on food labels with the Daily Values or DVs. The US Recommended *Daily* Allowance was a simplification of the RDA (Recommended *Dietary* Allowance) which was a set of guidelines by sex and age. The DVs are made up of two sets of references: the RDIs (Reference Daily Intake) and the DRVs (Daily Reference Values) for nutrients not covered by the RDIs (fat, saturated fat, cholesterol, carbohydrate, protein, fiber, sodium, and potassium). The RDIs are not meant to be recommendations but reference points so consumers can compare one food with another.

A single guideline given for a food is usually the Reference Daily Intake (RDI), while a set of guidelines by sex and age are the Dietary Reference Intakes (DRIs). The RDIs were developed for food labels, but they are used elsewhere and often confused with the DRIs. The similarity of the two names does not help. Both the RDI and DRI are reference points, not goals.

The word *vitamin* was coined in 1912 by biochemist Casimir Funk, whose research of deficiency diseases led to the discovery of vitamins. Originally, vitamins were recognized only for their ability to prevent deficiency diseases. For example, vitamin C (ascorbic acid) was discovered because of its ability to cure scurvy, and vitamin

B$_1$ (thiamine) cured beriberi. With time, this definition has proved too narrow. Vitamins are now known to serve many functions in the body besides preventing specific deficiency diseases. For example, many vitamins are also potent antioxidants, and some enhance absorption of other vitamins or minerals.

Role of Vitamins

Vitamins are essential to life. They regulate metabolism and assist in biochemical processes such as energy release from food in your digestive system. They are the coenzymes that activate the enzymatic pathways necessary for all bodily functions. Besides being needed for general health and well-being, vitamins can have an effect on diabetes by reducing the risk of hypertension and atherosclerosis, minimizing the side effects of diabetes medications, reducing the oxidative load caused by diabetes, and enhancing the body's ability to handle carbohydrates.

Your cell-citizens obtain vitamins in three ways:

- They can absorb vitamins from foods in the digestive tract.
- Some bacteria in the colon produce vitamins (such as vitamin K), and these can also be absorbed.
- The body is able to manufacture some vitamins, such as vitamin D.

Vitamins do not provide energy or contribute to cell mass. They prefer to be "the molecules behind the nutrients," so to speak—helper elements that enable other nutrients from the sidelines.

We tend to think of each vitamin as a single molecule, but nature is rarely that simple. Each vitamin is actually a family of related compounds, including those that are one step away from being the vitamin but are not quite there yet and forms that are bound to another molecule so that it can move through the body. Some substances, such as choline, carnitine, inositol, taurine, and pyrroloquinoline quinone, have vitamin-like properties and may be required at particular stages of growth. For classification purposes, vitamins are divided into two groups: those that dissolve in water and those that dissolve in fat.

Vitamin Deficiencies

Diabetes is not associated with any specific nutritional deficiency, and the American Diabetes Association does not recommend any particular supplement for diabetes patients. However, diabetes symptoms (high blood sugar, increased urination, and nerve damage to the GI tract), diseases associated with diabetes (heart disease, kidney disease, osteoporosis, and high blood pressure), side effects of the drugs used to treat them, and nutrient-deficient diets (for weight loss or from illness and/or refined, overly processed foods) all conspire to put the patient with diabetes at risk of developing nutrient deficiencies. Patients with diabetes who have had bariatric surgery are at greatest risk. They must commit to taking a quality multivitamin-mineral supplement daily to protect against the nutrient deficiencies so common with these procedures.

Nutrient deficiency diseases are rare in the United States. However, research has shown that even subclinical deficiencies can put a person at risk of developing a chronic disorder such as cardiovascular disease, high blood pressure, or osteoporosis.

What Vitamins Can and Can't Do

As we stated in the introduction to this chapter, there is considerable research on the use of vitamins in the treatment of diabetes, but there is not enough to prove that any one vitamin or mineral has a specific action. However, there is evidence that some nutrients can help your body return to health, and they do not need to be taken in large amounts.

These days, it can be difficult to get all the needed vitamins and minerals from food alone—as the many diet histories taken by both of the authors attest. So, we recommend that you fortify yourself with a comprehensive vitamin, mineral, and antioxidant supplement. Never take a single vitamin by itself unless you are told to do so by a knowledgeable physician; vitamins often depend on each other to be effective. A vitamin can also have a different effect when removed from its natural habitat in a food, and large doses of one vitamin can upset the balance of nutrients.

Water-Soluble Vitamins

Vitamins that can dissolve in water are called water soluble. The water-soluble nutrients include **thiamine (B_1), ribo-**

flavin (B$_2$), niacin (B$_3$), pantothenic acid (B$_5$), pyridoxine (B$_6$), cobalamin (B$_{12}$), folic acid, biotin, and vitamin C. Different vitamins are absorbed in different places along the small intestine and enter the portal blood system that connects the blood vessels of the digestive tract to those of the liver. This gives the liver first chance at them. None of your organs can store water-soluble nutrients for long periods of time like the fat-soluble, but they can be stored for the short term. You do not need to eat sources daily, but to keep optimal levels of these vitamins in circulation you do need to eat them frequently.

Thiamine (B$_1$), riboflavin (B$_2$), niacin (B$_3$), and pantothenic acid (B$_5$) are all involved in energy production through the citric acid cycle. As you read through these pages, notice how interconnected these vitamins are—they are needed for each other's absorption or are necessary for each other's activation. The **citric acid cycle** (also called the **Krebs cycle**) is a series of reactions, or steps, that releases the energy that is stored in the glucose bonds. Each reaction is made possible by a protein called an enzyme. Its job is to bring two molecules together and hold them there until they react and produce a third molecule. The enzyme then separates and floats off to find two more molecules. This makes an enzyme a kind of matchmaker for molecules. It also acts as a divorce lawyer by attaching itself to a molecule and making it into two separate molecules. Enzymes specialize in marrying and separating certain kinds of molecules.

For example, in some of the steps of the Krebs cycle, enzymes bring two molecules together and, as they react, two hydrogens (or electrons) are removed. The enzyme then hands these electrons over to a cofactor called **FAD** (**flavin adenine dinucleotide**), making it **FADH**, or to **NAD** (**nicotinamide adenine dinucleotide**) making it **NADH**. The flavin part of FAD is from the vitamin riboflavin, and nicotinamide, part of NAD, is from the vitamin niacin. The FADH and NADH carry these electrons to the electron transport chain in the inner membrane of the mitochondria, and energy is released. Without riboflavin and niacin to carry these electrons, energy is lost. These two cofactors are involved in many reactions, not just the Krebs cycle, so the body is thrown off balance when not enough is available.

Folate, pyridoxine (B_6), and cobalamin (B_{12}) are all involved in the breakdown of a chemical called **homocysteine**. Normally, homocysteine is broken down into the amino acid **taurine** (which requires pyridoxine) or recycled into the amino acid **methionine** (which requires B_{12} and folate), but when these vitamins are in short supply, it can stay around long enough to damage blood vessels and cause atherosclerosis. The Framingham Heart Study, an ongoing research project of the National Heart, Lung, and Blood Institute, confirmed the link between low pyridoxine levels and high homocysteine levels.

Vitamin B_1 (Thiamine)

During absorption, thiamine is converted to **thiamine pyrophosphate**, or **TPP**. In this active form, TPP is a cofactor for the enzyme system necessary for the production of energy and for the manufacture of fats. About 30 mg of thiamine can be stored in the body. Here are key facts you know about thiamine:

- Thiamine is occasionally low in people with diabetes.
- Some research found sensorimotor, or peripheral neuropathy, to be associated with thiamine deficiency.
- A synthetic form of thiamine called benfotiamine is used in Europe to prevent diabetic retinopathy. Animal research suggests it may block three of the four biochemical pathways leading to it.

Alcoholics are often deficient in thiamine, as alcohol prevents its absorption and storage. To correct a possible deficiency, take a multivitamin that includes thiamine; you will find it labeled as thiamine hydrochloride and thiamine mononitrate. It is available in multiple vitamins, as part of B-complex supplements, or as a supplement by itself.

The upper limit of safety for thiamine has not been determined due to lack of data. The DRI for adult males is 1.2 mg and for adult women 1.1 mg. Sources of thiamine include asparagus, peanuts, beans, peas, broccoli, rice bran, brussels sprouts, soybeans, cut oats, wheat germ, nuts, and whole grains.

Riboflavin and Riboflavin Phosphate

Riboflavin is a critical part of flavin mononucleotide (FMN) and flavin adenine dinucleotide (FAD), coenzymes involved in energy production. The production of these enzymes from riboflavin can be affected by hormones and drugs. Thyroid hormones and adrenal steroids enhance their production, and tricyclic antidepressants and phenothiazines inhibit their production.

The body is able to make niacin out of the amino acid tryptophan, but it needs riboflavin to do so. Riboflavin is also necessary to change the B vitamins folic acid and pyridoxine (vitamin B_6) into their active forms.

The need for riboflavin increases with energy intake and growth needs. Milk and dairy products make the greatest contribution to riboflavin intake in Western diets. It is degraded by light (up to 70 percent in four hours), so glass bottles of milk exposed to sunlight will provide less riboflavin. If you do not drink milk or regularly take a multivitamin supplement, you are at risk for a subclinical riboflavin deficiency. When B complex is taken as a food supplement, the breakdown products of riboflavin give the urine a bright yellow color and pungent odor; this is a sign that the riboflavin has been absorbed.

Sources of riboflavin include milk, yogurt, asparagus, currant berries, avocados, fish, beans, nuts, broccoli, spinach, and brussels sprouts.

Niacin (Nicotinamide and Nicotinic Acid)

Niacin is the generic word for **nicotinic acid** and its derivatives, the **niacinamides** (**nicotinamide** and **nicotinic acid amide**). Niacin is an essential component of the coenzymes NAD (nicotinamide adenine dinucleotide) and NADH, which are needed for metabolism. It is absorbed from the diet and can also be manufactured by the body from the amino acid tryptophan with the help of riboflavin, thiamine, and pyridoxine. Up to half of the DRI can be obtained this way. Therefore, a shortage of these three vitamins can lead to a shortage of niacin. Diabetes is associated with low levels.

Nicotinamide prevents autoimmune diabetes in animal models of the disease, so a large-scale study was done to test it on humans: the European Nicotinamide Diabetes Intervention Trial. Unfortunately, it found that nicotinamide did not prevent diabetes at the dose used (1.2 g/m^2). Several other facts should be noted:

- Niacin (nicotinic acid or nicotinate) taken in pharmaceutical doses (1 to 2 g three times a day) reduces high cholesterol, a major source of diabetic complications. Taken this way, niacin can be toxic to the liver, so periodic blood tests are necessary.
- Nicotinamide improved HbAlc levels in a two-year study of new type 1 diabetes patients.
- The position paper developed by a European consensus panel recommended the combination of nicotinic acid and one of the statin drugs, together with lifestyle modification, as a useful strategy to lower cardiovascular risk in patients with diabetes and the metabolic syndrome.

Niacin is more stable than the other B vitamins because so little is lost to food preparation and cooking. The upper limit of safety for niacin established by the Food and Nutrition Board of the Institute of Medicine is 35 mg daily for adults. The DRI for niacin is 16 mg for adult men and 14 mg for adult women. Common sources of niacin include chicken, peanuts, tuna, salmon, mackerel, sardines, whole

grain products, enriched cereals, brewer's yeast, and potatoes with skins.

Pantothenic Acid

Pantothenic acid is involved in the release of energy from
carbohydrate and in the breakdown and use of fatty acids.
It is obtained from food as part of coenzyme A (CoA), and
half of the available pantothenic acid is absorbed. It passes
into the blood as free pantothenic acid, and cells change
it back into CoA for use in the energy-producing Krebs
cycle.

As part of CoA, pantothenic acid protects cells against
oxidative damage by increasing the level of **glutathione**,
the body's natural free-radical defense system. Milling
cereal grains reduces their content of pantothenic acid by
50 percent.

The upper limit of safety for pantothenic acid has not
been determined due to lack of data The DRI for adults
is 5 mg. Sources of pantothenic acid include salmon, sunflower seeds, poultry, peanuts, avocado, mushrooms, low-
fat yogurt and milk, corn, and sweet potatoes.

Vitamin B₆ (Pyridoxine)

Vitamin B_6 is a family of chemically related compounds
that include **pyridoxal**, **pyridoxine**, **pyridoxamine**, and
pyridoxal 5-phosphate. In fact, all forms of this vitamin are converted to pyridoxal 5-phosphate, a coenzyme
needed for fat and protein metabolism and immune func-

tioning. It is a necessary part of more than one hundred enzyme systems. Pyridoxine helps the body absorb B_{12}. This conversion requires enzymes that contain riboflavin and magnesium. A pyridoxine deficiency may result in low blood levels of vitamin C; increased excretion of calcium, zinc, and magnesium; and reduced copper absorption.

Other considerations:

- A deficiency of pyridoxine reduces the number of disease-fighting lymphocytes and lowers the ability of other immune elements to respond to the chemical messengers sent by the lymphocytes.
- Supplementation of pyridoxine may prevent diabetic complications because it inhibits glycosylation of proteins responsible for diabetic complication.
- A study of diabetic neuropathy patients found that there was an inverse relationship between pyridoxine and C-reactive protein. This protein is an indication of inflammation that is associated with heart disease.

Pregnancy, lactation, an overactive thyroid, or a high intake of animal protein can necessitate extra amounts or pyridoxine. Food processing can destroy some of the pyridoxine present in foods.

The upper limit of safety for vitamin B_6 (pyridoxine) established by the Food and Nutrition Board of the Institute of Medicine is 100 mg daily for adults. The DRI is 1.3 mg for adults, 1.7 mg for men over 50, and 1.5 mg for women over 51. Sources of pyridoxine include: meat (organic grass fed), poultry (skinless), fortified cereals, vegetarian meat substitutes, skipjack tuna, salmon (wild), halibut, trout, herring, potato, sunflower seeds, oatmeal, peanut butter, and mackerel.

Folic Acid, Folate, Folacin, and Folinic Acid

Folic acid is the commonly used term for **pteroyl-polyglutamic acid**, or **PGA**, the precursor of a large family of folate compounds. Folic acid is the most stable form of the vitamin and is usually used in fortified foods and supplements. More than 90 percent of the folates present in foods occur as PGA. Folate metabolism depends on zinc, niacin, B_{12}, and vitamin C.

A deficiency of this vitamin causes megoblastic anemia and has been associated with a degeneration of the intestinal lining, which then further reduces nutrient absorption. The body cannot make any folate and therefore must obtain all it needs from the diet. Enough folate can be stored to prevent a deficiency from occurring for up to four months.

Folic acid is involved in the production of neurotransmitters, including serotonin and dopamine. When folate is present, it works with vitamin B_{12} to recycle homocysteine back to methionine. Increased levels of homocysteine in the plasma are associated with decreased levels of folate in the plasma, and oral supplementation of this vitamin will almost always lower plasma homocysteine levels. Elevated homocysteine is more common in people with diabetes and is a known risk factor in heart disease.

Folic acid should be taken as part of or with a vitamin B complex. Take a high-quality multivitamin that contains folic acid, B_6, and B_{12} in combination, because all three play important roles in homocysteine reduction. It is estimated that 400 micrograms (mcg) of folic acid daily could reduce the number of heart attacks in Americans by 10 percent. Metformin may inhibit the absorption of folic acid. So can antacids, cimetidine, and ranitidine, used to treat heartburn and ulcers.

Folates are sensitive to heat. Boiling, steaming, or frying for five to ten minutes may destroy up to 96 percent of the folate in a food. The maintenance dose is 400 mcg a day. Amounts recommended for heart disease range from 400 mcg to 1,200 mcg.

The upper limit of safety for folate established by the Food and Nutrition Board of the Institute of Medicine is 1,000 mcg daily for adults. The DRI is 400 mcg for adults. Sources of folic acid include brussels sprouts, turnips, beet greens, mustard greens, brewer's yeast, salmon, oysters, orange juice, split peas, avocados, bulgur wheat, milk, whole germ, white beans, lima beans, and mung beans.

Vitamin B$_{12}$ (Cobalamin)

Vitamin B$_{12}$ is available in several forms. **Cyanocobalamin** is the main synthetic form. **Methylcobalamin** is one of two active forms of B$_{12}$ and may be a more effective supplement. In the stomach, cobalamin is released from its dietary sources by digestive enzymes. Cells in the stomach lining produce a substance called intrinsic factor (IF), which binds to the vitamin, forming an IF-B$_{12}$ complex. This complex is resistant to digestion and is readily absorbed in the small intestine. Vitamin B$_{12}$ is involved in protein, fat, and carbohydrate metabolism. It aids in formation of red blood cells, antibody production, and cell respiration and growth.

Vitamin B_{12} works closely with folic acid and vitamin B_6 in a number of body functions. A vitamin E deficiency may reduce the conversion of vitamin B_{12} to its active form. A pyridoxine deficiency reduces vitamin B_{12} absorption. Large doses of vitamin C can increase excretion of vitamin B_{12}. In addition:

- Vitamin B_{12} works with pyridoxine and folic acid to decrease elevated homocysteine levels.
- There is some evidence that it might help relieve diabetic neuropathy.

Acids and alkalis, water, sunlight, alcohol, estrogen, and sleeping pills can destroy vitamin B_{12}. Antacids, antiepileptic drugs, cholestyramine, and colchicine (for gout) may decrease vitamin B_{12} absorption. Older people do not always produce enough intrinsic factor, making absorption difficult. Microorganisms are the ultimate source of all vitamin B_{12} in the diet. Strict vegans may have to supplement this nutrient.

The upper limit of safety for vitamin B_{12} has not been determined due to lack of data. The DRI for B_{12} is 2.4 mcg for adults. Sources of cobalamin include clams, mackerel, herring, nutritional yeast, kidneys, seafood, and liver.

Biotin

Biotin is essential for many enzyme systems and is related metabolically to B_{12}, folate, and pantothenic acid. The biological role of biotin is to attach a carbon and two oxygen molecules (a carboxyl group) to other molecules. This reaction is critical for the metabolism of carbohydrate and fat. Research findings suggest promise in several areas:

- Biotin is believed to be involved in insulin production and release, and serum biotin concentrations are lower in subjects with type 2 diabetes than in control subjects.
- Preliminary research on humans and animals indicates that it may help improve blood glucose control, particularly in those with type 2 diabetes. Every day for a month, Japanese researchers gave 9 mg biotin to eighteen people with type 2 diabetes. After thirty days, the participants' blood sugar had fallen to nearly half its original levels.
- There are reports that biotin can improve peripheral neuropathy. In one study, improvement was noticed in as soon as one to three months.
- There is evidence that biotin can increase the activity of an enzyme called **glucokinase**, which is low in most people with diabetes. It can also help reduce the excessive glucose produced by the liver and improve insulin sensitivity.

Low biotin levels have been found in elderly people, athletes, pregnant women, and smokers. Vegetarians are able to absorb more biotin than meat eaters. Biotin is present in most foods and can be made by bacteria in the intestine and absorbed from there. It is resistant to heat.

The upper limit of safety for biotin has not been determined due to lack of data. The DRI for biotin is 30 mcg for adults. Sources of biotin include brewer's yeast, soybeans and soy flour, other legumes (beans, black-eyed peas, peanuts), cooked eggs, walnuts, milk, whole grains, molasses, and cauliflower.

Vitamin C (Ascorbic Acid)

Perhaps the most famous vitamin is vitamin C. It enhances the absorption of iron and the bioavailability of stored iron. For example, when a vitamin C source such as orange juice is consumed with a slice of whole wheat bread, the iron in the bread becomes free for absorption. The amount of vitamin C in the body is estimated to be between 900 mg and 1,500 mg. Scurvy (a vitamin C deficiency) can occur when levels are decreased by two-thirds or more. Vitamin C's antioxidant properties are discussed in the next chapter.

Humans are among the few mammals unable to make their own vitamin C. Despite this fact, the glucose/insulin system still influences vitamin C metabolism. The absorption of vitamin C by cells is promoted by insulin and inhibited by high blood sugar levels. High blood glucose also increases vitamin C loss in the urine.

Vitamin C is associated with other significant effects in people with diabetes:

- Levels of vitamin C are reduced in diabetes. The emotional and physical stress of having diabetes may increase the body's use of vitamin C. The oxidative stress (attack by oxygen free radicals) can also increase use and decrease levels of this antioxidant.

- In comparison with a placebo, vitamin C (500 mg twice a day) had beneficial effects on glucose and lipid metabolism in older people with type 2 diabetes. It also decreased the amount of free radicals in the blood and increased glutathione levels.
- Vitamin C reduces sorbitol accumulation and therefore may be useful in preventing diabetic retinopathy complications.
- Vitamin C is important in manufacturing the protein substance collagen. Collagen is the building material for connective tissue, cartilage, and tendons. Therefore, low levels of vitamin C lead to poor wound healing, bleeding gums, and susceptibility to infection, already a concern because of the risk of gum infections in people with diabetes.
- Vitamin C can prevent the buildup of sorbitol, which can occur in the lens of the eye and cause cataracts. Sorbitol can also damage the kidneys and nerves.
- When sugars in the bloodstream bind with proteins, the result is known as **glycosylation**. This is a problem for diabetic patients because they can have high blood sugar levels. Glycosylation can dramatically change the structure and function of body proteins. In diabetes, glycosylation of the blood protein albumin results in damage to the lens of the eye and the myelin sheath of nerves. Vitamin C prevents this.
- Cholesterol particles can become glycosylated too. Glycosylated LDL particles do not bind to LDL receptors or shut off cholesterol synthesis in the liver. Therefore, diabetics often have elevated cholesterol levels and an increased risk of atherosclerosis.

- Vitamin C is necessary for a healthy immune system. It also helps build dense connective tissue, and research shows that it enhances antibiotic therapy. All of these are necessary to prevent gum disease common in diabetes and enhance its treatment.

The body can absorb only a limited amount of vitamin C at one time, and even large doses are eliminated from the body within twelve hours. Therefore, it is best to take a slow-release or sustained-release formula—500 mg once or twice a day.

You should be aware of the following interactions:

- For people who take diuretics (water pills) to treat high blood pressure or edema, animal studies suggest that vitamin C may strengthen the effects of furosemide.
- If you take beta-blockers for high blood pressure as well as vitamin C, take them at different times of the day. Vitamin C may decrease the absorption of propranolol, a beta–blocker.

The upper limit of safety for daily vitamin C intake established by the Food and Nutrition Board of the Institute of Medicine is approximately 1,000 mg for adults. The DRI is 90 mg for adult men and 75 mg for adult women. Sources of vitamin C include asparagus, lemons, avocados, mustard greens, beet greens, onions, berries, papaya, broccoli, parsley, brussels sprouts, persimmons, cabbage, radishes, cantaloupe, rose hips, cauliflower, spinach, citrus fruits, strawberries, collard greens, and sweet bell peppers.

Fat-Soluble Vitamins

Fat-soluble vitamins are intimately related to fats and lipids. There are four families: vitamin A, vitamin D, vitamin E, and vitamin K. These vitamins need to be dissolved in fat before they can be absorbed in the intestine. Low-fat and low-calorie diets, whether by chance or by purpose, may not provide enough of these vitamins.

Dietary fats and the fat-soluble vitamins are absorbed into the lymph vessels, bypassing the portal blood system that takes water-soluble nutrients to the liver. After a long climb up to your shoulder, they are dumped into the left subclavian artery.

Vitamins A and D can be toxic in large amounts when taken over a long period. They are stored in fatty tissues and the liver, and they can accumulate over time. Unlike vitamin C and the B complex, the fat-soluble vitamins are very stable. They are better able to stand up to the heat of cooking and processing. When supplementing any fat-soluble vitamin or oil, you must also take a vitamin E supplement to protect against oxidation.

Vitamin A, Retinol, Retinal, Retinoic Acid, and Retinyl Esters

The vitamin A, or **retinoid**, family contains several forms, natural and synthetic, that have vitamin A activity. They are measured in units called Retinol Equivalents, or RE. This vitamin is found only in animal fats. In addition, the body can convert some of the **carotenoids**, a group of red and orange plant pigments, into vitamin A. They are strong antioxidants and nutrients in their own right, with benefits unrelated to their association with vitamin A. They are discussed in detail in the next chapter.

Of particular note:

- Patients with poorly controlled type 1 diabetes sometimes have low levels of vitamin A and its carrier protein. Taking a vitamin A supplement in this case may not increase vitamin A levels and may instead put more stress on the liver.
- A compound derived from vitamin A, Retin-A (tretinoin), which is applied to the skin to treat acne, also shows promise in healing diabetic ulcers. A study was done on twenty-two volunteers with diabetic foot ulcers. When Retin-A was applied to the ulcers, it healed them completely in almost half of the treatment group, while in the untreated control group only 18 percent were healed.

A six-month supply of vitamin A is stored in the liver, but this supply can be depleted when a person is sick. Vitamin A can be toxic in dosages over 15,000 RE, but much of this toxicity can be prevented by also taking vitamin E. Vitamin E and vitamin A work together. Never take more than 10,000 IU (international units) of pure beta-carotene. In itself it is not toxic, but the carotenes compete for absorption, so taking more of one will reduce how much of the others your body will absorb. Blood tests have confirmed that taking large doses of beta-carotene decreases serum levels of the other carotenes.

Warning: If you are pregnant, you should not take any more vitamin A than is already in your prenatal supplement. Excess vitamin A taken during pregnancy is associated with birth defects.

The upper safety limit for vitamin A established by the Food and Nutrition Board of the Institute of Medicine is approximately 3,000 mcg daily when provided as retinol in animal foods, fortified products, or vitamin supplements. The DRI for vitamin A is 900 mcg in adult men and 700 mcg in adult women. Sources of Vitamin A include cod-liver oil, egg yolks, butter, liver, and leafy greens. Red-, orange-, and yellow-fleshed vegetables are sources of beta-carotene.

Vitamin D (Cholecalciferol, Ergosterol, and Calcitriol)

The vitamin D family includes **cholecalciferol** (vitamin D_3), **ergosterol** (vitamin D_2), and **calcitriol**. It has two possible sources: preformed from the diet and synthesized by the skin. Vitamin D is called the sunshine vitamin because there are large amounts of the precursor (**7-dehydrocholesterol**) in the skin. When the precursor is exposed to ultraviolet light, it is converted into cholecalciferol. It is estimated that up to 80 percent of the body's needs for vitamin D can be obtained this way.

Dark-skinned people and anyone who lives in low-sun areas (the Pacific Northwest or England, for example) probably cannot rely on manufacturing enough of their own vitamin D and are at risk for deficiency. Elderly people are also at risk, since they often cannot get out and do not eat fortified foods. Sunscreen "protects" against vitamin D formation, so if you wear it all the time, you are not making vitamin D. Vitamin D deficiency is much more common than was previously thought. It has been linked to musculoskeletal pain. When you eat foods that contain vitamin D, your liver and kidneys convert it to the active form, which aids in calcium and phosphorus absorption, hair growth, bone and teeth development, osteoporosis prevention, immunity enhancement, and prevention of **hypocalcemia** (calcium deficiency in the blood).

Vitamin D is a hormone that regulates mineral balance. It stimulates intestinal absorption of calcium and phosphorus, works with the parathyroid hormone to mobilize calcium from bone, and stimulates the reabsorption of calcium from the kidneys. Here are a few other reasons for ensuring sufficient levels of vitamin D:

- Vitamin D deficiency impairs the manufacture of insulin and its secretion in humans, suggesting a role in the development of type 2 diabetes.
- Researchers in Bulgaria showed that giving vitamin D supplements to diabetics during the winter markedly improved control of their blood sugar levels.

Other sources of vitamin D include eggs, salmon, fish-liver oils, halibut, and tuna.

Vitamin K (K_1, or phylloquinone, and K_2, or menaquione)

Vitamin K is a fat-soluble vitamin best known for its role in blood clotting. There are two types of vitamin K—vitamin K_1, which is found in green plants, and vitamin K_2, which is produced by bacteria in the colon. In the liver, vitamin K acts as a coenzyme in reactions that produce the clotting factors. Three functions merit particular attention:

- Vitamin K plays an important role in the conversion of glucose into glycogen for storage in the liver.
- Vitamin K is needed for bone formation and osteo-porosis prevention, along with regulation of blood pressure.
- Vitamin K also interferes with the action of warfarin (Coumadin), a blood-thinning drug that decreases the viscosity of the blood and prevents clots from forming; it is used by many diabetes patients to prevent heart attacks and strokes.

At the top of every list of foods containing vitamin K is green tea. Green tea *leaves* contain a lot of vitamin K, but green tea *brew* contains none. Being a fat-soluble nutrient, it does not dissolve in boiling water. However, if you brew loose green tea, you must be very careful not to let the leaves get in your cup. Too often warfarin users are given a list of vitamin K sources without being told how to use the information. As a result, they get the message that Vitamin K–rich foods and leafy greens are bad for them. Instead, patients on warfarin should avoid the foods highest in vitamin K and keep their intake of the rest the same week to week. Warfarin should be titrated to this base level of vitamin K and not the other way around. Vitamin K and the foods that contain it are too important for anyone to limit.

The upper limit of safety for vitamin K has not been determined due to lack of data. The DRI is 120 mcg for adult men and 90 mcg for adult women. Sources of vitamin K include green tea leaves, cabbage, broccoli, turnip greens, lettuce, wheat bran, cheese, and egg yolk.

Vitamin K is made by bacteria in the colon and absorbed through the intestinal wall. Anything that affects the bacteria will affect your vitamin K status. Elderly people are particularly at risk for low vitamin K levels.

6

Minerals, Antioxidants, and Diabetes

This chapter explores the role minerals and antioxidants play in the health of people with diabetes. For diabetes patients, minerals can help to reduce high blood pressure, normalize cholesterol, and minimize the side effects of medication. Antioxidant nutrients, including the antioxidant minerals, have been shown to help preserve beta-cell function, increase insulin sensitivity, protect the endothelial lining, and reduce nerve damage. Since a poor diet is the most common cause of micronutrient deficiencies, eating foods rich in the minerals and antioxidants covered in this chapter will help restore the optimum levels of nutrients and aid in blood-sugar maintenance. We included the richest sources of each nutrient determined by practical serving sizes, the upper limit of safety established by the Food and Nutrition Board of the Institute of Medicine and the DRI (Dietary Reference Intake).

First, some warnings: Before you try supplementing any of these nutrients, check with your doctor. Some people taking insulin or insulin-stimulating drugs might have to change their medication level. Test your blood glucose frequently until you know how your body will react to a particular mineral or antioxidant. Never take large doses of any one nutrient unless you are under the care of a knowledgeable physician. If you must take a supplement, it's always better to take small amounts of a large range of nutrients than large doses of one or two. Excess minerals are filtered out of the blood by the kidneys, so those on dialysis must reduce the amount of minerals they eat to take the pressure off their failing kidneys; these minerals include phosphate and potassium.

Minerals and Diabetes

Minerals are necessary for, among other things, bone and tissue growth, muscle movement, electrical impulses, enzymatic reactions, and oxygen distribution. They also play key roles in metabolizing blood sugar. Deficiencies in potassium and magnesium, and possibly zinc and chromium, may predispose a person to carbohydrate intolerance. Even though whole wheat products have the same glycemic index/glycemic load as refined wheat, only the whole wheat products promote insulin sensitivity. Researchers believe this is likely due to their mineral content. Refining strips wheat not only of its fiber but also of its minerals. Minerals can also be lost in the urine. When people with type 2 diabetes experience ketoacidosis, there is a marked loss of minerals this way. High blood sugar levels cause the kidneys to make more urine, which then takes minerals out of the body. Alcohol and the water pills (diuretics) used to treat high blood pressure and edema have the same effect.

The Electrolytes

The minerals sodium (Na^+), potassium (K^-), and chloride (Cl^-) exist in the body as charged atoms called ions and are collectively known as the electrolytes. Your cell-citizens need a source of electricity, and electrolytes act like batteries, generating the electrical current that runs along the wiring of your nervous system. They cause your muscles to move, your heart to beat, and, along with magnesium and calcium, they regulate your blood pressure. Vomiting and diarrhea can seriously deplete electrolytes and, in rare cases, cause life-threatening complications.

Phosphate and phosphorus. In the body, phosphorus (P) exists only in an ionic form as phosphate (H_2PO_4); in solution in the blood it acts as an electrolyte. It is part of the ADP (adenosine diphosphate) and ATP (adenosine triphosphate) molecules, the energy currency of the cells. It also helps to form the backbone of the DNA and RNA helix that forms our genetic material. Phosphate works closely with calcium, forming the calcium phosphate that hardens bone tissue. The high volume of urine produced as a result of high blood sugar takes this electrolyte, and the other three, out with it. However, many people get too much of this mineral. Prepared foods and soft drinks provide such a large amount of phosphate that it causes imbalances. Too much phosphate in your blood can lead to a calcium loss in the bones and eventually osteoporosis. Bone is continuously dissolved and reformed, and phosphate can cause more bone to be dissolved than formed, resulting in a net loss of bone density. This is not good, since diabetes already puts diabetes patients at risk for osteoporosis.

The upper limit of safety for phosphorus established by the Food and Nutrition Board of the Institute of Medicine is 3–4 grams daily for adults. The DRI for phosphorus is 700 mg. Common sources of phosphorus include pumpkin and sunflower seeds, yogurt, sardines with bones, salmon and halibut, milk, meat, almonds, legumes, oatmeal and grains.

Potassium. It has been known for decades that when people move from an area that has a high level of fruit and vegetable intake to an area with a low level, they develop high blood pressure. Some researchers believe this is caused by an imbalance in minerals. Western diets contain too much sodium and chloride from processed and refined foods and not enough potassium from fruits and vegetables. This mineral imbalance lies at the heart of high blood pressure. Too much caffeine, alcohol, and salt (sodium chloride) can also cause potassium loss. According to the National Dairy Council, more than 90 percent of adults are not getting the recommended amount of potassium.

Some diabetes patients take diuretics (water pills) for high blood pressure or for edema (excess water in the tissues). These cause potassium loss through the urine, and increasing the consumption of potassium-rich foods is necessary to restore normal levels. Potassium deficiency is a common cause of leg cramps. A potassium-sparing diuretic causes little potassium to be lost in the urine. In this case you may need to limit the highest potassium-rich foods because your kidney cannot get rid of any excess. If you do not know which kind of diuretic you are taking, check the label on the bottle, call the pharmacy that filled it, or call your doctor.

The Food and Nutrition Board of the Institute of Medicine set the Adequate Intake (AI) of potassium for adults at 4.7 grams a day. The DRI for potassium is 4,700 mg for adults. Common sources of potassium include orange juice, bananas, baked potatoes, winter squash, tomato juice, vegetable juice cocktail, avocados, cooked dried beans, and blackstrap molasses. Salt substitute is also a very rich source.

Magnesium

Magnesium is a cofactor in more than 300 enzymatic reactions and, among other things, is necessary for the secretion and action of insulin and the actions of many enzymes involved in carbohydrate metabolism. Both pyridoxine (vitamin B_6) and vitamin E are needed to get magnesium into cells. People with diabetes have a documented mild magnesium deficiency at diagnosis, and in one study those with severe retinopathy had the lowest levels. To make matters worse, an increased urinary loss has been documented in both type 1 and type 2 diabetes. Gastric juice is relatively high in magnesium, so a substantial amount of magnesium may be lost if any vomiting is prolonged.

Antioxidants may help to prevent loss of cellular magnesium or promote transport of magnesium into the endothelial, vascular, and heart cells. Magnesium may prevent some of the complications of diabetes, such as retinopathy, heart disease, and blood-vessel deterioration. Supplements have improved glucose handling in elderly men with type 2 diabetes.

The presence of calcium, fat, alcohol, phosphate, and phytates in food decreases magnesium absorption. Alcohol, diuretics, and sugar increase the loss of magnesium from the urine. The upper limit of safety for magnesium established by the Food and Nutrition Board of the Institute of Medicine is approximately 350 mg daily for adults. The DRI for magnesium is 400 mg for young men, 420 mg for men age 31 and older, 310 mg for young women, and 320 mg for women age 31 and older. Common sources of magnesium include pumpkin seeds, almonds, firm tofu, chili with beans, molasses, wheat germ, and sunflower seeds.

Calcium

Calcium is involved in nerve transmission and is necessary for normal heart rhythm. Increased calcium consumption has been associated with increased weight loss through improved energy metabolism. Calcium is needed for B_{12} absorption in the GI tract; supplements have reversed the low vitamin B_{12} levels caused by metformin. It also is necessary for dense healthy bone tissue. Adequate calcium, magnesium, vitamin K, vitamin D, and sunlight can help to strengthen bones. Calcium supplements have been shown to decrease high blood pressure, which is a problem for many people with diabetes.

Magnesium and calcium have similar functions and may oppose each other. In normal muscle contraction, calcium causes tightening and magnesium causes relaxation. Calcium and magnesium compete with each other for absorption; as a result, large amounts of one decrease absorption of the other.

High intakes of sodium and phosphates, excess alcohol consumption, and cigarette smoking all decrease calcium levels. Calcium carbonate is best absorbed under acidic conditions, so supplements should be taken with food. Calcium lactate and malate can be taken at any time during the day and are more appropriate for those with low stomach-acid levels. Vitamin D helps to stimulate calcium absorption. Coral calcium, which is touted as a cure for everything including diabetes, is just a fancy name for ordinary calcium carbonate (limestone).

The upper limit of safety for calcium established by the Institute of Medicine is approximately 2,500 mg daily for adults. The DRI for calcium is 1,000 mg for adult men and women and 1,200 mg for older men and women. Common sources of calcium include yogurt, canned salmon with bones, blackstrap molasses, milk and calcium-fortified soy milk or fortified rice beverage, sardines with bones, calcium-fortified orange juice, cottage cheese, spinach and tofu, amaranth, soy nuts, and collard greens.

Chromium

Chromium (Cr) is an essential trace element and cofactor required for normal carbohydrate and lipid metabolism. This was illustrated in a study that found men with both type 2 diabetes and cardiovascular disease had lower levels of chromium than healthy men. Chromium is the supplement most recommended for those with diabetes or insulin resistance. It is known to enhance the action of insulin, helping it to be absorbed and utilized by the cells. Researchers have not yet discovered the biologically active form of chromium and do not yet know how it works. One theory is that it may make the insulin receptor more responsive to insulin. People with a chromium deficiency develop severe signs of diabetes, including weight loss and high blood sugar.

Diets containing large amounts of simple sugars cause more chromium to be lost in the urine than do diets that are high in complex carbohydrates. This may be caused by the larger amounts of insulin released in response to these simple sugars when compared with the lesser amounts of insulin released in response to low-GI carbohydrates. But not only is more chromium lost in a refined diet; it contains less chromium to begin with, since chromium is stripped away in the refining process. Some of the research on chromium includes these studies:

- Chromium significantly improved blood sugar control in a study of 30 women with gestational diabetes mellitus (GDM).
- Patients with type 2 diabetes who were being treated with either sulfonylureas or a diet program were given 1,000 μg (1 mg) of chromium picolinate daily. The 16 patients who received chromium picolinate experienced a greater increase in insulin sensitivity than the placebo group did.
- Some studies have shown that chromium supplements can lower total cholesterol and LDL (bad) cholesterol levels and raise HDL (good) cholesterol levels in the blood, particularly in people with high cholesterol.

Despite all the positive studies, the overall results of research on chromium have been mixed. However, most positive studies on chromium used chromium picolinate rather than chromium chloride. The former is better absorbed than the latter. Positive studies were also more likely to involve higher than lower doses. This might account for part of the mixed results. Patients who had low chromium levels at the start had a more pronounced reaction to the supplementation. People who have adequate chromium and well-balanced diets do not always respond to supplementation.

The FDA recently stated that there is insufficient evidence to support any of the proposed health claims for chromium supplementation, including the claims made for weight loss. Although chromium is often recommended for weight loss and is an ingredient in many weight-loss products and pills, there is no evidence that it is effective. Chromium is not well absorbed, but vitamin C might be able to enhance this. Aspirin may also increase chromium absorption. High doses of chromium may compete with iron for absorption and can decrease zinc absorption. Clinical trials show that treatment with chromium at doses up to 1,000 μg/day for periods up to 64 months has not resulted in any toxic effects. However, if chromium supplementation is to have a positive effect, it should be observed within 6 to 12 weeks.

Because of its lack of toxicity, the upper limit of safety for chromium has not been determined. The Food and Nutrition Board of the Institute of Medicine recommends that intake of chromium be from food only to prevent high intake. Dietary sources of chromium include whole grains, potatoes, oysters, liver, seafood, cheese, meat, brewer's yeast, and acidic foods cooked in stainless steel cookware. This list is approximate, since many foods have not yet been tested for chromium.

Vanadium

Vanadium is a trace mineral. Its supplemental form is **vanadyl sulfate**, and it can act as an antioxidant in addition to its other roles. Vanadium appears to activate the insulin receptors and increase the number of GLUT-4 (glucose transporter) molecules in the cell membranes, thereby improving insulin sensitivity. You will remember from previous chapters that insulin prevents fat from being broken down (lipolysis) and burned for energy. In a study on moderately obese type 2 diabetes subjects, vanadyl sulfate enhanced insulin's ability to prevent fat breakdown and increase the insulin sensitivity of muscle and liver cells.

Vanadium may enhance the activity of digoxin and anticoagulant medications. Because vanadium can be toxic in low doses you should limit daily intake to less than 100 μg/day.

Zinc

Zinc supplementation may exert insulin-like effects and protect beta cells from oxidative damage. People with diabetes are often found to be deficient in zinc at the time of diagnosis, perhaps because they excrete too much of it in their urine. Both zinc and vanadium imitate insulin, reducing the excessive loss of insulin and decreasing the risk of developing diabetes. Zinc and vanadium may be depleted from the stress of beta-cell destruction, and low levels of zinc in drinking water have been linked to the development of diabetes.

Zinc is also needed for taste acuity. A home test kit to estimate zinc levels works by measuring your ability to taste a solution that you swish around in your mouth. You can find this kit at most health-food stores. Zinc supplements should be taken in a therapeutic dose of thirty milligrams a day with two milligrams of copper or a maintenance dose of fifteen milligrams a day.

The upper limit of safety for zinc established by the Food and Nutrition Board of the Institute of Medicine is 40 milligrams daily for adults. The DRI for zinc is 11 mg for adult males and pregnant women and 8 mg for women. Common sources of zinc include oysters, beef, crab, poultry, pumpkin seeds, wheat germ, yogurt, sunflower seeds, soy nuts, peanuts, and shrimp.

Antioxidants and Diabetes

The last group of nutrients is the antioxidants. Both vitamins and minerals can act as antioxidants, but most members of this group are plant substances. The most commonly recognized antioxidant nutrients are beta-carotene (a precursor to vitamin A), vitamins C and E, and selenium. They are, however, but a tip of the iceberg. Antioxidants come packaged in bright colors, delicious flavors, and tempting aromas. They are so common in whole foods that they have not all been identified. Unfortunately, we tend to eat refined foods stripped of most of their antioxidants and few of the antioxidant-packed fruits and vegetables. Antioxidants are responsible for protecting the body; when they are plentiful, the body is better able to withstand the metabolic changes caused by diabetes. The bodies of people with diabetes are under attack from much higher than normal levels of free radicals, yet they have lower levels of antioxidants to fight them off. The result is damage to the eye, kidney, nerves, and the digestive system.

Free Radicals and Oxidation

Free radicals are the terrorists of the body; they do damage to anything they touch. Some free radicals are made by the immune system, which uses them to kill invaders. Others are generated as a part of normal metabolism, and yet others attack us from our environment.

A free radical is simply a molecule that lacks an electron in its outer shell. Electrons have a violent compulsion to travel in pairs. When an electron is pulled away from its partner—a process called oxidation—it starts a chain of reactions. The molecule that has taken the electron is now happy, although damaged, and settles down. But the molecule that has lost the electron is now a free radical itself, and it goes to the closest vulnerable molecule and steals another electron. In this way a single free radical "ricochets" all around the immediate area, damaging (oxidizing) everything the process touches. It can punch holes in membranes by destroying their essential fatty acids and damage your genetic material and cause cellular mutations.

The most dangerous free radicals are the ones that contain oxygen. Because they react so easily with molecules, they are called **reactive oxygen species**, or **ROS**. Luckily, the body has two main mechanisms for ridding itself of free radicals: it can manufacture antioxidants and get them from the diet, or it can use the body's own system of enzymes. Although antioxidants can neutralize ROS, the body's primary defense against free radicals is its enzyme systems. These systems produce the weapons with which the immune army attacks invaders and insurgents. The major enzymes used by the body are glutathione peroxidase, superoxide dismutase, and catalase. The best way to strengthen these enzymes is to give your body all the nutrients it needs to build them.

Antioxidants and Oxidative Stress

Antioxidants are simply molecules that stop oxidation. The antioxidant nutrients have an electron that is very easy to remove—more easy to remove than any of the free radicals' or ROS's usual targets. If you have ever made a fruit salad, you know that when the surface of certain fruits is exposed to air, oxidation occurs and the cells become brown from the oxygen damage. This can be prevented by adding a few drops of lemon juice, which is rich in vitamin C. Now, when an ROS approaches the fruit looking for an electron, vitamin C throws itself in front of the ROS and offers its electron instead. Since it will be easier to take the electron from the self-sacrificing vitamin C, the ROS obliges. Now the free radical is no longer dangerous, and the reaction stops there.

When there is more oxidation than antioxidant protection, the result is called oxidative stress. Oxidative stress is common in our free-radical-ridden environment, particularly among people who have a chronic disease. People with diabetes are under oxidative stress (as are people who are overweight), and a body under oxidative stress is more likely to experience diabetic complications. There is evidence that oxidative stress is involved in retinopathy, and studies in lab animals have shown that antioxidant treatment can inhibit the early stages of diabetic retinopathy. Oxidative stress is suspected of being involved in the development of insulin resistance. A growing body of evidence suggests that oxidative stress resulting from increased free-radical formation and/or defects in antioxidant defense systems is implicated in the development of diabetic neuropathy.

Antioxidant Nutrients

Recent studies have found that patients with diabetes who were given 1,250 mg of vitamin C and 680 IU of vitamin E for four weeks or 1,000 mg of vitamin C for nine months or 1,800 IU of vitamin E for four weeks showed decreased evidence of kidney damage. Another recent study found evidence that a combination of magnesium, zinc, and vitamins C and E resulted in an improvement of renal function in type 2 diabetic patients. Although this might tempt some of you to run out and buy a bottle of antioxidants, we suggest you get most of yours from your diet. A good multivitamin mineral supplement should already contain the antioxidant vitamins and minerals; the rest can only be obtained from the diet. There is no substitute for fresh fruits and vegetables and a variety of whole grains. The various antioxidants work together synergistically. Too often we take large doses of a single antioxidant. Not only is this less effective; it can even be dangerous. Under certain conditions antioxidants can "flip" and become pro-oxidants that cause free-radical damage rather than protect against it.

Carotenoids

The carotenoids are a huge family of more than 600 yellow to red pigments, of which beta-carotene is the most famous. Other powerful carotenoids include alpha-carotene, lycopene, lutein, and cryptoxanthin. Many health professionals have recommended high doses of beta-carotene for antioxidant protection because it is nontoxic even at high doses. However, you must keep in mind that

Table 6.1 Carotenoid food groups

ALPHA- AND BETA-CAROTENE	BETA-CRYPTOXANTHIN	ZEAXANTHIN
Carrots	Oranges	Peaches
Sweet potatoes	Grapefruit	Corn
Pumpkin	Lemons	Tangerines
Winter squashes	Tangerines	
Yams		

LUTEIN AND BETA-CAROTENE	LYCOPENE	ASTAXANTHIN
Deep-green leafy vegetables	Tomatoes	Salmon
	Watermelon	

just because something is nontoxic does into mean it will not have a negative effect on your health. For example, high doses of beta-carotene decrease the serum levels of other carotenoids, some of which are more powerful than beta-carotene. This is because the carotenoids compete for absorption. When you saturate all the transport sites with beta-carotene, not much alpha-carotene from your diet is going to get through. We strongly suggest that you consume small amounts of many antioxidants and avoid large single doses.

Each carotenoid is unique, so different carotenoids are preferred by different organs. For example, the cells in your liver, heart, thyroid gland, kidneys, and pancreas prefer beta-carotene and lycopene equally; the cells of the adrenal glands and testes mainly prefer just lycopene. Zeaxanthin and beta-carotene are favorites in the ovaries; in the macula of the eye, lutein and zeaxanthin predominate.

Polyphenols

These chemicals are found in a wide variety of colors in fruits and vegetables, from the colorless **flavonones** in citrus fruit to the bright red and dark blue **anthocyanins** found in berries to the astringent **tannins** found in tea and wine. They appear to work synergistically with vitamin C and stimulate the detoxification of drugs by the liver enzymes. Polyphenols are usually concentrated in the peel, skin, or outer layer of the plant. One of the most potent "miracle" foods you can buy is a bottle of organic purple grape juice; blueberry juice is good too.

The Vitamin C and Vitamin E Team

In addition to the other roles they play in the body, these two vitamins also function as antioxidants. Often, they work together as a team.

The vitamin E family is a group of four related compounds called **tocopherols**. They act as bodyguards for cells in fatty deposits, the liver, and muscle tissue by attaching themselves to the cell membrane. Vitamin E will save a membrane by offering the ROS one of its own electrons before the oxygen can steal one from the cell. But vitamin E only has one electron it can spare—once that is gone, it can no longer function as an antioxidant. Vitamin C to the rescue! It recharges vitamin E with one of its own electrons. Armed anew, vitamin E can now protect the lipid areas again. In this way vitamin C indirectly protects the fat-soluble areas it cannot reach by recharging vitamin E. This is why vitamin C is so important: it spares vitamin E, which is usually hard to get in the diet. When vitamin E is needed, vitamin C molecules can keep recharging the same vitamin E molecule until it wears out. A number of antioxidants are able to recharge vitamin E.

Data shows that monocytes, a type of white blood cell, are very active in people with diabetes. They increase inflammation and generate free radicals and cytokines. Diabetic monocytes also stick to the endothelium (wall of the artery), a necessary step toward plaque lesion formation. Researchers found that in people with type 2 diabetes a high intake of vitamin E could reduce the inflammation caused by these monocytes and possibly help discourage plaque formation. Vitamin E might also be able to prevent the glycosylation (addition of glucose molecule) to protein after three months.

One human study suggests that supplementation with vitamins C and E could play an important role in the health of the eye surface in type 2 diabetes patients. In rats, vitamin E supplementation significantly improves glycemic control, possibly by minimizing free radical damage to the pancreatic ß-cells.

Vitamin E occurs naturally as **d–alpha–tocopherol**. The synthetic version is the **dl-tocopherol isomer**, which has 25 percent less activity than the natural isomer. Since vitamin E is a fat-soluble vitamin, it requires fat in the meal to be properly absorbed. As with all antioxidants, large doses should be avoided. The upper safety limit for vitamin E intake established by the Food and Nutrition Board of the Institute of Medicine is 1,000 mg daily (as a–tocopherol in food or supplemental form) for adults. The DRI is 15 mg. Vitamin E is measured in milligrams, but on food labels it is measured as IU (international units). One IU of vitamin E is equivalent to 0.67 mg of vitamin E. Vitamin E is commonly found in sunflower seeds and oil, peanuts and peanut oil, almonds and almond oil, wheat germ, whole grains, and avocados.

Selenium

Selenium is one of the few minerals with antioxidant power. It is a part or cofactor of glutathione peroxidase, one of the enzymes that make up the body's free radical defense system. It protects cell membranes and has a synergistic effect with vitamin E. By protecting lipids, selenium indirectly promotes the production of the helpful prosta-glandins (series 2) rather than the damaging prostaglandins (series 3). In this way it helps to prevent inflammation and inappropriate blood clotting. The amount of selenium in foods is determined by the selenium content of the soil in which it grew.

The upper limit of safety for selenium established by the Food and Nutrition Board of the Institute of Medicine is 400 mcg daily for adults. Selenium is commonly found in Brazil nuts, oysters, clams, meat, poultry, whole grain pasta, sunflower seeds, oatmeal, soy and other nuts, black-strap molasses, eggs, and low-fat dairy products.

Coenzyme Q10 (Ubiquinone)

Coenzyme Q10 belongs to a family called the ubiquinones. It is a coenzyme that works in mitochondria of the cell to produce energy (ATP—adenosine triphosphate). Without CoQ10 no cell could survive. CoQ10 supplementation has been used successfully in Japan to treat heart disease and high blood pressure and to enhance the immune sys-tem. In addition to being a coenzyme, ubiquinone is also a very powerful antioxidant that helps to recycle vitamin E. Studies have shown that people with diabetes have a greater incidence of CoQ10 deficiency.

CoQ10 is manufactured by the body but is also found in many foods. The average person obtains about 5 mil-ligrams from the diet each day. CoQ10 levels decline with age, so a lack of it may contribute to aging. Synthesis of CoQ10 is complicated and requires pantothenic acid, pyri-doxine, niacin, folate, and vitamins C and B_{12}. All plant foods contain some CoQ10, but in insignificant quantities. The therapeutic dose is 120 milligrams a day. Being fat soluble, CoQ10 should be eaten with a fat-rich meal for best absorption. There is no DRI set for CoQ10.

Alpha-Lipoic Acid

Alpha-lipoic acid (**ALA**, or **thioctic acid**) is a sulfur-containing fatty acid that appears to be one of the most promising supplements for diabetes. All cells contain ALA; it is vital for the oxidation of energy, and under normal circumstances, our bodies make all of this nutrient they need. ALA is also a powerful antioxidant that appears capable of scavenging a wide range of reactive oxygen species and protecting the body from oxidative stress. Unlike other antioxidants, it works in both fatty and watery areas of the body. We do not make the amounts of ALA necessary for it to work as an antioxidant, so it must be taken as a supplement. More than seven controlled randomized clinical trials have been completed using ALA in patients with diabetic neuropathy. Other research includes these studies:

- Recently a meta-analysis of 1,258 patients, the largest sample of diabetic patients ever to have been treated with a single drug or class of drugs to reduce symptoms of diabetic neuropathy, confirmed the favorable effects of ALA based on the highest level of evidence. In Germany, alpha-lipoic acid is approved as a drug for the treatment of polyneuropathy.

- Researchers with the DEKAN (Deutsche Kardiale Autonome Neuropathie) study followed 73 people with diabetic neuropathic damage to the heart. Treatment with 800 mg/day of lipoic acid showed statistically significant improvement when compared with a placebo. There is also research that suggests ALA can help improve kidney function in patients with diabetes.
- ALA lowers blood-sugar levels in patients with diabetes by inhibiting the production of glucose by the liver, and a placebo-controlled study of type 2 patients found that lipoic acid significantly increased insulin-caused glucose uptake, presumably by increasing insulin sensitivity.

ALA indirectly helps to recharge vitamin E and directly recycles and can prolong the life of vitamin C, glutathione, and coenzyme Q10. ALA is found in small amounts in foods such as spinach, broccoli, beef, and yeast.

PART II

TREATING DIABETES AND ITS COMPLICATIONS

Diabetes brings with itself a number of complications. Not only must you learn to deal with short-term problems such as high blood sugar, low blood sugar, and ketoacidosis, but you must also learn how to protect yourself from the long-term complications such as diabetic nerve disease (neuropathy), diabetic kidney disease (nephropathy), diabetic eye disease (retinopathy and more), atherosclerosis, heart disease, and hypertension. Even obesity can be considered a complication of diabetes.

Almost all of these complications are traceable to two culprits: sugar (glucose) and fat (lipids). Our tissues were just not designed to handle

. . . . .
171

long-term exposure to the glucose molecule. Insulin is supposed to be quickly removed from circulation before the glucose can get into any trouble, but when you have diabetes, it lingers. Like a delinquent, the glucose molecule lurks in a dark alley, waiting for trouble to find him.

To avoid the complications described in this section, you must have the knowledge of how to avoid high blood sugar levels. People with type 2 diabetes can test their levels one hour and two hours after a meal, first thing in the morning, and just before bedtime. This schedule may seem excessive if you are not accustomed to tight glucose control, but adhering to it is the only way to learn what you should eat. Once your glucose levels are under control, you can eliminate the test one hour after meals. The glycemic charts can tell you what happens when the average person eats a particular food; when you have a glucose meter, you can tell what happens when you eat that food. Test, listen, and learn the rhythms of your own body.

If you have type 1 diabetes, you first test before meals so that you know how much insulin to inject. You also test two hours after meals to make sure the amount of insulin you injected was not too little or too much.

The other offender is fat—the fat in and around your belly. Fat is one of those tissues that scientists once took for granted. Adipose cells just sat around on their collective cellular butts doing nothing all day. What else was there to say about a cell that was almost all lipid droplets? Quite a bit, as it turns out, and it led to the discovery of a whole new class of messenger molecular called adipokines. Those bulging fat cells were not so lazy after all. In actuality, they were so busy churning out message molecules that adipose tissue is now considered a gland. This is why it can be incumbent on people with diabetes to lose some weight. Get rid of the tissue that is stirring up serious trouble. Lose 10 percent of your body weight, and your risk of developing any of the complications in this section will be greatly reduced. This weight loss might even be enough to resolve your problem.

7

Non-Insulin Diabetes Medications

Type 2 diabetes is now recognized as a progressive disease. The United Kingdom Prospective Diabetes Study determined that by the time the patients in the study group were diagnosed with type 2 diabetes, their insulin production had already decreased by 50 percent. This decline is ongoing. As insulin-producing beta cells in the pancreas continue to die and natural insulin production falls, diet and lifestyle modifications alone are no longer enough to control the body's blood sugar. This is when your doctor will recommend that you start taking one or more of the diabetes drugs. Needing medications or insulin is not a sign that you have failed in any way. If you have type 2 diabetes, medication of some sort is eventually inevitable.

Sometimes people need a particular medication for just a short while after they are diagnosed, and it can be discontinued when the diet has had a chance to work or when sufficient weight has been lost and insulin sensitivity increases. Nevertheless, as times goes on, chances are it will be necessary to take one oral drug or a combination of drugs. An injectable drug can be added if oral drugs, diet, and lifestyle changes still cannot control blood sugar. As you read the information in this chapter, you will see how some classes of drugs complement other classes. Combinations of certain drugs yield better results than can be gained from each drug by itself. The drugs may even be combined in the same pill.

Whatever your medication schedule, don't make the mistake of thinking drugs alone can control your blood sugar. When you have diabetes, diet and lifestyle changes are not a choice; they are a necessity, part of your prescription. In addition, no matter how many medications you take, you must test your blood sugar frequently. Glucose meters continue to get smaller and to require less blood, so they can be used on less sensitive areas of the skin. Some do not require a blood sample at all, and even those that do are barely felt. With the choices available today, you have no excuse for not testing frequently.

A caution: These medications were developed to treat type 2 diabetes and are not appropriate for people with type 1 diabetes.

Oral Medications

Oral medications are not insulin pills; they are drugs that can help you control your blood glucose levels. Different drug classes work in different ways and have different potential side effects. A medication that is right for you may not be right for someone else. For example, metformin and the thiazolidinediones decrease the body's need for insulin, while the sulfonylureas, epaglinide, and nateglinide increase the amount of insulin in the blood. Oral medication can help control blood sugar only in combination with the right lifestyle changes. You must still follow a diabetic diet, exercise regularly, not use tobacco, and test your blood sugar often.

When your medications are prescribed, your doctor should tell you when to take them, what potential side effects you may have, and how to report any unusual side effects. Several oral drugs can cause hypoglycemia, or low blood sugar. This is a dangerous state that leads to weakness, shaking, trembling, and, if prolonged, mental confusion and even coma. (We discuss this condition more in the next chapter.)

Sulfonylureas

The sulfonylureas are the oldest category of oral drugs used to treat type 2 diabetes and are often the first drugs prescribed for lean patients. They are **insulin secretagogues**, drugs that increase insulin secretion. They allow the pancreas to release insulin with less stimulation than normal. The increased level of insulin then helps to make up for the cells' resistance to it: despite insulin resistance, glucose levels fall. In theory, the sulfonylureas target post-meal blood glucose levels, but most clinical trials suggest that these drugs improve fasting blood glucose more, and in that way reduce glucose levels after a meal. The possible nutritional side effects of these drugs take three principal forms: hypoglycemia (low blood glucose), stomach upset, and weight gain.

Take a sulfonylurea thirty minutes to one hour before meals. You should not miss meals, but if you do, the pill for that meal should be skipped too. Missing meals or taking extra pills can cause hypoglycemia. The new "second-generation" sulfonylureas (glipizide, glyburide, and glimepiride) have fewer side effects than those associated with the first-generation products. Glimepiride is taken with the first meal of the day. The sulfonylureas can be taken alone or combined with metformin, the glitazones, or acarbose.

The following list shows the major brand names and corresponding generic names for the sulfonylureas:

Orinase (tolbutamide)
Tolinase (tolazamide)
Diabinese (chlorpropamide)
Glucotrol (glipizide)
Micronase (glyburide)
Amaryl (glimepiride)
Prandin (repaglinide)
Starlix (nateglinide)

Biguanides (Metformin)

Metformin is in a class by itself. It can be prescribed on its own or with a sulfonylurea as part of a combination pill. Metformin decreases the amount of glucose released by the liver and improves glucose tolerance. It is often the first drug prescribed for the newly diagnosed overweight type 2 patient because it does not cause weight gain, and in some people it leads to weight loss, which in itself improves glucose tolerance.

Metformin can carry the following nutritional side effects:

Folic acid deficiency
Vitamin B$_{12}$ deficiency
Nausea and vomiting
Diarrhea
Metallic taste in the mouth

Metformin interferes with vitamin absorption from the gut. The symptoms cited usually occur only when you start taking the drug and decrease with time. However, if you have vomiting and diarrhea and are not able to keep down fluids, call your doctor. Dehydration can have serious side effects. If you consume more than two to four alcoholic drinks a week, you should probably not take metformin.

Metformin can be taken alone or with acarbose as part of a combination pill. Unlike some other oral diabetes drugs, metformin does not cause low blood sugar when taken on its own. There are two popular drugs that contain metformin: Glucophage (metformin) and Glucovance (metformin plus glyburide).

Alpha Glucosidase Inhibitors

The alpha glucosidase inhibitors (AGIs) work by blocking the enzymes in your gastrointestinal tract that break down carbohydrates—delaying, but not preventing, their digestion. They also slow the rate at which food leaves the stomach. The two drugs in this class are acarbose (the generic form of Precose) and miglitol. An AGI should be taken with the first bite of a meal.

Possible nutritional side effects include the following:

- Abdominal pain
- Diarrhea
- Flatulence (intestinal gas)
- Delayed gastric emptying
- Modest weight loss in overweight diabetics

These side effects lessen with time and can be reduced or prevented by starting with a low dose and gradually increasing it. Beneficial effects of acarbose can include decreased levels of glycosylated hemoglobin (HbAlc), triglycerides, and low-density lipoprotein (LDL, the bad cholesterol) and increased levels of high-density lipoprotein (HDL, the good cholesterol).

An AGI can be prescribed alone with either a sulfonylurea or metformin or as part of a combination pill with sulfonylurea or metformin. When taken alone, it does not cause low blood sugar, but if taken in combination with a sulfonylurea, low blood glucose is a possible side effect. In this case, the hypoglycemia should be treated with glucose tablets or gel, since some sugar digestion is delayed by the AGI, and hypoglycemia needs immediate treatment.

The over-the-counter AGI acarbose was one of the original "starch-blocker" products that were supposed to allow dieters to have their starchy foods without the pesky calories. However, further research showed that acarbose did not prevent starch breakdown; it just delayed it. There is currently no evidence that acarbose causes significant weight loss in overweight diabetics or any weight loss in people who are overweight but not diabetic.

Thiazolidinediones

The thiazolidinediones are commonly shortened to "**gli-tazones**" because the names of the drugs in this class end in "glitazone" (rosiglitazone and pioglitazone). It takes several months for a thiazolidinedione, or TZD, to reach full effectiveness, so this class of drugs is not usually prescribed for people with very high blood sugar. A TZD can be prescribed on its own or with a sulfonylurea as part of a combination pill, and it can be taken with or without food. This class of diabetes drugs has a unique mechanism of action that is not completely understood. Its main effects are to increase the amount of glucose absorbed by muscle cells and to decrease the amount of glucose made by the liver. Research has shown that it also reduces a number of cardiovascular risk factors.

Nutritional side effects include:

• Weight gain
• Water retention (edema)

When a TZD is taken alone, it does not cause low blood sugar.

Meglitinides

The meglitinides class comprises two drugs: epaglinide and nateglinide. The **meglitinides** are rapid-acting insulin secretagogues. As with the sulfonylureas, they stimulate the pancreas to release more insulin, but they are metabolized faster and so are active for a shorter period. This action allows the meglitinides to be used to control glucose levels after a meal when glucose is elevated. Because these drugs disappear from the blood after several hours when glucose levels have returned to normal, there is a decreased risk of hypoglycemia.

Possible nutritional side effects include:

- Hypoglycemia
- Nausea
- Weight gain

These drugs must be taken frequently with meals, which makes them a poor choice for some people.

Injectable Incretin Mimetics

Not all of the drugs used to treat diabetes are taken as pills. There is a new class of injectable drugs called **incretin mimetics**, or **synthetic extendin-4**. They are the first drugs to imitate what happens inside the body naturally. Incretin mimetics are added to your oral medication regime when the pills can no longer control your glucose levels. Incretin mimetics are not insulin, although they may be taken like insulin.

The first drug in this class approved by the Food and Drug Administration is exenatide, trade name Byetta. It is a synthetic version of a hormone (incretin hormone GLP) naturally found in the body. Exenatide stimulates insulin production after a meal, but only when glucose levels are high. It also prevents glucagon release after meals and slows the rate at which the stomach empties. In animal studies, exenatide helped animals with diabetes to keep the beta cells they had and helped them to form new ones.

Possible nutritional side effects include:

- Weight loss
- Mild to moderate nausea
- Decreased appetite

The nausea caused by this drug is mild and usually occurs during the start of treatment. Exenatide is taken in addition to your oral medication regime and is given by injection.

Monitoring Your Medications

You are the person who is most knowledgeable about your health and the one most closely tracking your drugs. This puts a lot of responsibility on you. All medications have some effect on the body, so it is a must to know what you are taking and why. Some of your diabetic medications can also interact with other drugs you take, so all doctors who care for you and all pharmacists who fill your prescriptions must know all the drugs you take—even if they did not prescribe or supply them. Not all doctors will ask what other physicians have prescribed for you, so it is your duty to bring up the subject. Even when your doctor has an up-to-date list of your drugs, if he or she gives you a new prescription, you should ask if that drug will react with any of the others you are using. Also, if you consume alcoholic beverages, let your doctor and pharmacist know how much. Alcohol can interact with a wide range of drugs, increasing their side effects, decreasing the effectiveness, and even contributing to liver damage.

Following are questions to ask about a medication that is prescribed for you:

- What is the name of the drug—and its generic equivalent, if applicable?
- Why is it being prescribed?
- What are the short-term and long-term side effects?
- What are the nutritional side effects?
- Does it require any lifestyle or meal-planning changes?
- What drug-drug and/or drug-nutrient interactions are associated with it?
- When and how often should it be taken?
- Should it be taken with food or on an empty stomach?

To help you remember what you're told, it's a good idea to write it down in note form immediately. As time passes, it is easy to forget exactly why you are on a particular drug and who prescribed it, especially when multiple medications are involved.

Keep a list of all your medications in your medical and health file at home. For each medication, record who prescribed it and when, the date you stopped taking it and the reason, and any side effects you had. Always read through the inserts and drug information sheets that come with your medications, and retain them in your file. Inserts are the sheets with fine print that are supplied by the drug manufacturer. Your pharmacist may also distribute a more patient-friendly drug information sheet, but you should ask your pharmacist about insert information if it is not provided to you.

Your list should be updated at each doctor's visit and when your prescriptions are filled. Leave nothing out when drawing it up. All over-the-counter meds, herbs, vitamins, and similar supplements should be included, because they can interact with other substances. When there are changes, make sure all your caregivers know about them.

Make several copies of your medication list, and keep one with you at all times. In case of an emergency, medical personnel need to know what drugs you take. Partners or family members may be forgetful when they are worried about you.

It is a wise practice to have all your prescriptions filled at the same pharmacy. The more drugs you take, the more important this becomes. It is not rare for a person with diabetes to take one drug for high blood pressure, another for high cholesterol, and a combination of one or more drugs for diabetes itself; and the more drugs you take, the greater the chance of interactions.

Your pharmacist should be able to tell you if any of your medications can block nutrient absorption. In such cases, you will need to take them separately from your food and/ or vitamin and mineral supplements (which will also be an integral part of your program).

In the end, it is not *how* you control your blood glucose levels that is important; what matters is just that you do so. To avoid the devastating complications of diabetes, add insulin injections to your treatment plan when your doctor wants you to add insulin. Some people with poorly controlled type 2 diabetes see having to start insulin as a failure, so they postpone it as long as they can. Sometimes no matter what pill you take or how closely you follow your diet, you simply can no longer control your glucose levels. This is not a personal failure, and you have done nothing wrong. Doctors now realize that type 2 diabetes is a progressive disease. As the years go by, less and less insulin is produced despite the patient's best efforts. Too many patients with type 2 diabetes put off starting insulin and pay for it later with their eyesight or feet.

8

Managing Low Blood Sugar, High Blood Sugar, and Ketoacidosis

Hypoglycemia occurs when the body's blood sugar levels drop too low. In the case of diabetes, hypoglycemia happens when there is too much insulin in your blood and not enough sugar. The high level of insulin removes too much glucose from the blood, leaving not enough for the nerves and brain to function. If you take insulin or a drug such as one of the sulfonylureas, which stimulate insulin production, episodes of low blood sugar are going to be a fact of life, so plan ahead for them. Having one low blood sugar response puts you at risk for another the same day.

When glucose levels in the blood rise after a meal, the body responds by releasing insulin. Sometimes, however, the body does not secrete enough insulin to return glucose levels to normal. This results in hyperglycemia, a blood-sugar level of more than 180 milligrams of sugar per deciliter (mg/dl). If not treated, high blood sugar can progress to an emergency life-threatening condition known as **dia-**

betic ketoacidosis, or DKA. Ketoacidosis can result in coma or death.

This chapter will help you to recognize the symptoms and causes of some of the most dangerous diabetic complications, including hypoglycemia, hyperglycemia, and keto-acidosis. It will also provide you with helpful suggestions for managing these illnesses and emergency situations.

Low Blood Sugar

Many of the symptoms of low blood sugar are caused by epinephrine (adrenaline), a stress hormone that tells your liver to release more glucose so your blood sugar returns to normal. Because hypoglycemia can be so dangerous, you must learn how to recognize the early symptoms (Table 8.1, left-hand column). Make sure your family is familiar

Table 8.1 Early and late symptoms of hypoglycemia

EARLY SYMPTOMS	LATE SYMPTOMS
Sweating	Confusion
Pale skin	Blurred vision
Shaking	Impaired coordination
Pounding heart	Personality change
Hunger	Numbness in mouth
Headache	Seizures
Dizziness	Fainting
Irritability	Agitation
Weakness	
Frequent sighing	
Nausea/vomiting	

Table 8.2 Nighttime and morning-after symptoms
of hypoglycemia

NIGHTTIME SYMPTOMS	MORNING-AFTER SYMPTOMS
Insomnia	Headache/hangover upon
Nightmares	waking
Sweat-filled sheets or	Difficulty waking up
nightclothes	Unusually high blood sugar
Waking up with	after breakfast
pounding heart	Small amount of ketones with no
Restlessness and inability	glucose in morning urine
to go back to sleep	

with the late symptoms (Table 8.1, right-hand column)
and that they know what to do to help. A severe hypoglycemic episode can make you appear to be drunk, even
violent, when you are really in serious need of medical
help. Because the brain is so dependent on glucose, low
blood-sugar levels can even cause a coma.

Hypoglycemia can also occur during the night when
you sleep unaware of the symptoms. If you have any of
these symptoms at night or in the morning, the real problem might be nighttime hypoglycemia (Table 8.2).

Causes of Hypoglycemia

Blood sugar levels drop when you:

- Overestimate how much insulin you need and take
  too much
- Do not eat enough food to compensate for the
  amount of insulin you took

- Take too many epaglinide or nateglinide pills (sulfo-nylureas), which stimulate your pancreas to produce insulin
- Get more exercise than usual, which decreases your blood sugar
- Eat later than usual or miss a meal or snack
- Have an overactive thyroid
- Drink alcohol on an empty stomach

When your stomach empties too fast, before the carbo-hydrate in it has had a chance to be released, insulin goes unopposed and blood sugar levels drop. Some research has found that the stomachs of people experiencing hypogly-cemia emptied three times faster than the rate for peo-ple who were not hypoglycemic. Since it takes longer for carbohydrate to be released from whole and unprocessed produce and grains than from refined and fully processed food, unprocessed and fiber rich-foods can actually make hypoglycemia worse. There is still too much insulin and not enough glucose to match it. If you have problems con-trolling your blood sugar (Table 8.3), a stomach that emp-ties too fast might be the reason.

Table 8.3 Recommended ranges for blood sugar

TIME OF TEST	NORMAL (MG/DL)
Before breakfast	70–120
1 hour after eating	Less than 180
2 hours after eating	Less than 150
At bedtime	120–140
At 3:00 a.m.	More than 65

Table 8.4 Ketone testing*

AMOUNT	URINE TESTING (MG/DL)	BLOOD TESTING (MMOL/L)
Small	More than 20	Less than 0.6
Moderate	30–40	0.6–1.5
Large	More than 80	More than 1.5

* Urine ketones lag behind blood ketone levels. At the start of ketoacidosis, the blood ketone level will be much higher than urine levels. Testing for ketones in the blood allows them to be detected two to four hours earlier than with urine testing.

Call your doctor if you have a moderate to high amount of ketones in your urine (see Table 8.4), as detailed in the final section of this chapter, or if you have a blood-sugar reading in any of the following danger categories:

- Less than 70 mg/dl three days in a row
- More than 180 mg/dl three days in a row
- 300 mg/dl or more even once

When you determine your blood sugar is too low, you should take these steps immediately.

In a low-blood-sugar emergency (readings of less than 70 mg/dl), eat one serving of carbohydrate from the following list, wait fifteen minutes, and recheck your blood-sugar level. Each serving contains about fifteen grams of sugar.

- One-half cup orange
- One-third cup apple juice
- One tablespoon honey, molasses, or corn syrup
- Three glucose tabs, each 5 mg (check the dose—not all glucose tabs are made for diabetics)

- One small tube (single serving of 15 grams) of glucose gel or one-third of a large tube (45 grams) of glucose gel.
- One rounded tablespoon of table sugar
- Four to six pieces of hard candy (depending on size)

Other guidelines for blood-sugar control:

- If after eating one serving of carbohydrate your blood sugar is still less than 80 mg/dl, eat one more serving.
- If you are sitting down to eat, have one serving of carbohydrate before you begin your meal. Don't depend on the meal to bring up your blood sugar— it will take too long.
- If your next scheduled meal is more than forty-five minutes away, have the one serving and then some protein-containing snack such as peanut butter and bread or cheese and crackers. This should prevent another low-blood-sugar reaction.
- If you are having nighttime symptoms, set your clock and test at 2 a.m. for a few nights.
- When someone suggests that you check your blood-sugar levels, do not resist.

How to Prevent and Prepare for Hypoglycemia

If you take insulin or a sulfonylurea, the question is not *if* you will have hypoglycemia but rather *when*, so you will need to plan ahead. Here are some recommendations:

- Make it easy for others to help you when you can't speak for yourself by carrying a medical ID of some sort that identifies you as having diabetes. Don't depend on an ID card hidden away in your purse or wallet; they are easily misplaced and often the last place that is checked. A medic-alert symbol on a bracelet or neck chain is best.
- When you take a chromium supplement, closely monitor your blood sugar levels and adjust your medication accordingly. Chromium may enhance the effect of your medication and can make it work *too* well.
- Limit alcohol intake, and don't drink on an empty stomach.
- Exercise cautiously until you are more knowledgeable about how your body and blood sugar reacts. Eat extra carbs before doing physically demanding household chores such as lawn work.
- Learn from your episodes. Soon after a low blood sugar reaction, look back at how you might have recognized it so you will recognize it next time.
- Carry an emergency kit. You might find yourself in a situation where you cannot get home or find food.

Hypoglycemia Unawareness

The longer you have diabetes and the more frequently you have hypoglycemia, the less able you are to recognize low blood sugar. It is as if your body becomes so used to the condition that it no longer bothers to give you warning

signs. This is a condition called hypoglycemia unawareness. People with this condition can pass out without even
knowing their blood-sugar level is low.

Hypoglycemia unawareness can happen to people who
are on intensive insulin therapy. Because their glucose
levels are kept within a tight range, glucose does not fall
fast enough for epinephrine to be produced. Nerve damage (neuropathy), depression, and stress can also decrease
production of epinephrine and lead to hypoglycemia
unawareness. Beta blockers can block the symptoms of
hypoglycemia, and alcohol can prevent the mind from
recognizing symptoms.

Hypoglycemia unawareness happens to almost 20 percent of type 1 diabetes patients and is more common in
women than in men. It can happen to pregnant women
and people who have had frequent bouts of hypoglycemia. Never assume you are able to sense your blood-
sugar level. The only way to know your levels is to test.
If you develop hypoglycemia unawareness, follow these
guidelines:

- Before taking part in any activity that requires your
  full attention—for example, before driving your
  car—test your blood sugar.
- Reduce how frequently you have low blood sugar
  episodes. Especially try to prevent having episodes
  within two days of each other.
- Set your target blood-sugar levels higher so you
  have no more than one or two low levels per week.
  Discuss this with your endocrinologist or diabetes
  educator first.
- Ask your doctor about prescribing acarbose (Precose) or Glyset (miglitol) to delay absorption of car-

bohydrates. This has been shown to reduce risk of hypoglycemia.

Preventing all lows for two weeks increases symptoms of hypoglycemia; preventing them for three months lets symptoms return to nearly normal severity.

Emergency Kit

Be prepared for any crisis—always carry an emergency kit with you that contains the following items:

- **Glucose.** Keep one or two 15-gram servings of carbohydrate with you at all times to bring up your blood-sugar levels. Keep a serving or two in your car, and more where you work. Glucose gel and glucose tabs take up the least space.
- **Food.** An aseptic carton of milk (does not need refrigeration) and a snack-size pack of peanut butter and crackers or cheese and crackers. Keep additional food in your car and where your work.
- **Insulin.** Have enough insulin and syringes to last several days.
- **Glucose meter.** Never leave the house without your glucose meter so you can test your blood-sugar levels away from home. Be sure to include any extra supplies, such as alcohol pads, testing strips, and lances.
- **Water replacement.** You need to keep yourself hydrated if you are in a situation where water is not available. A glass bottle of water will keep indefinitely if unopened. Keep one with you, one or more in your car, and one at work.

- **Emergency phone numbers.** Include numbers for your family doctor, your endocrinologist, the hospital where they have privileges, and your next of kin.
- **Your medication list.** You will find information on preparing a list in Chapter 7.

Alcohol and Hypoglycemia

Alcohol is quickly absorbed through the stomach; it does not require digestion as do other nutrients. Once in the blood, it can enhance the effects of insulin and other diabetic medications and put you at risk for hypoglycemia for up to several hours. If your blood sugar levels are under control, drinking one serving of alcohol with meals will have minimal consequences. However, if you are having problems keeping your blood sugar levels within range, skip the alcohol. No matter what kind of diabetes you have or how well it is controlled, never drink alcohol on an empty stomach. The faster and harder a drink "hits" you, the greater the risk of hypoglycemia. The symptoms of hypoglycemia are the same as those of intoxication, so a blood-sugar emergency could be mistaken by you and by others as your having had too much to drink.

Exercise and Hypoglycemia

Exercise burns energy, so it decreases the glucose levels in your blood. If you do not adjust your medication when you exercise, glucose levels can drop too low and bring on hypoglycemia.

- You must learn how your blood sugar levels react to the different types of exercise you do, and the only way you can be sure is by testing. Test both before you start to exercise and after you finish. If your blood glucose levels are lower than 100 mg/dl, eat a carbohydrate-containing snack before you begin exercising.
- Keep an exercise log that documents the type of exercise, length of exercise, and your glucose levels before and after. Reviewing your log will help you learn how to anticipate your body's needs.
- Always have an emergency source of carbohydrate close at hand in case your glucose levels drop too low during exercise.
- Never exercise alone, and always carry a medical ID that identifies you as having diabetes.

High Blood Sugar

Hyperglycemia can be a sign that your present treatment plan is no longer working and that you need to change your medication regime and/or diet. Type 2 diabetes is a progressive disease, and your treatment plan will need to be altered accordingly from stage to stage. If you have type 2 diabetes, your blood sugar could be elevated because you are not eating enough carbs. Consuming too few carbs in the evening can lead to low blood sugar the next morning after a long overnight fast. Your liver tries to compensate for this state by "dumping" its store of glucose into the blood, elevating glucose levels, and in the morning the body overreacts to your usual number of carbs.

Hyperglycemia can also be caused by other circumstances. Be on guard for these potential triggers:

- The dietary prescription was not followed.
- An insulin injection or oral medication was skipped or forgotten.
- Injected insulin may no longer be reaching its target. If you have recently gained fat mass, the insulin needle may not be long enough to reach through the fat layer.
- There is a blockage in your insulin pump tubing, or the pump infusion set is disconnected.
- You have a cold, the flu, or some other infection and/or illness.
- You're experiencing increased stress.
- Your activity level is lower than usual.

Symptoms of hyperglycemia vary and include thirst (polydipsia), frequent urination (polyuria), blurred vision, fatigue, sugar in the urine, weight loss, increased appetite, repeated vaginal and skin infections, and slow healing of cuts and sores.

What You Can Do

When you determine your blood sugar is too high, don't delay in taking action. Your behavior can have a profound effect on your health and safety. For example:

- Test your blood sugar frequently: when you get out of bed (fasting), before you go to bed, and two hours after every meal. If it's over 240 mg/dl, test your urine for ketones, per the guidelines in the following section.

- Call your doctor if your blood sugar before breakfast is more than 180 mg/dl three days in a row.
- Choose whole fruits and vegetables over fruit juices and sweet vegetable juices. An apple will increase insulin levels only slightly, versus the rise induced by a glass of apple juice.
- Don't eat sweet foods on an empty stomach. The stomach quickly empties, and the sugar is immediately absorbed.
- Eat foods rich in vitamin C, which may help to keep glucose production by the liver within normal bounds.
- Incorporate fish in your diet. Dutch researchers at the National Institute of Public Health found that eating one ounce of fish (lean, fatty, or canned) a day protected against the development of glucose intolerance.
- Eat brown rice, brown bread, and whole grains. Not only are they sources of chromium, but they also contain fiber, which will extend the amount of time food spends in your stomach.
- Consume foods rich in chromium. Refer to Chapter 6 for more information on the benefits.

To avoid raising insulin levels when eating carbohydrates, base your food selections on these guidelines:

- Emphasize starches that have a high amylopectin content. A diet rich in amylopectin starch has been shown to improve insulin tolerance and decrease triglyceride levels. Foods high in amylopectin starch such as new potatoes, legumes, and basmati rice are absorbed more slowly.

- Choose acidic foods, such as fruit and tomatoes; fermented foods, such as buttermilk, yogurt, and sourdough bread; foods preserved with vinegar; and foods seasoned with acid, such as salads with lemon juice or vinegar-based dressings. Acid in food slows down digestion.
- Do not overcook pasta and starchy vegetables such as potatoes and yams. Cooking food softens the cells that contain starch, bursting them open and making starch more available to the digestive enzymes of the gastrointestinal tract. The longer a starchy food is cooked, the faster it will elevate glucose and insulin levels.
- Because large pieces of food take longer to digest and absorb, it's best not to mash or puree starchy foods. Serve potatoes in slices or smashed rather than whipped. Choose larger sizes of pasta.
- Eat whole, unrefined starchy foods such as brown rice and oats. Their fat and fiber slow digestion and absorption and blunt the insulin response. By contrast, instant white rice and highly processed breakfast cereals elevate blood sugar levels too quickly.

Ketoacidosis

When there is too much sugar and not enough insulin, your cells are forced to burn fatty acids for fuel. This process creates chemicals called **ketones** (acetone, beta hydroxybutyrate, and acetoacetate) as a by-product. Ketones not only are toxic but also make the blood dangerously acidic. Ketones appear first in the blood and then in the urine (where they can be detected with a urine test). **Ketoacidosis** is a complication of type 1 diabetes; it rarely occurs in people with type 2, even if they are on insulin. Low levels of ketones are common in women with gestational diabetes. The causes of ketoacidosis are the same as those of hyperglycemia. Ketoacidosis can occur in type 2 diabetics who are seriously ill and in women with gestational diabetes who have been vomiting. Nausea and vomiting can throw off meal plans, causing ketoacidosis, which in turn causes more nausea and vomiting. It becomes a vicious circle. Morning ketones can also be a sign of low blood sugar during the night. In the morning, the body rebounds and bounces back to normal.

Signs that hyperglycemia has progressed to ketoacidosis are a fruity odor to the breath (not everyone can detect this odor); nausea and vomiting; deep, rapid breathing; abdominal pain, and shortness of breath. If you have any of these symptoms, test both your blood-sugar level and urine for ketones.

What You Can Do

Today there are two ways to test for ketones: urine testing and blood testing (Table 8.4). Both can be done at home. A normal result is negative—there should be no ketones in either the blood or the urine.

Test your urine for ketones if any of the following applies:

- You don't feel good or you have the flu or a cold. When you are sick, ketones can be present even when blood sugar levels are not high.
- You have unexplained nausea and vomiting.
- You are pregnant.
- Your fasting blood sugar level is over 240 mg/dl.
- Your daytime blood sugar level is over 300 mg/dl.

This is not a condition you can treat yourself. You must contact your doctor and follow the directions you're given. If your ketone level is moderate or large, you must call your doctor immediately, day or night. After contacting your doctor, you will need to take specific actions:

- Drink water to prevent dehydration.
- Monitor your blood sugar levels. Your doctor may tell you to give yourself a small amount of very rapid acting insulin.
- Go to the emergency room if directed by your doctor. You may need intravenous fluids and insulin therapy.
- If you have gestational diabetes, your doctor may have you drink a glass of milk before you go to bed and another at 3 a.m. You should not go more than eight or nine hours between snack and breakfast.

To prevent ketoacidosis, contact your doctor as soon as you have even a low level of ketones in your urine, if your blood sugar is more than 240 mg/dl, or if you have any symptoms of the illnesses. If your blood ketones are above 3 millimoles per liter (3 mmol/L), have someone take you to the emergency room.

9

Dealing with Oral Complications and Motility Disorders

You depend on your teeth and gums to start processing the food you eat for digestion. When the tissues of your mouth become diseased or painful from cavities, gum disease, or infections, eating and processing good food becomes difficult, and getting all the nutrients you need becomes challenging. Your oral health is tied to the health of your body, and the health of your body is affected by diabetes. Oral complications of diabetes and insulin resistance include periodontal disease, inflammation of the gums, dry mouth (xerostomia), burning mouth syndrome, poor wound healing, cavities, candida, and other oral infections.

Your gastrointestinal tract is a thirty-foot muscular tube that runs through the center of your body. Its purpose is not only digestion but also absorption of what is digested, storage of what is not, and excretion of waste products and undigested food. The movement of this tube is called **gastrointestinal motility**. Food is squeezed through the alimentary canal via a series of rhythmic muscle contractions called peristalsis. When these muscle contractions are abnormal, motility in the digestive system is affected. Motility disorders from diabetes can cause peristalsis to increase, decrease, or become uncoordinated.

This chapter will educate you about symptoms, causes, and solutions related to oral complications and motility disorders that can affect you when you have diabetes.

Dental Care and Diabetes

Diabetes afflicts the body in numerous ways. When your blood sugar level is elevated, so is the glucose level in your saliva. This excess sugar feeds the bacteria and fungi growing in your mouth and puts you at risk for developing infections that cause cavities, gum disease, and oral candidiasis. Because of this, controlling your blood glucose levels is the single most effective thing you can do to prevent infections and maintain good oral health.

At the same time, diabetes weakens the neutrophils, a type of white blood cell that is responsible for defending your body from infections. This adds another risk factor for the development of infections. Blood flow to the tissues of the mouth can also be decreased, which can make the tissues slower to heal after dental surgery.

Research has shown that the health of your heart is related to the health of your mouth. People who have aggressive gum infections also have higher cholesterol levels.

Guidelines for Oral Hygiene

As soon as you are diagnosed with diabetes, insulin resistance, or the metabolic syndrome, you need to commit to a thorough program of oral hygiene.

- Have your teeth cleaned and examined by a dentist every six months. If you have some of the dental problems mentioned here, you may require more frequent treatment. Ask your dentist how often is right for you.
- Brush your teeth gently after each meal, using a soft-bristle toothbrush with rounded ends. Brushing removes the sticky bacterial plaque that causes cavities.
- Brush your tongue and your gums when you brush your teeth. Bacterial deposits can build up on the tongue too.
- Floss your teeth every day. Flossing removes plaque and trapped bits of food from between your teeth and under your gums where the toothbrush cannot reach.
- Use toothpaste that contains fluoride, which can help kill bacteria in addition to making your teeth stronger and more cavity resistant. This is especially important if the water in your area is not fluorinated.
- If your gums become too sore to brush, clean around gums with a soft cloth. Use nonirritating toothpaste. A paste of baking soda and water makes a gentle but refreshing cleaner.
- Rinse your mouth with water after consuming sweet foods or juices.

- Make sure your toothbrush does not become a breeding place for germs. Replace it every three to four months, and always rinse it well and leave it to air-dry before putting it away.
- Invest in tools such as electric or sonic toothbrushes, floss holders, irrigators, stimulators for gum tissues, and special rinses to reduce bacterial levels as well as protect eroded enamel. Ask your dentist or hygienist which tools are appropriate for you.

Guidelines for Office Visits

Your dentist and/or oral surgeon should have a record of all the prescription medication, over-the-counter drugs, and food supplements that you take and their dosages. In case there are questions about your treatment, your dentist needs to have a record of the name and phone number of your family doctor and endocrinologist. Likewise, all your doctors should have the name and number of your dentist and/or oral surgeon. Each time you see your dentist, be prepared to give a status report on your health, including your latest glycosylated hemoglobin (HbAlc) level and whether you have had a recent hypoglycemic episode.

Other suggestions to remember:

- Before scheduling oral surgery, ask your endocrinologist if you need to take any presurgical antibiotics, change your meal schedule, or change the timing and dosage of your insulin, if applicable.
- If you use insulin, schedule dental work in the morning, after you have eaten.

- If you are being treated for a dental infection, your insulin dosage may have to be adjusted.
- If your blood sugar levels are out of control, put off dental work until it is back in range. If the dental work is an emergency, it may have to be done in a hospital setting.
- Before your dental appointment, stay on your usual medication schedule—unless your dentist tells you otherwise.
- Be sure to eat before having dental work, so your blood sugar level is in a normal range.
- After dental work, stay on your usual meal plan. Use your sick-day meal plan if necessary.

The Mouth-Body Connection: Oral Complications to Watch Out For

Along with a diagnosis of diabetes comes the possibility of a number of additional oral problems.

Cavities (Caries)

While sugar does not directly cause cavities, it greatly contributes to the environment that causes them. **Streptococci mutan** are bacteria growing in the mouth that form a film that sticks to the teeth, called plaque. The bacteria make acids out of the sugars in your mouth that are strong enough to eat through the enamel surface of your teeth, causing cavities.

Plaque is constantly being formed, not only on your teeth but also on your gums. It hides bacteria and other infective factors. If it is not removed, it builds up, forming a hard material called calculus or tartar. Brushing and flossing can remove plaque, but they cannot remove calculus. It can be removed only during a professional cleaning.

Periodontal Disease and Periodontitis

The word *periodontal* means "around the tooth." Each tooth is rooted in the gum tissue, or gingiva, and attached to the bone of the jaw with connective tissue. Healthy gums surround your teeth like a turtleneck sweater; the fit is snug, with barely any space separating the gum, tooth, and bone. Periodontal disease is a chronic bacterial infection that affects the gums and the bone that holds the teeth in place. It is more common in people with uncontrolled blood sugar levels.

In people with diabetes, gum infections have consequences that extend far beyond the mouth. Studies have shown that periodontal disease actually makes diabetes worse, and successfully treating periodontal disease makes glucose control easier. When you have diabetes, infections take longer to treat and are harder to stop, so you must start treatment as soon as gum disease is diagnosed. Don't wait to see if the disease gets better on its own; it won't.

The first stage of gum disease is **gingivitis**, or inflammation of the gums. It begins when the bacteria in plaque cause the tissue along the gum line to become inflamed and start to pull away from the teeth. At this stage, there is no damage to the connective tissue or bone. Symptoms include bad breath and red, swollen, and sore gums that may bleed when you brush your teeth. Healthy gums do not bleed, so see your dentist if you notice pink marks on your toothbrush or in the sink after you brush.

With time, plaque spreads below the gum line. Toxins made by the bacteria it carries irritate the gums and cause inflammation that soon spreads to the underlying bone anchoring the teeth. Plaque that is not removed hardens into calculus, which makes the condition worse. Gum tissue continues to pull away from the teeth, forming pockets that become infected. Over time, the pockets deepen, and more gum tissue is destroyed. Bone that supports the teeth is broken down, loosening them so that teeth may have to be removed. As painful as the process sounds, often the symptoms are mild. Following are warning signs:

- Your gums bleed easily and/or are red, swollen, or sore.
- Your gums pull away from the teeth.
- There is pus between your teeth and gums.
- There is pus when your gums are pressed.
- You have a persistent bad taste in your mouth or bad breath.

If you suspect you have gingivitis, see your dentist immediately. Therapy for periodontal disease may involve surgery, antimicrobials such as Listerine and chlorhexidine gluconate (Peridex), or a combination of both. If you smoke, stop. The chemicals in smoke reduce blood flow to tissues that desperately need it. Patients with diabetes who smoke have a greater risk of developing gum disease than nonsmokers.

Can Gum Disease Cause Diabetes?

Which comes first, the gum disease or the diabetes? According to some researchers, you shouldn't be too sure it is the diabetes. The common theory is that changes caused by diabetes lead to an increased risk of infection. But what if it started with a bacterial infection that causes gum disease and the release of bacteria into circulation? The body would respond with inflammation, sending cytokine messages that are destructive. This damage can cause type 2 diabetes in people who have no other risk factors for diabetes.

Xerostomia

Diabetes can impair the ability of the salivary glands to produce saliva, a condition called **xerostomia**. So can age and a number of over-the-counter drugs. A dry mouth makes chewing and swallowing difficult, and since saliva keeps the mouth clean, a dry mouth is a haven for bacteria. Xerostomia can lead to cavities, inflammation of the tongue, bad breath (halitosis), cracking of the oral tissues, salivary gland infection, yeast infections (oral candidiasis), and ulcers of the tongue.

Combating xerostomia requires several actions:

- You must be extra vigilant in your oral hygiene. Keep your teeth clean and flossed, your tongue brushed, and your mouth tissues rinsed.
- Between meals or at night, use a wetting agent such as Salivart or Xero-lube to prevent dryness.

These products can be purchased in drugstores and pharmacies.

- During meals, take small sips of water to help you swallow food.
- To keep your saliva flowing, chew sugar-free gum or drink a small glass of water with a tablespoon of lemon juice before meals.
- To relieve mouth irritations and sores, apply vitamin E or tea tree oil to the area.
- Carry a small water bottle with you and take frequent sips between meals to keep oral tissues hydrated. Keep a glass of water on your nightstand for when you wake up with a "cotton" mouth.
- If you smoke, stop. Smoking will make xerostomia worse.
- Reduce the amount of alcohol that you drink. Alcohol will also make xerostomia worse and further dehydrate your tissues.

Candidiasis (Thrush)

Oral candidiasis, also called **thrush**, is a fungal infection caused by the yeast *Candida albicans*, an otherwise normal inhabitant of the mouth. This yeast loves mucous membranes and other warm, moist areas of the body. In healthy people, the growth of candida in the mouth is held in check by the immune system, a limited amount of food (sugar) to feed on, and the cleansing action of the saliva. All three are out of balance in people with diabetes, so they stand a greater chance of developing an oral candida infection.

If the sugar level in your blood is elevated, you are going to have a high sugar level in your saliva too. Sugar feeds yeast. When you have diabetes, your body is also less able to fight off infections caused by microorganisms. All of this adds up to an environment that can allow candida to thrive. The free flow of saliva is one way your body protects the tissues in your mouth, so xerostomia also puts you at risk of developing oral candidiasis.

Candidiasis produces white (sometimes red), velvety patches in the mouth that slowly increase in size and number. They can be painful or can cause no discomfort at all. These lesions can spread down the esophagus too, making swallowing painful. Left untreated, they can grow into ulcers. Candidiasis can also cause the tongue to burn painfully, a condition called **burning mouth syndrome**. **Angular chelitis** is another complication that happens when candida takes up residence in the deep folds that some people have in the corners of the mouth. It causes skin cracking and pain when the person smiles or talks.

If you have candidiasis, eat at least one serving of yogurt a day. Choose a yogurt with live cultures (it should be marked on the label). If you drink milk, switch to a brand that contains acidophilus. Eating yogurt and the bacteria it contains increases the competition of yeast for food. Also, lightly crushing fresh garlic produces allicin, a natural antifungal. Along with the appropriate drugs, this might prevent or slow the yeast from spreading to the gut.

Gastroparesis (Delayed Gastric Emptying)

One cause of motility disorders is diabetic autonomic neuropathy, or DAN. It can affect the stomach and cause gastroparesis; it can also affect the colon and cause constipation and diarrhea.

Gastroparesis, or delayed gastric emptying, is a motility disorder in which food remains in the stomach too long. The word literally means "stomach paralysis." It is a chronic condition that occurs in about 20 percent of people with type 1 diabetes, but it also occurs in type 2 diabetes.

The healthy stomach collects food coming in from the esophagus and pulverizes it into a semiliquid, much the way a blender operates. The valve at the bottom of the stomach then opens every few minutes, and the muscles squirt a few milliliters of the pulverized food through it into the first part of the small intestine (the duodenum), where absorption continues.

When a person has gastroparesis, the stomach is not able to contract normally. It cannot crush food or propel it into the small intestine properly. This can stop the stomach from digesting food. A doctor may need to prescribe medication to regulate muscle contractions.

The following are questions to consider if you think you have gastroparesis. Discuss your answers with your doctor.

- Has your appetite changed recently?
- Do you feel full after eating a small amount of food?
- Do you have unexplained nausea?
- Have you vomited undigested food, especially in the morning?
- Have you felt bloated?
- Do you have heartburn?
- Do you have abdominal cramping or pain?
- Have you had any difficulty controlling your blood glucose recently?

- Have you gained or lost any weight recently?
- Have you had diarrhea or constipation recently?

The vagus nerve controls the movement of food through the digestive tract. As with all other nerves, it is vulnerable to damage from high glucose levels caused by diabetes. The vagus sends a message to the smooth muscle of the stomach, telling it to contract and move the food forward. When the vagus nerve is injured, the movement of food through the stomach and intestine is slowed. For more on neuropathy refer to Chapter 2.

Be aware that any medicine that slows the movement of the muscles of the digestive system can mimic the symptoms of gastroparesis. This includes narcotic pain medications, tricyclic antidepressants, calcium channel blockers, clonidine, dopamine agonists, lithium, nicotine, and progesterone-containing medications. However, don't assume the problem is neuropathy until your doctor has reviewed your records and run some tests.

Treating gastroparesis calls for certain adjustments:

- If you take insulin, you may need to take it more often.
- You may need to take your insulin after you eat instead of before.
- Check your blood glucose levels frequently after you eat and administer insulin whenever necessary.

In addition, diet modification is one of the most frequently prescribed treatments for gastroparesis. Try the following suggestions:

- Avoid foods that are hard to digest. This includes fibrous foods such as raw fruits and vegetables.
- If you are not already eating small meals, start now. Eat six small meals a day, and avoid large ones. If less food enters the stomach each time you eat, the stomach may not become overly full.
- Substitute liquid meals until your blood glucose levels are stable and symptoms go away. They provide all the nutrients in solid foods but can pass through the stomach faster.
- Avoid fatty foods. Fat decreases the rate at which food leaves the stomach.
- Avoid carbonated beverages, such as soft drinks and sparkling cider and water.
- Avoid foods that contain large amounts of cellulose, such as oranges and broccoli. Cellulose is an insoluble fiber that the human body cannot digest. If it remains in the stomach for too long, it can cause a solid mass, or bezoar. This can be dangerous if the bezoar causes a blockage.
- Cook fibrous foods until they're soft, and chew them well.

Motility in the Colon: Constipation and Diarrhea

The large colon is divided into four sections: ascending, transverse, descending, and sigmoid. The ascending colon receives the watery chyme with undigested fiber from the small intestine. Together with the transverse colon, it reabsorbs electrolytes and water at the rate of two liters per day. How fast the chyme moves through these sections determines its water content. If the chyme moves too slowly, more water is absorbed, and the feces are very dry (constipation). If it moves too fast, the water does not have time to be reabsorbed, and the feces are too watery (diarrhea).

As the peristaltic movements of the colon propel the dehydrating mass along, water is trapped by the undigested fiber (primarily insoluble fibers) in the chyme, preventing the stool from becoming too dry. Other undigested fibers (primarily soluble fibers) are eaten by the many species of "friendly" bacteria that live in the colon, causing a population explosion that contributes additional bulk to the dehydrated feces, making it easier to pass.

The descending and sigmoid colons are used for storage. When fecal matter is pushed into the rectum, the distention stimulates the reflex to defecate.

Constipation

Constipation is a common side effect of neuropathy. As the liquidlike remnants of a meal pass through the large intestine, water is absorbed, producing a solid mass. The longer the mass stays in the colon, the more water is removed. When peristalsis slows, too much water is removed, and a dry, hard stool is produced.

Constipation can also be the result of insufficient fiber in the diet. Water can be trapped by the undigested fiber (primarily insoluble fibers) from fruits, vegetables, and whole grains, preventing the stool from becoming too dry.

Causes of constipation include the following:

- Treatment side effects. Some of the oral drugs used to treat type 2 diabetes can cause nausea and lack of appetite. These side effects often lead the sufferer to greatly reduce the intake of fibrous foods, thus bringing on constipation.
- Decrease in activity. Diabetes often leaves a person feeling drained and tired. Exercise becomes a low priority, and all of the muscles in the body suffer, including those responsible for colonic movement.
- DAN, or neuropathy. The high blood sugar common in both types of diabetes and the high insulin level common in type 2 diabetes and insulin resistance can damage delicate nerves.

The following dietary suggestions can help prevent or treat constipation:

- Incorporate bran into your diet. Wheat bran is the usual recommendation for increasing fiber intake, but rice bran tastes and works better. For a morning treat, sprinkle wheat or rice bran or ground psyllium seed on cooked or cold breakfast cereals, nonfat yogurt, or fresh fruit. Start with one teaspoon, and gradually work up to a tablespoon. These foods are concentrated sources of insoluble fiber, which will increase the bulk and frequency of bowel movements by attracting water into the feces. Wheat bran holds three times its weight in water, and rice bran may hold even more. Soluble bran, such as oat bran, also may be effective.

- Increase the amount of water you are drinking to at least eight glasses a day. This is particularly important if you are supplementing with cereal brans. Measure out the water in the morning so you will know how much you need to drink.

- Increase dietary fiber. Substitute whole grains for refined grains, including brown rice for white rice and whole-grain bread for white bread. Eat a variety of grains, including oats, barley, and quinoa. Each grain has a unique blend of fibers with unique advantages. The brans in these grains are also important sources of valuable minerals.

- Increase the amount of raw vegetables you eat. Take small bites, and chew them thoroughly. If chewing is a problem, grate or blend raw veggies. Monitor your blood sugar closely, since processing vegetables this way decreases the amount of time it takes for the carbohydrates in them to reach your blood. In addition, eat more vegetables in the cabbage family (including bok choy, brussels sprouts, cauliflower, collards, and broccoli) and in the legume family (including beans and lentils). The gas they produce will help to increase the volume and softness of bowel movements.

- Eat more nuts and seeds. Nuts and seeds not only are high in fiber but also are rich sources of healthy fats. If you need to increase calories and fiber, eat at least two servings a day. Nuts can be whole or ground into nut butters. Take a pass on the salted or oil-roasted varieties. Nuts fresh from the shell are always best.

- Add laxative foods to your diet. Prunes are well known for their laxative abilities. They are also high in fiber, which will also help. Apple juice and pear juice contain sorbitol, another natural laxative.

- Limit coffee to one or two cups a day. One cup of coffee in the morning may act as a laxative, but too much can overstimulate the muscles of the colon, leaving them sluggish. Moderation is the key here.
- Try removing or decreasing the amount of milk and cheese you eat. These foods can cause constipation in some individuals.
- Drink hot or warm liquids before a meal to stimulate gastrointestinal-tract movement.
- Lighten up! Laughing is a wonderful source of exercise. A deep belly laugh not only stimulates abdominal muscles but also increases endorphins, the feel-good chemicals in the brain.

Diarrhea

Diarrhea occurs when food moves though the digestive tract too quickly. Sever or prolonged diarrhea not only causes the loss of water from the body; it can also seriously deplete the body of electrolytes and minerals. Some oral diabetes medications—Metformin and Precose (acarbose)—can cause diarrhea.

Avoid foods that may aggravate diarrhea. This list can guide you:

- Hot foods stimulate muscle movement and may increase diarrhea. Try foods and beverages that are cold or at room temperature.
- Milk and other dairy products can cause diarrhea due to a temporary absence of lactase, the enzyme

that digests lactose (milk sugar). Take lactase in pill form (available at your pharmacy or local health-food store) before eating.

- Avoid raw foods. Steam or pressure-cook vegetables.
- Avoid irritating foods such as coffee, alcohol, sweets, carbonated drinks, and highly spiced foods.
- Calorie-free carbonated drinks are not good sources of liquids, since they contain no energy sources or minerals to replace those lost in fluids. Sports drinks and fruit juices contain too much sugar, which can aggravate diarrhea.
- Avoid prunes and prune juice, apple juice, and pear juice. They all can have a laxative effect.
- Avoid foods that contain sorbitol, a natural laxative, including sugar-free and dietetic candies.
- Avoid foods that cause gas and are not well absorbed, such as beans and vegetables of the cabbage family (broccoli, cauliflower, kale, cabbage, and so on).

The following recommendations can help you choose foods to eat when you have diarrhea:

- Drink or eat starchy liquids such as split-pea or potato soup, rice or oat porridge, and mashed ripe bananas.
- The recommendation for diarrhea used to be a clear diet to rest the bowel. However, we now know that, instead of resting the bowel, this advice starves the bowel and therefore the body. Stimulation from food is necessary to keep the colon working.
- Eat a cup of nonfat yogurt. Yogurt is a natural source of friendly bacteria and a natural antibiotic.

Make sure that the yogurt contains live cultures.
This will be stated on the container.

- Nutmeg reduces peristalsis. Add a liberal sprinkle to a cup of yogurt or a mashed banana.
- To replenish lost potassium, eat more high-potassium foods, such as bananas and potatoes.

10

Gestational Diabetes

Gestational diabetes mellitus (GDM) is defined as any degree of glucose intolerance that happens during pregnancy or is first recognized during pregnancy. It is not really diabetes, but rather an increase in blood glucose that usually goes away after the baby's birth. A doctor may call it increased blood glucose or blood sugar, insulin resistance, or decreased insulin sensitivity. Each year, according to the Department of Health and Human Services, nearly two hundred thousand women in the United States get gestational diabetes, making it one of the major concerns of pregnancy. GDM happens when the cells of the liver, muscles, and fatty tissue do not respond to insulin in the way that they should. They are resistant or not sensitive to insulin.

In the first trimester, the body is more sensitive to insulin because this is when the mother needs glucose to build her body and prepare it for the pregnancy. It is also normal for a woman to become insulin resistant during her final two months. This process shifts food (glucose) from being available for Mom to being available for the baby. This is the period when the baby needs it the most, for it is during the last part of pregnancy that 70 percent of fetal growth occurs.

Women with GDM have another problem: in addition to being insulin resistant, they make less insulin than they should. This combination of reduced insulin production and insulin resistance is the same abnormality found in type 2 diabetes. Researchers think that the stress of pregnancy may be uncovering a hidden genetic susceptibility to diabetes. Together, the insulin resistance and reduced insulin secretion cut glucose transport into muscle by 25 percent.

A baby needs calories and carbohydrates to grow, but a woman with GDM is providing way too much sugar. This excess sugar puts both at greater risk.

The mother with GDM and her baby are more likely to develop certain complications after birth:

- After pregnancy, women who had GDM have a greater chance of developing diabetes. Research has shown this risk factor to be greatest for those who are glucose intolerant early in their pregnancy and who have an elevated fasting glucose level. The greatest longtime risk factor for developing diabetes is being overweight. If you have ever had GDM, make sure your doctor screens you for diabetes at each yearly physical.
- Babies of GDM mothers stand a greater chance of being very large (macrosomia) as well as having low blood sugar, and jaundice.
- The babies of women with GDM have more body fat at birth than babies of normal women, but they weigh the same as the babies of normal pregnan-

cies by their first birthday. During early childhood, however, the fat can return and can make it more likely they will be overweight as adults.

Evaluating Your Risk for GDM

During your first prenatal visit, your doctor should evaluate your personal and family medical history for risks of GDM. If you are obese, if you had GDM with a prior pregnancy, if members of your family have a history of GDM or diabetes, or if you have sugar in your urine, you are at high risk of developing GDM with this pregnancy. You should have a glucose test as part of your first visit and again at twenty-four to twenty-eight weeks. Women with average risk should be tested at twenty-four to twenty-eight weeks.

Know these benchmarks:

- A fasting plasma glucose level greater than 126 milligrams per deciliter (mg/dl)—7 millimoles per liter (7 mmol/L)—or a nonfasting plasma glucose of greater than 200 mg/dl (11.1 mmol/L) meets the threshold for the diagnosis of diabetes.
- A fasting blood glucose level greater than 105 mg/dl (5.8 mmol/L) may be associated with an increased risk of fetal death during the last four to eight weeks of pregnancy.

A moderate exercise program can help reduce your high blood sugar levels. You should see a nutritionist, preferably one who is also a certified diabetes educator, for counseling about your diet.

If your body mass index (BMI) is greater than 30 (see Chapter 12 for information on how to calculate your BMI), your carbohydrates may be restricted to 35 percent to 40 percent of calories. A low-carbohydrate diet can decrease your risk of having a large baby and of having the cesarean section that goes along with large babies. It also helps control blood glucose and decreases your risk of needing insulin.

The metabolism of chromium, magnesium, and zinc is not normal in women with GDM. However, researchers do not yet know how changes in nutrient levels affect the growth of the baby or the mother's health. We suggest that you take chromium and zinc supplements as part of your prenatal vitamins, but do not take high levels (more than the daily values, or DVs) of any mineral unless you are under the care of a knowledgeable doctor who prescribe them. Do not restrict the salt in your diet. Season food to taste. Your baby needs the sodium.

Here are highlights of the research being done on GDM:

- Researchers believe that chromium plays some role in how insulin works in the body, but the specifics remain a mystery. Several investigators have found that chromium levels decline during pregnancy and more so in women who had repeated pregnancies in four years. When chromium supplements were given to women with GDM, the subjects had lower fasting and peak blood glucose levels. However, chromium did not prevent women with severe glucose intolerance from needing insulin.

- Some researchers have reported decreased levels of serum magnesium, which may be a sign of lower levels of magnesium in tissues. They also reported that more magnesium was lost in the urine in women with GDM. This decrease in magnesium persisted even when glucose levels were well controlled. Magnesium depends on insulin for entry into cells. If your prenatal supplement does not contain magnesium, you may want to add a magnesium malate supplement.

- Zinc is required for normal glucose metabolism. It appears to have an insulin-like effect on glucose transport into fat cells. A normal pregnancy causes insulin resistance and higher glucose levels, and a zinc deficiency may put the mother at risk for GDM.

Watch Out for Mercury

While fish oil is an important part of a healthy diet for a pregnant woman, the U.S. Food and Drug Administration advises pregnant women, women of childbearing age, nursing mothers, and small children to avoid eating shark, tuna, swordfish, king mackerel, and tilefish. These are large fish that have lived long enough to accumulate substantial amounts of mercury, which could harm the baby's developing nervous system.

If You Have Gestational Diabetes

When you have gestational diabetes, you should test your first morning urine for ketones. This helps you to understand what has been happening at night. You may not be eating enough to sustain both yourself and your baby. Your evening snacks should be substantial—two starches, one milk, and one to two proteins. Remember that your baby will not be getting any food overnight. Eat every three to four hours so that your cells have a constant supply of glucose.

Women with gestational diabetes who are nauseated should still try to eat, even though they may not feel like it. Take small portions of food so that your stomach is not overloaded.

Test your blood sugar one hour, two hours, and three hours after you have eaten. If there is a big drop in blood sugar after hours two and three, you may have reactive hypoglycemia. This happens when your beta cells have a strong reaction to carbohydrates and produce too much insulin in response to a meal, which causes a corresponding drop in blood sugar. Stick to your regular medication, mealtimes, food quantities, exercise, and blood-sugar-testing plans. Make sure to record your ketone levels with your glucose readings.

11

High Blood Pressure and High Cholesterol

High blood pressure, or hypertension, is found in 20 percent to 60 percent of patients with diabetes. Even in patients without diabetes, the effects of hypertension on tissues can be devastating. Not only does it accelerate atherosclerosis, but also it is a leading cause of strokes, kidney disease, and congestive heart failure. Worst of all, hypertension does all this damage silently with no pain or discomfort. Typically, there are no symptoms at all. When a person does finally experience difficulties, the disease has already severely damaged tissues and vessels. High blood pressure significantly raises your risk of developing the small-blood-vessel damage that causes eye, kidney, and nerve damage and the large-blood-vessel damage that causes heart disease, stroke, and peripheral artery disease. The increased pressure that hypertension exerts on the kidneys, heart, and blood vessels puts people with diabetes at greater risk of developing complications. Aggressive medical and dietary treatment reduces this risk.

In addition, many forms of heart disease are caused by high cholesterol—another risk factor for diabetes patients. Therefore, your lipoprotein profile is one of the best indicators of how your body handles lipids. Management of blood lipoproteins (often shortened to "blood lipids") by diet is one of the most basic habits you can acquire to recover from heart disease and to prevent the recurrence of heart attacks and strokes.

This chapter will help you understand your risk for high blood pressure and high cholesterol as well as the ways to get these two nemeses in hand.

Managing High Blood Pressure

Hypertension is not a disease, but rather a disorder. Once it is established, it changes the structure of the arterioles—the small, muscular arteries. The smooth-muscle cells in the arterial wall multiply and enlarge, so that the walls become thicker and the opening becomes smaller. They also contract, further constricting the opening. Think of your arteries as a simple garden hose: When water comes out the end of the hose, it continues on for an inch or two and then drops straight to the ground. You can't water a bush at the other end of the garden with just a hose. For that, you need to attach a nozzle—a tube that is narrower than the hose. When the water goes through the constricted nozzle, it is under greater pressure. It shoots out the end, easily reaching a bush ten feet away. And the narrower you make your nozzle, the farther the water goes. Aim your nozzle at the ground, and it will rip away part of your lawn if you are not careful.

If the pressure in your arteries gets high enough, it too can rip things. High blood pressure can peel the lining off artery walls and otherwise inflict trauma on these delicate cells. There is no clear-cut threshold of blood pressure above which damage occurs. The detrimental effects of hypertension increase continuously as pressure increases.

African Americans and Hypertension

In the United States, rates of diabetes, obesity, heart disease, and hypertension are higher among African Americans, particularly African-American women. High blood pressure develops earlier in African Americans when compared with Caucasian Americans; average blood pressures are much higher too. According to a report issued by the National Heart, Lung, and Blood Institute (part of the National Institutes of Health), this translates into an 80 percent higher rate of death from stroke, a 50 percent higher rate of death from heart disease, and a 320 percent greater rate of hypertension-related end-stage renal disease than those in the general population.

Researchers from Meharry Medical College and Vanderbilt University wanted to know if these differences were due to genetics or lifestyle. To answer this question, they studied the nutrition and exercise habits of 223 members of the African Hebrew Israelite community, a group of African Americans who had emigrated in the early 1970s from the United States to Israel. This group was of interest because they are the first group of African Americans to have actually emigrated from the United States in large numbers and changed their entire lifestyle. The group had virtually no health problems despite the fact that 43 percent reported a family history of hypertension and/or coronary artery disease. Questionnaires showed that they had a vegan diet (ate no meat or animal products), and more than 80 percent reported at least one session of exercise per week, with 53 percent reporting three or more exercise sessions per week. Participants also did not use tobacco and reported no alcohol or drug abuse.

The research team concluded that African Americans are not necessarily genetically predisposed to hypertension and that hypertension, obesity, and high cholesterol can be prevented with a drastic change in lifestyle.

Understanding Your Blood Pressure Numbers

Your blood pressure is stated as two numbers. For example, let's say that your blood pressure is 110/70 mmHg, which is read as 110 over 70 millimeters of mercury. This means that the pressure inside the blood vessel being measured is strong enough to force a column of mercury up to a level of 70. The first number, 110, is the *systolic* pressure. This is the pressure taken when the ventricles of the heart are pushing blood into the arteries. The second number, 70, is the *diastolic* pressure. This is the pressure taken when the ventricles are relaxed. The diastolic pressure is the least pressure that is exerted on the arterial walls. It is the most useful in assessing an individual's risk for heart disease or stroke.

Hypertension occurs when either one or both of these numbers is out of range (Table 11.1). *All* elevated readings, whether systolic or diastolic, should receive prompt attention.

Table 11.1 American Heart Association blood
pressure ranges

BLOOD PRESSURE CATEGORY	SYSTOLIC (mmHg)	DIASTOLIC (mmHg)
Normal	Less than 120 *and*	Less than 80
Prehypertension	120–139 *or*	80–89
High stage 1	140–159 *or*	90–99
High stage 2	160 or higher *or*	100 or higher

Dietary Recommendations for Hypertension

It is clear that diet affects blood pressure. Vegetarians, for example, tend to have lower blood pressures than nonvegetarians. When groups of people move from an area that has a low incidence of high blood pressure to one that has a high incidence of high blood pressure, they gradually assume the blood pressure incidence of the new area as they adopt the new diet.

Just how effective are diets in controlling blood pressure? The American Heart Association Nutrition Committee estimates that a reduction in diastolic blood pressure of just 2 millimeters of mercury could lower a person's stroke risk by as much as 15 percent and lower heart disease risk by 6 percent. Talk to your doctor if your blood pressure is above 130 over 85. Insulin resistance increases the amount of sodium excreted in the urine. This results in an increase in blood volume, increasing blood pressure.

Small dietary changes can often translate into large drops in blood pressure. If you are overweight, lose 10 percent of your body weight. When you have done this, recalculate the percent and make that your new goal. This may be enough to decrease your blood pressure. You do not have to get down to your "ideal" weight, which is often unrealistic. Weight loss will also enhance the effects of your medications.

You can also take an arginine supplement. Constricted arteries are dilated by **nitric oxide**, also called **endothelial-derived relaxing factor**. You cannot supplement nitric oxide, but you can take arginine, an amino acid that is a precursor to the enzyme that produces it. By increasing arginine, you produce more enzyme and therefore more nitric oxide. Arginine supplementation has been shown to reduce blood pressure. Since lysine, another amino acid, competes for absorption with arginine, the two should not be taken together. Supplementing lysine can also cause a decrease in arginine, for the same reason.

The sodium in salt is not the only mineral implicated in hypertension. The Western diet contains insufficient amounts of the other electrolyte minerals such as potassium, calcium, and magnesium. Several studies have shown that people who eat diets rich in potassium-containing foods tend to have lower blood pressure, while other studies have found this association in diets rich in calcium. Instead of blaming any one mineral, it may make more sense to consider hypertension to be a result of mineral imbalance.

Here are related ways to improve your diet:

- Limit alcohol. Alcohol can reduce the ability of your heart to pump and can reduce the effectiveness of medications.
- Choose fruits and vegetables that are rich in potassium, magnesium, and calcium.

- Reduce the amount of caffeine and sugar in your diet. Both can increase the amount of potassium that is excreted by the kidney.
- Take a comprehensive mineral supplement that contains calcium, magnesium, and potassium.
- Eat fatty fish at least twice a week, and take a fish oil supplement with it.
- Get enough exercise. Moderately intense physical activity, such as thirty to forty-five minutes of brisk walking most days of the week, has been shown to lower blood pressure.

Salt-Sensitive Hypertension

A higher intake of salt is related to higher blood pressure, and there is credible evidence that certain people with hypertension can lower their blood pressure by lowering their salt intake. If you suffer from high blood pressure, ask your physician if you are salt sensitive. African Americans are at greater risk for this kind of hypertension.

The American Heart Association recommends that healthy American adults reduce their sodium intake to no more than 2,400 milligrams (mg) per day. This is about one and a quarter teaspoons of sodium chloride (salt). When you add salt to your diet, these are the amounts of sodium you are adding:

¼ teaspoon of salt = 500 mg of sodium
½ teaspoon of salt = 1,000 mg of sodium
¾ teaspoon of salt = 1,500 mg of sodium
1 teaspoon of salt = 2,000 mg of sodium
1 teaspoon of baking soda = 1,000 mg of sodium

What to Look for on the Label

Claims on the labels of prepared food must conform to the following guidelines set by the Food and Drug Administration. The amounts listed here are for *one serving*, so be sure to read the labels to determine the specific serving size referenced for a given product.

- **Sodium-free** means less than 5 mg of sodium per serving
- **Very low-sodium** means 35 mg or less per serving
- **Low-sodium** means 140 mg or less per serving
- **Unsalted, no salt added,** and **without added salt** mean exactly what they say: no salt is *added* to the food. Note that these foods are not necessarily low in sodium, since some sodium may naturally be present in the ingredients.
- **Healthy** means less than 360 mg of sodium per serving, or no more than 480 mg per meal for meal-type products.

Choose foods that are naturally low in salt, such as fresh fruits and vegetables. You should also limit excessively salty foods such as smoked, cured, or processed meat; some convenience foods such as frozen meals and regular canned soups; certain spices such as regular soy sauce, garlic salt, and other salted condiments; highly salted snacks such as salted crackers, chips, pretzels, popcorn, and nuts; and many sauces, mixes, and "instant" products.

Controlling Cholesterol

Cholesterol is made in the liver, but almost every cell in the body also can make it. In fact, most cholesterol is made outside the liver. A diet rich in saturated fat causes an increase in fat storage in the liver. This fat provides the raw materials for cholesterol production, which can increase from 15 percent to 25 percent. Highly unsaturated fatty acids decrease cholesterol concentrations.

Cholesterol is manufactured from acetyl CoA molecules by an enzyme called HMG CoA reductase. When cholesterol levels in the plasma rise, this enzyme is inhibited. The amount of cholesterol manufactured is determined by the amount of available HMG CoA reductase. Less HMG-reductase translates into less cholesterol production. Agents that decrease the amount of HMG-reductase are called HMG-reductase inhibitors. HMG-reductase inhibitor drugs are the statins—drugs whose names end in "statin."

Your lipoprotein profile is one of the most reliable indicators of how your body handles lipids. Management of blood lipoproteins (often shortened to "blood lipids") by diet is one of the most important things you can do to protect your cardiovascular system and all the organs that it feeds.

Understanding Cholesterol Readings and Test Results

There are two types of cholesterol tests: screening tests and lab tests. Cholesterol screening tests are becoming more common. These are the finger-stick tests often done in shopping malls and health fairs. Since these tests are not that accurate and do not measure HDL (high-density lipo-protein) and LDL (low-density lipoprotein), you will need to have more complete testing done at a lab.

Standard cholesterol testing is done in a lab or doctor's office by drawing several tubes of blood. If you have had these blood tests done recently, contact your physician's office for a copy of the results. Put them in the same jour-nal where you will record your blood sugar levels, ketones, and diet. Your blood test should at least measure your total cholesterol and HDL cholesterol. LDL and triglyceride tests may also be performed, but they involve fasting nine to twelve hours before blood is drawn. Typically, they are done early in the morning.

The usual cholesterol test performed at your doctor's office measures total cholesterol. This a number that reflects the amount of cholesterol present in both your HDL ("good") and LDL ("bad") particles. A more accu-rate version is a **fasting blood test** (no food is eaten for nine to twelve hours before your blood is drawn). This test can differentiate between HDL cholesterol and LDL cholesterol.

Total cholesterol is made up of your LDL, HDL, and other blood cholesterol particles. Normal cholesterol is the level at which atherosclerosis does not occur. Animal and population studies suggest that this is about 160 milligrams per deciliter (mg/dl). In the Framingham Heart Study, an ongoing research project of the National Heart, Lung, and Blood Institute, subjects who had a cholesterol level lower than 160 mg/dl suffered no heart attacks no matter what their HDL, LDL, or triglyceride levels were.

The LDL reading measures your level of LDL cholesterol. This is the cholesterol contained in the LDL particle, which is vulnerable to oxidation. Oxidized LDL particles deposit cholesterol in your arteries. The lower this number is, the better. Some laboratories measure LDL directly, as part of the blood test. However, some doctors calculate your LDL levels using the following formula:

$$\text{Total cholesterol} - (\text{HDL} + [\text{triglycerides} \div 5]) = \text{LDL}$$

The HDL reading measures your level of HDL cholesterol, the cholesterol contained in the HDL particle, which removes cholesterol from your arteries. The higher this number is, the better. Research shows that even people with desirable levels of total cholesterol are at greater risk if their HDL levels are low. An HDL level below 35 mg/dl puts you at risk of heart disease. Table 11.2 gives you an idea of the different cholesterol classifications.

Triglycerides and Ratios

The **triglycerides** (also called tri*acyl*glycerides or **TAGs**) reading measures the fat in your blood that is being distributed to your tissues. High triglyceride levels are associated with cardiovascular disease. TAGs must be measured after an overnight fast; otherwise, the test will pick up triglycerides absorbed from a meal.

In addition to your LDL level, your doctor may calculate the ratios between your total cholesterol and HDL. As the levels of "helpful" HDL increase, the ratio decreases, and as HDL decreases, the ratio increases. As "bad" LDL

Table 11.2 Cholesterol classifications

CLASSIFICATION	TOTAL CHOLESTEROL LEVEL	HDL LEVEL	LDL LEVEL
Desirable	Less than 200	More than 35	130 or less
Borderline high	201–239		131–159
High	240 or higher		160 or higher

levels decrease, the ratio decreases, and as the LDL levels increase, the ratio increases. The goal is to keep the ratio below 5:1, with the optimum ratio being 3.5:1.

Here is an example:

- If a person has a total cholesterol of 200 mg/dl and an HDL cholesterol level of 50 mg/dl, the ratio would be stated as 4:1.
- If that HDL level *decreased* to 40 mg/dl, the ratio would now be 200 to 40—or 5:1. This increase of 10 mg/dl of HDL has unfavorably increased the ratio (and the risk) from 4:1 to 5:1.
- Now if that same person's total cholesterol increased to 240, the ratio would be 240/40—or 6:1.

While ratios can be helpful, they cannot substitute for knowing the actual numbers.

What You Can Do

HMG CoA reductase, the enzyme that makes cholesterol, also makes coenzyme Q10, a molecule needed to produce energy in muscles, especially in the heart muscle. Therefore, when you block HMG-reductase, you lower CoQ10 levels as a side effect. Some studies have found that CoQ10 in patients with heart disease is already low before they even start to take a statin. For this reason, if you take one of the statin drugs (HMG-reductase inhibitors), you should consider a CoQ10 supplement.

In addition, consider a red yeast rice supplement. Many doctors do not consider a cholesterol level between 200 and 240 mg/dl high enough to treat with a statin. Red yeast rice is a natural source of lovastatin, the first statin developed. It is made by growing a red yeast on rice, killing the yeast, grinding both yeast and rice into a powder, and then putting that powder in capsules. By controlling the temperature at which the rice grows, manufacturers are able to control the amount of lovastatin produced by the yeast. However, you cannot take red yeast rice when you are pregnant, because your baby needs cholesterol to grow brain tissue. You also cannot take this supplement if you are already taking a statin.

Benefits of fish oils and fiber. Numerous studies have shown that fish oil supplementation lowers the levels of very low-density lipoprotein (VLDL) and triglycerides but has little effect on LDL levels and total cholesterol. There were also some reports that supplementation with fish oil may worsen blood-sugar control. This led researchers at Case Western Reserve University to test a regime of soluble fiber and fish oil. Their experiment involved fifteen nonobese type 2 diabetic patients aged thirty-two to seventy-four. The patients continued their usual diabetic diet and medication during the entire study period. For the first four weeks, the patients were fed twenty grams of fish oil each day. During the next four weeks, all patients received the fish oil plus fifteen grams/day of soluble apple pectin. Findings included these outcomes:

- Fish oil supplementation alone lowered the levels of triacylglycerol by 41 percent and VLDL cholesterol by 36 percent.
- When apple pectin was added, triglyceride and VLDL cholesterol levels were both lowered by 38 percent. Total cholesterol levels also decreased by 13 percent, and LDL cholesterol decreased by 7 percent. There was no significant change in HDL cholesterol levels.

The researchers concluded that a combination of fish oil supplementation and increased fiber intake (up to forty grams/day total) may be a beneficial addition to the conventional treatment of high cholesterol levels in patients with type 2 diabetes. Table 11.3 provides some fiber sources that can help decrease cholesterol.

Table 11.3 Fiber sources that decrease cholesterol

FOOD	DECREASE IN TOTAL CHOLESTEROL
Beans	16%
Oat and rice bran	13–19%
Psyllium supplements	13%
Pectin supplements	12%
Guar supplements	11%
Fruits and vegetables	7%
Soy fiber	6.6%

12

Obesity, Overweight, and the Weight-Loss Equation

If you have type 2 diabetes, chances are you are over-weight. In fact, the vast majority of people with type 2 diabetes are overweight. Diabetes mellitus is increasing in the adult population, and the age of onset of adult type 2 diabetes is becoming lower. It is now commonly found among adolescents, and children as young as eight years are being diagnosed with type 2 diabetes.

Losing weight can reduce your likelihood of developing heart disease and high blood pressure and help to stabilize your blood sugar. No matter what kind of diet or how loudly the diet doctor/nutritionist/former dieter proclaims that his or her diet is something different, it isn't. Our favorites are the diets that claim not to be diets but are just a "lifestyle" change that involves a diet. A diet is the food you eat. Everyone alive is on a diet.

The weight-loss equation is this: For a person to maintain the same weight, the amount of calories eaten must equal the amount of calories burned. To lose weight, you can change two factors: you can take in less, and you can burn more. Eat less and exercise more, and you will lose weight. You have probably heard this particular piece of advice so often that you have tuned it out. Please tune it back in.

There is no way around this equation; it is how all weight-loss diets work, no matter what they claim. Of course, the numbers are approximate; it's impossible to know exactly how many calories a person is burning without some pretty expensive equipment. Not everyone will lose one pound of fat from burning 3,500 calories; some may have to burn more, and some may burn less. Different people burn calories more efficiently than others. We all know skinny gluttons who eat a large amount of food and never gain weight. We also know, or perhaps even are, a person who gains weight on far fewer calories.

Fat Weight or Water Weight?

Some diabetes medicines can cause edema, or water-weight gain. So can the heart failure that may accompany diabetes. A sudden weight gain is a sign that heart failure is worsening, and you need to let your endocrinologist or cardiologist know about it.

How can you tell water-weight gain from fat-weight gain? Water weight can be gained quickly—overnight, in some instances. If you gain or lose three pounds overnight, it is not your new eating habits. Your metabolism can burn fat only so fast; it can burn five pounds in a month but not three pounds overnight. Edema also causes "pitting"—when a swollen area is pressed, the depression stays for longer than a few seconds. Your doctor needs to be aware of any edema.

In general, to lose one pound of body weight, you must cut 3,500 calories from your diet. A net loss of 500 calories/day is usually enough for a one-pound-per-week loss. Any more than that and you are not losing fat: you are losing water and muscle. Since muscle tissue burns more calories than fat cells, you are only sabotaging yourself when you burn muscle tissue for the sake of a quick weight loss. When the weight is regained, it is regained only as fat.

People on the lower-carb diet (Chapter 16) will lose a few pounds more at first. This weight loss is really a water loss. The body needs that water; your body therefore will acclimate to your new diet and eventually regain it. Then the water-weight gain will offset your fat-tissue loss, and you will think your diet is not working when it is. Or your muscle tissue from exercise gain offsets your fat-tissue loss. Your muscles are larger and your waist is smaller, but your weight is the same. See why a tape measure is a better indicator of health than a scale?

What You Can Do to Lose Weight

We suggest you initially try the diet without cutting back on calories. When people first eat a whole-foods diet, they often lose weight because of the greater volume of food. Instead of counting calories, count your carbohydrates, practice portion control, and concentrate on the quality of food. Reevaluate your weight and caloric intake in two months. If you need to lose weight, then subtract 500 calories (as further explained in Chapter 14) and recalculate your diet plan. This amount of calories should result in a loss of four pounds a month. Don't try to lose more than ten pounds a month. Remember: the body can burn fat only so fast. Any more and you risk losing muscle mass too. All of a weight loss is not fat; some is muscle and water.

Setting a Weight-Loss Goal

Your first step to losing weight is to set goals. If you don't know where you are going, you won't know when you get there. Set goals that are specific, small, and sensible. Your goal should not be to "lose weight"—your goal should be to lose a specific amount of weight. It should be a small amount, and it should be sensible. To control blood sugar, the food choices you make to lose that weight are just as important as the weight loss itself. A good first goal is to switch to a whole-foods diet.

A 10 percent weight loss is a good second goal. To determine how many pounds this is, drop the third digit of your present weight. For instance, if you weigh 200 pounds, your first 10 percent is 20 pounds. Your second 10 percent is 18 pounds. However, after that first 10 percent, your risk of developing many diseases has fallen substantially.

Additional weight loss goals include these big three:

- Reduce the circumference of your waist. If you are a man, reduce it to below forty inches, and below thirty-five inches if you are a woman. To measure your waist, use a tape measure, and be careful to hold the tape level and not to pull it too tight. Measure your waist at the narrowest point on your torso.

If you cannot find your natural waist, don't worry about getting an exact measurement. Under the folds, your waist is probably more than forty inches. You may want to get an approximate measure to use for motivation. Nothing is as motivating as watching a waist shrink.

- Reduce your hip measurement so that it is equal to or greater than your waist measurement; this is another way of decreasing abdominal fat.
- Reduce your body mass index (BMI) to 30 or below. You can use the chart in Table 12.1 to determine your body mass index. Your BMI tells you

Table 12.1 BMI (body mass index) table

Height (inches)	Normal 23	24	Moderately Overweight 25	26	27	28	29	Markedly Overweight 30	31	32	33	34	Obese 35	36	37	38	39	40
BMI								*Body Weight (pounds)*										
58	110	115	119	124	129	134	138	143	148	153	158	162	167	172	177	181	186	191
59	114	119	124	128	133	138	143	148	153	158	163	168	173	178	183	188	193	198
60	118	123	128	133	138	143	148	153	158	163	168	174	179	184	189	194	199	204
61	122	127	132	137	143	148	153	158	164	169	174	180	185	190	195	201	206	211
62	126	131	136	142	147	153	158	164	169	175	180	186	191	196	202	207	213	218
63	130	135	141	146	152	158	163	169	175	180	186	191	197	203	208	214	220	225
64	134	140	145	151	157	163	169	174	180	186	192	197	204	209	215	221	227	232
65	138	144	150	156	162	168	174	180	186	192	198	204	210	216	222	228	234	240
66	142	148	155	161	167	173	179	186	192	198	204	210	216	223	229	235	241	247
67	146	153	159	166	172	178	185	191	198	204	211	217	223	230	236	242	249	255
68	151	158	164	171	177	184	190	197	203	210	216	223	230	236	243	249	256	262
69	155	162	169	176	182	189	196	203	209	216	223	230	236	243	250	257	263	270
70	160	167	174	181	188	195	202	209	216	222	229	236	243	250	257	264	271	278
71	165	172	179	186	193	200	208	215	222	229	236	243	250	257	265	272	279	286
72	169	177	184	191	199	206	213	221	228	235	242	250	258	265	272	279	287	294
73	174	182	189	197	204	212	219	227	235	242	250	257	265	272	280	288	295	302
74	179	186	194	202	210	218	225	233	241	249	256	264	272	280	287	295	303	311
75	184	192	200	208	216	224	232	240	248	256	264	272	279	287	295	303	311	319
76	189	197	205	213	221	230	238	246	254	263	271	279	287	295	304	312	320	328

Source: National Heart, Lung, and Blood Institute (nhlbi.nih.gov/guidelines/obesity)

your weight status—if you are underweight, just right, or overweight.

What will prevent you from reaching your goal? What are the obstacles that stand between your present position and your goal? For a moment, stop and think what has prevented you from being healthy in the past:

> What behavior has led to a weight gain?
> What has prevented you from exercising?
> What has prevented you from eating a healthier diet?
> What caused you to fail in your last attempt to diet?
>   Was it poor food choices?
> If so, what caused you to eat the wrong foods? Were
>   poor choices more convenient? Better tasting?

Only when you know what caused the problem can you effectively change it.

Write your weight-gain behavior at the top of a page. Ask why this happened. With each answer, ask yourself why again. For example:

> I gained weight because I ate too much food.
> Why did you eat too much food? Because I eat too
>   much fast food.
> Why do you eat too much fast food? Because I hate to
>   cook, fast food is convenient, and I like the taste.
> Why do you hate to cook, why is fast food convenient,
>   and why do you like the taste?

Continue until you get to the very core reason for your past failure.

What will make it easy to reach your goal? Your goals now will be to take whole-foods cooking lessons, identify close-by restaurants that serve healthier food, and identify healthy fast-food choices. Now when you get hungry and are short of time, you will know how to whip up a quick meal or find a restaurant that will serve you one. Making a healthy food choice will have become just as easy as (if not easier than) ordering a triple bacon burger.

Repeat the preceding exercise with ways to increase energy output. Your goals may be to join the YMCA, take adult swimming lessons, and enroll in the program for new exercisers. Now you will want to exercise, because you have always wanted to learn how to swim and you enjoy the companionship of others in the same exercise program.

Make the TV Work for You

Marketing departments have learned how to manipulate your mind, and research departments have learned how to manipulate your stomach. There is one thing you can do to avoid them: turn off the TV. This will help you in two ways, The ads will have less access to your head, and having no TV will make you bored. Boredom, it is hoped, will get you involved in some activity outside the house that will help burn calories, not put them on. The key to a healthy body is an active mind.

When you plant your butt in front of a TV screen, you can't be surprised when that body part starts to grow. Uproot that butt and take it someplace that the airwaves can't reach. Almost anything is better for your health than watching mindless TV. Pick two or three shows a week that you really want to watch, and record them. This puts you in control of what's going into your head. Later when you watch them, fast-forward through all those food commercials. They are not there just to fill up space. Each has been crafted with one thing in mind: stimulating hunger in someone whose body is not hungry. If the techniques did not work, companies would not pay the millions it costs to make and air those advertisements.

Choose TV shows that stimulate your mind in some way. Watch the latest watercooler show so that you can discuss it with coworkers and friends. Be an active participant in the program. If a TV show doesn't raise your heart rate or make you laugh, turn it off. Never, ever get into the habit of watching daytime TV. If you watch the same talk show every single day, you will see the host as a friend instead of seeking real friends elsewhere.

Build a Support System

Once you have cut the cord to the TV, get out of the house and involved in some activity. If it's an election year, volunteer to work for your party. This can be a lot of fun even if you just stuff envelopes at first. You are meeting new people and developing new interests. Go further:

- Surround yourself with people who are what you want to be. We don't mean your friends should be a size 4. We mean you should seek the company of active, upbeat people of all sizes who care about their health. Some people who need to lose weight find it helpful to join a weight-loss group of some kind. At this point, don't join a group that focuses on weight loss. Your primary goal is to make your body healthy, not to make it thin. The two are not synonymous.

- If you are newly diagnosed, joining a diabetic support group can be helpful, especially if you are using insulin. It's one thing to read tips about eating out in restaurants, but it's quite another to actually eat out with several other people who use insulin.
- Get involved with a religious organization. These institutions can offer a solid support system and a structure for change from within. Organizers of religious activities always need volunteers.
- Join the YMCA or a comparable gym in which to exercise. Choose a place where you will see people of all shapes and sizes: if you are overweight, no one is going to look twice.

Portion Control for Weight Control

In the first systematic, controlled study of the response to portion size in adults, researchers at Penn State's College of Health and Human Development found that the larger the portion of food, the more the participants ate. On average, they ate 30 percent more from a five-cup portion of macaroni and cheese than from a portion half its size. Participants did not report feeling any fuller after eating the larger size than they did from eating the smaller one. It didn't matter if they were normal weight or overweight; all responded by eating more.

At first, instead of counting calories, try controlling your portion sizes. Supersizing is a major cause of obesity, and portion control, as follows, can help you control your weight:

- Buy yourself a set of measuring cups and spoons. For one month, measure everything you eat. This will teach you how to estimate portion sizes.
- Most restaurants serve patrons double serving sizes. Eat half your entree, and take the other half home for a subsequent meal, or split a meal with your partner. Entrees on the luncheon and senior-citizen menus are usually smaller (and cheaper) than the same entrees on the dinner menu. Ask your waitress if you can order from them rather than from the full dinner menu.
- Don't serve meals family style at the table, with each person filling his or her own plate. Instead, measure food in the kitchen for the adults, and allow no seconds.
- Let young children determine how much they want to eat. Adults often overestimate a child's energy needs and offer too much food. Children need to learn how to listen to their body's needs. Encouraging children to finish all the food on their plates is the same as encouraging them to overeat.
- Divide your plate into quarters. One quarter should be filled with a protein food, another quarter should be a whole-grain starch or starchy vegetable, and two quarters should be vegetables. In at least one meal each day, half of the vegetables should be raw, as in a salad or raw vegetable appetizer. For dessert,

you should choose a serving of fruit. Most of all, you should be able to see your plate under the food. If you like the sight of your plate piled high, start eating dinner on a luncheon plate. Of course, lunch should always be served on a luncheon plate.

Make Wise Snack Choices

The need to crunch and chew is compelling, and lots of low-calorie foods meet this need. Lots of high-calorie foods do also, and the challenge is to make the switch. Find a snack with the following properties:

- Hard to eat—requires some effort to extract the food
- Low in fat, high in volume
- Low in calories, high in crunchiness
- High in fiber, more than six grams per serving

Desirable snacks include the following:

- Peel-and-eat shrimp and crab in the shell. Both are low in fat but are high in cholesterol, so limit how often you eat them. Skip the melted butter, and flavor with lemon juice.
- Three cups of air-popped popcorn or a single-serving bag of light microwave popcorn. Season with nutritional yeast.
- Sunflower seeds in the shell. Measure out one-fourth cup.
- A small handful of shelled peanuts
- Shelled walnuts—eight whole nuts

- Raw veggies. Buy them already cut up for a no-fuss snack.
- Soybean pods (edamame)
- Apple slices. You can also buy these precut and packaged for work-time snacks.
- High-fiber cold cereal and low-fat milk

Weight Reduction and Exercise

From the weight-loss equation, you learned that you must change two factors to lose weight: you must decrease energy in and increase energy out. How are you going to increase energy output? Exercise? A more active lifestyle?

Getting regular exercise is a priority for improving glucose levels and preventing heart disease, stroke, hypertension, and obesity. It goes hand and hand with proper diet: your body needs both to keep healthy. There is no substitute for vigorous exercise, just as there is no substitute for good food. The more active you are, the more weight you will lose. The more weight you lose, the greater your LDL reduction and HDL increase. Weight-bearing exercise is integral to building and keeping bone density, thereby preventing osteoporosis. Exercise can even help to reduce insulin resistance and improve your sex life. It will also do wonders for your mental health. There is no better stress reliever than exercise.

To incorporate more exercise into your regular routine, give these suggestions a whirl:

- Walk ten thousand steps a day. Get yourself a pedometer—a nifty and cheap little device that counts the number of steps you take. You will likely not be able to walk the full amount when you start, but you can add a hundred steps each day to slowly build toward your goal. The 10,000 Steps Program is put together by Shape Up America, a nonprofit organization dedicated to raising awareness of obesity as a health issue. See the organization's Web page at shapup.org for more information.

- Find an aerobic exercise you enjoy. Consider running, jogging, biking, cross-country skiing, and even vigorous walking. If you don't like your exercise program, you are not going to keep with it, so put some thought into choosing activities.
- Start slowly and build. Gradually increase how long you spend exercising, until you reach thirty to forty-five minutes at least three times a week. The higher your level of exercise, the greater your weight loss and health benefits. If you are obese or have been inactive for many years, it may take months before you can exercise this much. That's OK. Just take it slowly, and don't quit.
- Be persistent, and don't get discouraged. Find a friend to accompany you or join an exercise group to keep you motivated and committed to exercise.

....

PART III

DIET PLANS: DEVELOPING YOUR NUTRITIONAL THERAPY REGIMEN

We live in a time of the diet wars. Periodically, one side launches a study at the other, and after a spirited exchange of flying references, shooting editorials, and exploding expert opinions, both sides claim victory. On one extreme, firmly entrenched, are the high-carbohydrate proponents. By default, this type of diet is low in fat. Some interested parties believe it is the carbohydrates that make this diet a success, while others think it is the low-fat aspect. On the other end, just as firmly entrenched, are the low-carbohydrate proponents. By default, this type of diet is high in protein. Low-carb diets have been around for a long time under one name or another.

As often happens when two groups are polarized, new information has caused these camps to inch closer to each other. The low-carb diet took a step toward the center when it recognized that some types of fat are not good for your health. Now all of the low-carb diets recommend decreasing both cholesterol and saturated fat and increasing monounsaturated fat. The high-carb camp took a step toward the center when it recognized that some types of carbohydrates are not good for your health. Now most high-carb diets recommend decreasing processed carbs and increasing low-glycemic-load carbs.

The fact is that there is no one best diet for everyone. A recent analysis of four popular weight-loss diets found that all were equally effective. The reviewers concluded that it was not the diet that determined success; it was sticking to the diet. No one can deny that some people just seem to lose weight and keep it off more easily on some diets than on others. They are just better able to handle hunger or perhaps do not feel hunger on one type of diet.

All popular diets today are defined by their carb/protein/fat percentages. But the diet must be more than the sum of its macronutrient-level percentages. Weight loss is good, but the diet must also reduce inflammation by being low in animal foods and fat and rich in oily fish. It must be able to reduce oxygen damage (oxidation) by being rich in fruits, vegetables, and whole grains. It must be easy to follow and must contain enough food so that the dieter is not hungry.

The two diets that follow in Chapters 15 and 16 try to give you the best of the high- and low-carb worlds. Many people find they get tired of the low-carbohydrate diet after a few months and quit. To help prevent this reaction, we have increased the carbs a bit to bring in more variety. Our higher-carbohydrate diet is naturally low-glycemic and does not have as many carbs as some other high-carb diets. Its carbs come packaged with lots of fiber and nutrients.

Both diets in this book are whole-foods diets. They have a minimum of packaged and processed items, no bakery products made with refined flour and sugar, no candy bars or other sweets, no high-fat meats or deep-fried food, and no high-saturated-fat sauces. Both diets stress portion control as a way of losing weight. A whole-foods diet does not rely on artificial sweeteners but instead uses natural noncaloric and low-caloric sweeteners. We have included recipes for using these sweeteners and information on what types are available. Of course, there are times when people need to feast. Feast foods and treats always have their place, and you shouldn't feel guilty about indulging in them now and then. Just be careful that the occasional treat does not become the weekly habit.

13

Climbing the
Food Pyramid

This chapter will help you to prepare for your new way
of eating. Before beginning your individual diet plan,
it's important to have an understanding of the various food
groups. We give you serving sizes, suggestions, and preparation tips for the foods that will add nutritional therapy to
your treatment plan.

The food pyramid is one way to visualize a dietary plan.
It is not a complete diet, and it is not necessarily the best
configuration for all individuals, but it is a starting point.
The foods are placed in the pyramid by amounts of each
category that should be eaten every day or week. They are
not placed by quality; that is, good foods are not on the
bottom, and bad foods are not on the top. The difference
between top and bottom is how much should be eaten.
The food pyramid tells us that fats need to be eaten in
smaller amounts than starches—not that starches are better
than fats.

Each level of the pyramid contains good and poor food
choices. Good health depends on how often you select the

good choices. When you have diabetes and are at risk of cardiovascular disease, you want to pick foods that are rich in fiber and as close to their natural state as possible.

Forming the base of the pyramid is the starch group. It contains breads, cereals, beans, lentils, rice, potatoes, and pastas. When eaten whole, these foods provide you with energy in the form of carbohydrates, the B-complex vitamins, and minerals. On the next level up are the fruit and vegetable group. When many of today's adults were children, fruits and vegetables each formed a single group. As our understanding of the roles these foods play in good health has increased, so has the recommended number of servings. Fruits and vegetables now occupy a much more prominent position. On the third level is the protein group. At the top is the fats, oils, and sweets group. At each level of the pyramid, there are foods that will stabilize your blood sugar and strengthen your cardiovascular system as well as foods that will cause your blood glucose levels to put your cardiovascular system at risk.

Some of the foods in the "avoid" groups are there because they have a high glycemic load. These foods can increase your blood sugar and damage your small blood vessels and nerves, causing eye disease, kidney disease, impotence, and amputation, among other serious problems. Other foods are there because they contain a lot of fat and calories. These foods can increase your cholesterol and damage your large blood vessels, causing cardiovascular disease, heart attacks, and strokes. Some contain too much salt. If you are salt sensitive, too much of these foods can increase your blood pressure and damage the lining of your arteries, causing cardiovascular disease and stroke.

Starch Group: Grains, Legumes, and Cereals

The wide base of our food pyramid is the largest group, the starches, comprising cereals, breads, pasta, peas, beans, lentils, rice, and other grains. These are the foods that should form the "foundation" of your diet. They should be eaten every day and at every meal of the day. Unlike the food groups on higher levels of the pyramid, the foods at the bottom contain all the nutrients your body needs to thrive: carbohydrates, protein, fat, vitamins, minerals, and fiber. Although you may think of these foods as carbohydrate sources, they also contain protein. In fact, together, these foods account for two-thirds of the world's protein intake. Most are rich in fiber, particularly soluble fiber, which makes them a natural for blood glucose control.

Starch Group Serving Sizes

Each of the following serving sizes contains approximately 15 grams of carbohydrate:

- 1 slice bread
- ½ a bun, bagel, or English muffin
- ¾ cup dry ready-to-eat cereal
- ½ cup cooked cereal, rice, corn, pasta, yams or potatoes (white, yellow and sweet)
- ⅓ cup cooked beans, peas, or lentils or bean spread
- 3 cups popcorn

When you think of grains, too often you may think of bread made of wheat, pasta made of wheat, cold cereals made of wheat, and bakery products made of wheat. Grains are more than just wheat. Expand your culinary horizons and get acquainted with all the varieties that are available to you. Each has its own benefits to your health.

Choose your starchy foods from the following list:

- Steel-cut oats, scotch oats, rolled oats, pearl barley, and rolled barley. These are sources of beta-glucan, a soluble fiber that can help to keep your glucose levels even by decreasing how quickly food leaves the stomach. Choose long-cooking oats (those that require five or more minutes of cooking) over instant oatmeal.
- Amaranth, buckwheat, millet, quinoa, rye, and wild rice
- Brown rice, and white rice varieties with a low glycemic index or load. These types of white rice have higher levels of amylopectin, which blunts blood-glucose response.
- Wheat germ, wheat bran, rice bran, and oat bran. These are concentrated sources of fiber.
- Whole-grain breads and sourdough bread, especially those made of stone-ground wheat, those made of several types of grain, and those that include nuts and seeds and/or contain an acid (such as sourdough). Whole grains are also a good source of chromium, a mineral necessary for proper glucose control.
- All legumes. Legumes are the perfect food for people with diabetes.

The following foods are treats, so have them rarely, and in small amounts:

- Baked desserts. Baked goods such as cakes, pies, doughnuts, cookies, brownies, and muffins are treats, not sources of grain. They not only contain large amounts of sugar but contain fat too. Most of the cholesterol-raising trans fats in your diet come from commercial baked goods such as cookies. A small treat once or twice a week is fine, but be careful that eating treats does not become habitual.
- Instant or quick-cooking starches. This category includes instant potatoes, instant rice, and presweetened instant oatmeal. They are more likely to have a higher glycemic index/load and are likely to raise your glucose level.
- Refined grains. Products made with refined grains such as white flour and white rice usually have a higher glycemic load in addition to having had most of their nutrients (and taste) stripped away.
- Sugared cold cereals. These are the cereals marketed to children; they are no more than sugar-coated refined wheat. Think of them as a type of candy. Even if you removed the sugar from some of them, they would still have a high glycemic load. Cereals in this category include all sugar-coated cereals and flaked cereals.
- Snack chips. Most of these snacks are little more than salt-coated fried wheat.
- Some potatoes. Avoid mashed potatoes (which can elevate your blood sugar), french fries, and potato chips.

- Prepared bean products. If you are buying a prepared bean product, check the label to see what
  else has been added. Some types of baked beans are
  packed in a sugar-rich sauce; drain away as much of
  the sauce as you can. Some bean dips have added fat,
  often hydrogenated fat, the kind that can increase
  your cholesterol. Read the label so you know what
  you are getting, and make sensible selections.

Cooking with Starch

This section offers some basic buying and cooking instructions for grains and vegetables. We strongly suggest that
you invest in new cookware, as needed, to make preparing
these foods convenient and easy. Your kitchen should be
equipped with the following aids:

- Pressure cooker. When you have type 2 diabetes,
  you need to eat more legumes and fiber-rich whole
  grains to lose weight. A drawback is that most
  legumes and whole grains take a long time to cook.
  The solution is a pressure cooker. Pressure cookers turn beans and whole grains into fast food. We
  use our pressure cookers to make low-fat vegetable
  stew in less than fifteen minutes. Moreover, when
  used properly, pressure cookers keep food aromas to
  a minimum. This is a benefit to people for whom
  food smells are too much of a trigger for eating.
- Slow cooker. The opposite of a pressure cooker is a
  slow cooker, popularly known by the brand name

Crock-Pot. Use it to cook whole grains, legumes, and lean meats while you sleep or while you are at work. Put steel-cut oats, salt, and water in the pot before going to bed, and when you get up in the morning, breakfast is waiting. All you have to do is ladle the porridge into a bowl and add a drizzle of molasses or honey. It's faster than instant oatmeal and vastly superior in taste and texture. Likewise, before leaving for work, you can throw stew meat, vegetables, water, half a cup of red wine, and seasonings into the pot, and when you come home, dinner will be waiting for you.

- Microwave oven. If you have a microwave oven, you can buy specially designed cookware that will turn it into a pressure cooker, slow cooker, or rice steamer.
- Rice cooker/steamer. Rice steamers appear on store shelves under a variety of names; they can be called food steamers, vegetable steamers, or rice cookers. A rice steamer does much more than cook rice—it also steams other grains and vegetables. Grains prepared in a steamer come out fluffy, separate, and light. Delicate vegetables such as leafy greens and tender asparagus do not overcook and never turn out mushy or watery. Neither nutrients nor flavors get washed away. Just put the ingredients in the cooking bowl, turn on the machine, and forget about it. The cooking food needs no supervision because the steamer turns itself off when the water boils away, so you can never burn either the steamer or your food.

- Juicer. If you don't like vegetables, some of your recommended vegetable servings can be juiced. Never drink juices of any kind on an empty stomach, however. Always drink juices with meals for better absorption of nutrients and to keep blood sugar levels even. This is especially advisable for sugar-rich juice such as carrot juice. Dilute fruit juices.
- Bread machine. Prices have come down, so that almost anyone can now afford the luxury of freshly baked bread. By using a bread machine, you can have control over all the ingredients that go into your loaves. Set a small loaf to bake overnight so that you awake to the aroma of fresh bread.

Adding Legumes to Your Diet

Most food pyramids put legumes near the top level with meat and fish or as part of a group called "meat substitutes." While legumes are rich protein sources, they are also excellent sources of soluble fiber and low GI/GL carbohydrates, so they belong at the base of the pyramid as part of the everyday diet. Eating legumes (Table 13.1) will help you to control your blood sugar levels, so eat at least two servings a day.

Cooking tips for legumes. First, place the desired amount of dried beans (except lentils and split peas) in a pressure cooker along with two cups of water for every cup of beans and two teaspoons of salt. Bring the contents to high pressure for five minutes; remove the pot from the heat, and let the pressure fall on its own. Drain off the salted water, and

Table 13.1 Legumes

Lentils (including red, brown, yellow, green, and black)
Fresh snap beans
Fresh peas
Peanuts
Adzuki beans (including red and black)
Anasazi beans
Black (turtle) beans
Black-eyed peas
Brown (Egyptian) beans
Chickpeas (garbanzo)
Fava (broad) beans
Great Northern beans
Lima (butter) beans
Mung beans
Navy (Boston) beans
Pink (chili) beans
Pinto beans
Red kidney (rajma) beans
Red (Mexican) beans
Soybeans (edamame)
White kidney (cannelloni) beans
White beans
Peas (dried, split)

pressure-cook the beans for the amount of time listed in Table 13.2. If you prefer to soak beans overnight, add three to four minutes to the cooking times listed.

The cooking times in the table are approximate. The actual cooking times will depend on the type of cooker, growing conditions, storage conditions, and age of beans.

Table 13.2 Bean-cooking timetable for pressure cookers

LEGUME	COOKING TIME AT HIGH PRESSURE (MINUTES)*
Adzuki beans	2–3
Black beans	5–8
Black-eyed peas**	10
Cannellini beans	5–8
Chickpeas (garbanzo beans)	10–13
Cranberry beans	5–9
Great northern beans	4–9
Kidney beans	4–8
Lentils**	9–12
Lima beans	1–3
Navy beans	3–5
Pinto beans, pink or white	1–3
Small white beans	10
Soybeans	35
Split peas**	6–10
Whole dried peas	4–6

* These cooking times are approximate. Actual cooking times vary according to type of cooker, growing and storage conditions, and age of beans.

** These legumes do not need to be presoaked.

Never fill the cooker more than half full. Beans will expand during cooking and can block the pressure vent.

Eating the Right Grains

People with diabetes need to eat foods that will keep their blood sugar levels even. The key is to emphasize starches that are not refined, that are only minimally processed, and that have a low glycemic load; and avoid refined wheat products that contain lots of sugar and fat.

The starch group is the greatest victim of supersizing, so consumers these days need to learn how to recognize the normal-size baked good. Measure! Giant cookies, muffins, bagels, and brownies were once considered an outrageous indulgence, but today the supersize is the new normal. What you consider one cookie may be your diet's equivalent of three.

Here are a few guiding rules to remember when you're shopping to stock your grain pantry:

- Buy natural ingredients whenever possible. For example, many soy sauces contain MSG (monosodium glutamate), which causes a reaction in some people. Fortunately, soy sauce can also be purchased in a natural form with no artificial additives, and there are varieties now available in a low-sodium form.
- Buy organic whenever possible. Organic produce has not been treated or sprayed with any pesticides or fungicides. Our environment is contaminated enough already; give your body a break and buy pure foods. If your store does not carry organic foods, request them. Pester managers so that they understand there is a market for them.
- Buy in bulk whenever possible. Bulk buying from a bin makes sense both economically and ecologically.
- Do not, however, buy from bulk bins if you have grain allergies or intolerances. The scoops in containers are easily cross-contaminated.

These few tips will help to turn grain novices into grain gourmets:

- Rinse raw grain in cold water if it looks dirty or if you see foreign particles. If you have purchased the grain from a bin, it is always a good idea to rinse it well.
- Rinsing grain also removes excess starch clinging to the surface, which can make the grain sticky instead of fluffy and separate.
- Add spices in whole form to the cooking water for flavored rice. For example, you can use peppercorns, cinnamon sticks, cloves, and bay leaves for an Indian pilaf.
- Substitute nonfat chicken broth or vegetable broth for water when cooking grains. The flavor of the broth will be imparted into the grain.
- To dry-roast amaranth, rice, bulgur, or buckwheat, put the grain in a dry frying pan and stir over medium heat until the color deepens. Add liquid and cook as usual.

Cooking with Grains

Grains are so versatile that they can be presented in many enticing ways (see Table 13.3 for a grain-cooking timetable). You are limited only by your imagination. Instead of mounding cooked grain on a plate, change the shape: sticky grains such as rice and millet can be formed into balls after cooking and then rolled in toasted sesame seeds. Or you can pack cooked grains into a bread pan and slice

Table 13.3 Grain-cooking timetable for steamers

GRAIN (1 CUP)	COOKING TIME AT HIGH PRESSURE (MINUTES)	YIELD (CUPS)
Barley, pearled	17–20	3½
Barley, unhulled	50–60	3
Buckwheat	0–1*	2
Kamut	30–35	2
Kasha	0–1*	2
Millet	5–8	3
Oats/groats	25–30	2
Quinoa	5–6	2½
Rice, brown long-grain	35	2
Rice, brown short-grain	25	2½
Rye, berries	30–35	2
Spelt	30–40	2
Teff	6–8	3
Wheat, berries	35–40	2
Wheat, bulgur	5	2½
Wild rice	25–30	3½

* Bring to high pressure and immediately remove from heat.

the servings; top each slice with a drizzle of dressing or sauce. Medium- and short-grain rice and some of the smaller grains such as quinoa and millet can be spooned into molds for a more formal presentation. Use your small measuring cups as handy molds. Sprinkle fresh herbs on top. Of course, grains can also be stuffed into vegetables such as peppers, tomatoes, eggplant, and mushrooms. Use seasonings such as saffron and turmeric to color grains. These spices, when used in small amounts, will not change the flavor of a dish, but they will add an interesting color and important nutrients.

Here are some stove-top cooking instructions for grains:

1. Rinse grain under cold water to remove surface starch and debris.
2. Bring liquid to a boil in a heavy saucepan with a tight-fitting lid.
3. Add grains and heat to boiling again.
4. If you are cooking rice or millet, let grains cook for fifteen minutes before adding any salt. (Salt increases the cooking time of these grains.)
5. Reduce heat, and simmer for the recommended time, being careful not to remove the lid. For chewy grains, cook a few minutes less. For a softer grain, cook for a few minutes longer.
6. Add water if the grain is not cooked when all the liquid is absorbed.

Fruits and Vegetables

As we continue our climb up the pyramid, we come to the second level, which is shared by fruits and vegetables. Both fruits and vegetables are important sources of the antioxidant nutrients. Those who eat the fewest fruits and vegetables run the greatest risk of developing almost every disease when compared with those who eat the most fruits and vegetables. The two most powerful things you can do for your body when you have diabetes, or any other disease, are to have an active lifestyle and to eat more fruits and vegetables. This secret to better health is so simple that most people give it little thought. You cannot replace produce in your diet with supplements. Supplements have a place, but as their name says, they should supplement the diet, not replace it.

Vegetable Group

Vegetables are wonderful sources of vitamins, minerals, soluble and insoluble fiber, antioxidant nutrients, and various phytonutrients. For purposes of this discussion, there are two kinds of vegetables: those that contain a lot of starch (and therefore carbohydrate) and those that don't. Most of the starchy vegetables are technically fruits but are used as culinary vegetables. This includes potatoes, corn, lima beans, avocados, and winter squashes.

The green leafy vegetables contain almost no digestible carbohydrate or fat. Other vegetables such as the cruciferous family contain small amounts. It's not practical to look up the carbohydrate content of each vegetable you eat, so use the carbohydrate serving sizes to simplify the process. The carbohydrate content of any given plant food naturally varies, so the numbers in related tables reflect estimates.

High-carbohydrate vegetables include avocados, potatoes, yams and sweet potatoes, winter squashes, corn, and lima beans. Potatoes have gotten a bad reputation as a result of the glycemic index. We still read websites that claim eating a potato is like pouring sugar into your veins. It is not quite that simple. If you eat mashed potatoes on an empty stomach, it will increase your blood glucose as high as eating candy, so no diabetic should eat mashed potatoes as a snack. Then again, how often do you eat potatoes by themselves like that? It's typical to eat them as part of a meal, and it is the fiber content and glycemic load (GL) of the meal that count, not the GL of individual courses of a meal. When the meal contains another carbohydrate that has a low glycemic load, the GL of the meal decreases too. Refer to Chapter 3 for an in-depth discussion of the glycemic index and glycemic load. Note that potatoes are at the top of the satiety index, a rating of how well a food reduces hunger. Adding potatoes can make smaller meals more satisfying.

Vegetable Group Serving Sizes

Only count a vegetable as carbohydrate if you have three or more in one meal. Each serving size below contains approximately 5 grams carbohydrate:

- 1 cup raw vegetables
- ½ cup cooked vegetables
- ½ cup chopped vegetables
- 1 medium vegetable
- ⅛ medium avocado
- 10 small or 5 large olives
- 1 cup tomato/vegetable juice cocktail or clamato juice (clam juice mixed with tomato)
- 2 tablespoons tomato sauce
- 1 cup canned tomatoes or tomato sauce
- 1 small whole potato

Guidelines for choosing vegetables. All vegetables have some benefit; only the intervention of humans can make them bad for your health. Vegetables to incorporate into your diet include the following:

- All fresh vegetables. There are no bad vegetables.
- All frozen vegetables except those packed in fat-rich sauces (read the label).
- Yellow potatoes such as Yukon gold
- Sweet potatoes and yams. The yams widely consumed in the United States are not true yams; they are a variety of sweet potato. Yams are a good source of carotenes, an antioxidant family of pigments.

Vegetables to avoid include the following:

- High-glycemic-load vegetables—especially mashed potatoes, baked potatoes, and white potatoes.
- Fried eggplant. Eggplant soaks up a tremendous amount of oil, so beware of calories.
- Frozen vegetables that contain high-fat sauces

Cooking with Vegetables

The best way to cook nonstarchy vegetables is to steam them. Nutrients do not wash away during steaming, and flavor is not diluted. There are several ways to do this. Perhaps the easiest is to purchase a vegetable or grain steamer as described earlier. It will prevent your vegetables from being overcooked and prevent the pan from going dry and burning. Vegetables steamed this way do not need to be watched as with stove-top steamers, and you have the option of using the same machine to steam grains.

If you do not have a steamer machine, put a metal steamer basket inside a large saucepan. Add water, being careful that the level does not touch the basket. Lay the food to be steamed in the basket, and cover with a tight lid. Make sure the water does not boil away.

If you are not fond of vegetables, a dressing can make all the difference. Keep a bottle of thawed frozen lemon juice in the fridge for those times when you're out of fresh lemon. This type of juice does not taste as lively as fresh juice, but it is a close second and definitely much better than the preserved juices that need no refrigeration.

Fruit Group

Sharing the second level with vegetables is the fruit group. Originally, the word fruit meant an edible plant and was used to describe both fruits and vegetables. Because the botanical definition of fruit is so broad, we will discuss only culinary fruits in this section.

Fruits provide carbohydrates, vitamins, minerals, antioxidants, and other nutrients. They contain almost no protein or fat. Some types of fruit are rich in soluble fiber, especially apples, pears, strawberries, and citrus fruits (oranges, lemons, grapefruit, tangerines). Berries (blueberries, blackberries, cherries, and raspberries) are rich in flavonoids. Orange and red fruits are good sources of carotene, including apricots, cantaloupe, mangoes, papayas, peaches, and watermelon.

Be on guard if you're not buying fresh. Some fruit packed in juice actually contains more sugar than those packed in light syrup. Always read package labels for carbohydrate content. You can decrease some of the carbs of

juice-packed fruit by draining it and applying the carbohydrates you save to something more solid. Fruit packed in
individual half-cup servings is more expensive than larger
cans, but the single servings can be a great convenience,
and you do not have leftovers to throw away. Or you can
make your own. Buy reusable half-cup glass containers
and fill them with fruit from a larger container. Keep these
snack cups in the fridge so they're available when you want
a healthy way to bring up low blood glucose levels or just
for a quick refreshment.

Fruit Group Serving Sizes

Each of the following serving sizes contains approximately
fifteen grams of carbohydrate. For packaged fruit, check
the label for carbohydrate content.

- 1 cup raw fruit
- ¾ cup berries
- ½ of a large fruit—pear, grapefruit, papaya, mango,
  pomegranate, banana
- ½ cup (four ounces) of applesauce or juice-packed
  fruit
- ½ cup (four ounces) of fruit juice
- ¼ cup (two ounces) of dried fruit
- 1 small to medium fruit—apple, peach, nectarine,
  orange, kiwifruit
- 2 canned peach halves
- ⅛ of a melon

Each of the following half servings contains approximately 7.5 grams of carbohydrate:

- 2 apricots or dried prunes
- 1 small tangerine
- ¾ cup strawberries or watermelon cubes

Guidelines for choosing fruit. These fruits should be incorporated into your diet:

- All fresh fruit. As with vegetables, there is no bad fruit.
- Frozen fruit without added sugar or syrup
- Dried fruit such as figs, dates, raisins, and prunes
- Fruit canned in juice or water (or light syrup when juice is not available)
- Stewed fruit such as applesauce without added sugar
- Fruit juice without added sugar and juices fortified with calcium. Make sure juice drinks are 100 percent juice—many sound as if they are all juice but actually contain very little.

These fruits should be avoided:

- Frozen fruit that is presweetened or packed in heavy syrup
- Canned fruit packed in heavy syrup
- Juice drinks with added sugar

Protein Group

The third level of the food pyramid is the protein group, which includes milk and dairy foods, eggs, noncarbohydrate soy foods, red meat, poultry, fish, and nuts and seeds.

This group supplies protein, a nutrient that is necessary for the repair and maintenance of tissues. Protein is present in almost all foods, but the richest source is muscle from red meat, poultry, and fish. Although people tend to think of animal protein as superior to plant protein, this is not true. Animal protein comes packaged with lots of fat, few vitamins and minerals, and no fiber; plant protein, on the other hand is accompanied by lots of vitamins, minerals, and fiber.

Dairy foods also contain milk sugar, or lactose, so they must be included if you count carbohydrates.

Protein Group Serving Size

Each serving size below contains approximately 15 grams of carbohydrate:

- 1 cup milk or yogurt
- ½ cup ice cream or frozen yogurt
- ½ cup evaporated milk
- ⅓ cup dry nonfat milk
- 1½ ounces cheese

Each of the following protein serving sizes below does not contain carbohydrate. If you count carbs, they are free foods. If you count calories or fat, they are not.

- 3 ounces meat or fish (about the size of a deck of cards)
- 3 ounces tofu
- 3 ounces nut butter
- ½ cup cottage cheese

- 1 egg
- 2 tablespoons of peanut butter (1 T is 1 protein exchange)

Dairy Guidelines

The following dairy products should be incorporated into your diet:

- Low-fat yogurt. This includes nonfat as well, and both plain and flavored, but especially brands that are made with live cultures. The bacteria used to make yogurt are beneficial to your digestive tract. The carbohydrate content of flavored yogurt varies greatly; some naturally sweetened products may be lower in carbs than artificially flavored "light" yogurts.
- Low-fat milk. This includes 1 percent and skim milk, especially brands with acidophilus (a type of bacteria beneficial to the digestive tract), and buttermilk.
- Low-fat milk products. This includes low-fat cheeses; flavored and plain nonfat or low-fat cottage cheese; low-fat and nonfat sour cream; and nonfat powdered or instant milk and milk products (check the label to be sure no fats have been added).

These dairy products should be avoided:

- Desserts made with dairy foods. These are more sweets than they are nutrient sources. Limit your intake of puddings, frozen yogurt, and ice cream.

- All dairy products sweetened with artificial sweeteners, colored with artificial colors, or flavored with artificial flavors.
- Whole milk and cream. Avoid whipping cream, sour cream, coffee cream, full-fat yogurt, and whole milk and foods made with whole milk. These can be a source of calories and saturated fat, which can increase your cholesterol levels.

Ice cream, cheesecake, custard, and other full-fat desserts also contain large amounts of sugar. A dab or tablespoon of cream now and then won't hurt you, but if you make these foods a habit, they will expand your waistline and possibly put you at risk for heart disease.

Guide to Fish and Seafood

Fish not only are sources of protein but also bring the healthful omega-3 fatty acids.

The advice for fish is the opposite of that for meat: eat as much fish as desired. It is rich in protein, minerals, and vitamins and low in saturated fat as long as it is cooked using low-fat methods: baked, broiled, grilled, or steamed. Fatty fish are rich sources of omega-3 fatty acids, which can reduce inflammation in the body and help prevent heart disease, strokes, and hypertension. Shellfish do not contain omega-3 fatty acids but are low in fat and high in protein unless they are deep-fried or dipped in butter. It is a myth that lobster is high in cholesterol. The meat in a one-pound lobster has only ninety-eight calories and thirteen milligrams of cholesterol, which is less than an equivalent portion of skinless chicken.

Here are some suggestions for choosing fish:

- Choose cold-water fish as often as you can, including herring, sardines, anchovies, mackerel, wild salmon, and trout. Always eat the skin, as it contains valuable oils.
- With regard to tuna fish, do not eat albacore, yellow-fin, or any other large, fresh tuna. Instead, chose skipjack tuna, a small fish with less contamination, and limit consumption to two servings a week. Buy canned tuna that is identified as 100 percent skipjack; light canned tuna has lower mercury levels because it contains a high percentage of skipjack tuna. Canned tuna is not a source of omega-3 fatty acids.
- Pregnant women should not eat shark, swordfish, king mackerel, tilefish, or farmed fish and should limit tuna to one serving of skipjack a week, due to concerns about contamination.
- Drain fish canned in oil—it is vegetable oil, not fish oil. Or buy water-packed fish.
- Avoid deep-fried fish, shellfish, and other seafood. Fish and shellfish that are deep-fried or baked in butter and frozen breaded seafood contain carbs and often contain fat.
- Shrimp is high in cholesterol (but low in fat), so do not eat eggs the same day you have shrimp. In addition to shrimp, other good seafood choices include calamari, clams, lobster, and scallops.
- Choose fatty fish over leaner species. High-fat fish are sturdier and can stand up to broiling or grilling much better than lean and delicate whitefish can.

Fatty fish include herring, mackerel (northern or Atlantic mackerel and Spanish mackerel), halibut, lake trout, whitefish, salmon, and sardines.

Guidelines for Eating Meats

You should limit the amount of red meat you eat to once or twice a week. The majority of the fat in both of these diets is monounsaturated, and the least amount is saturated (7 percent for both diets in this book). Animal products, especially red meat, contain too much saturated fat. Always cut off any visible fat. Poultry should always be served without its skin. The skin does not have to be removed before cooking; leave it on until you are ready to serve, to keep the flesh from drying out.

Here are other meats to include in your diet:

- Poultry such as chicken, duck, pheasant, game hen, emu, quail, and ostrich served without skin
- Ground poultry made from white meat only
- Lean beef such as round, sirloin, chuck, and loin
- Leaner "choice" or "select" grades of beef
- Lean or extra-lean ground beef (no more than 15 percent fat)
- Lean ham and pork such as tenderloin and loin chops
- Lean lamb such as leg, arm, and loin
- Wild game such as rabbit and venison

The following meats should be avoided or limited to special occasions:

- Marbled cuts of beef such as tenderloin and prime rib
- High-fat pork products such as bacon, sausage, and ribs
- High-fat lunch meats such as bologna and liverwurst
- Salted and high-fat canned meats such as Spam, canned meat spreads, and chicken canned in oil
- Organ meats such as liver, heart, tripe, sweetbreads, and pigs feet, and foods made from them such as pâté
- High-fat hamburger meat, hot dogs, beef jerky, salami, and pepperoni
- High-fat poultry such as duck, goose, and any poultry with skin
- Pan-fried or deep-fried chicken, deep-fried breaded meat patties (such as chicken-fried steak), and other fried or deep-fried meat products
- Chicken cordon bleu and other chicken-cheese combinations
- Ground chicken made with skin and dark meat

Defatted ground beef. Cooking will remove more than half the fat from ground beef, even high-fat ground beef. You can remove half of the remaining fat by following these instructions. Since much of the flavor of ground beef is in its fat, this beef is best used in recipes that require crumbled ground beef. It will not form patties or loaves. It contains much less fat and fewer calories than regular ground beef.

1. Start with the ground beef of your choice. Don't use the leanest beef (which is the most expensive) or beef with the most fat (it's hard to remove that much fat). We like to buy organic hamburger from a local farm.

2. Crumble it into small pieces, and cook well.
3. Place the cooked meat in a strainer, and press out all the fat you can.
4. Rinse the meat with hot (not boiling) water.
5. Season to taste.

Add crumbled meat to soups, salads, casseroles, tacos, sloppy joes, and spaghetti sauce.

Soy Foods, Nuts, and Seeds to Emphasize

Soy milk—especially brands fortified with calcium—as well as tofu, tempeh, soy nuts, and miso are products that will not raise your blood glucose levels. Nuts and seeds are good sources of protein, but since they are also rich in oil and calories, you should limit their consumption to a palmful unless you are trying to gain weight. Nuts are good sources of fiber and heart-healthy fats.

Recommended nuts include the following:

- All fresh and dry-roasted nuts such as almonds, Brazil nuts, cashews, filberts, pecans, pine nuts, pistachios, and walnuts
- Fresh, unseasoned seeds such as pumpkin seeds, sesame seeds, sunflower seeds, and flaxseed
- Nut and seed butters such as tahini and sesame seed butter, walnut butter, almond butter, hazelnut butter, cashew butter, and sunflower butter
- Nut milks such as almond and cashew milk
- Psyllium seed husk powder. This is an especially rich source of soluble fiber; however, it must always be mixed with a liquid. It is tasteless, so it mixes easily.

Nut and seed butters with hydrogenated oils that contain trans-fatty acids should be avoided, as should nuts cooked in hot oils.

Fats and Oils

At the very top of the pyramid sit the most concentrated sources of energy—fats and oils. These foods are not at the top because they are necessarily bad for you. They are there because they are so energy rich, and you need very few servings of them a day. It is easy to overindulge in these foods and thus gain weight or sustain an unhealthy weight.

Fats and oils come packed in molecules called triglycerides. A triglyceride is a molecule that resembles a ladder. From each rung hangs a fatty acid. The health-promoting versus health-damaging properties of a fat are determined by the nature of the fatty acids that hang on it. Saturated fatty acids are associated with heart disease, whereas mono-unsaturated fatty acids (MUFAs) are associated with a decreased rate of heart disease. Polyunsaturated fatty acids (PUFAs) are also good for your heart but do not have the power of the MUFAs. Most of the fats in your diet should be rich in MUFAs.

A serving of fat equals each of the following:

- 1 teaspoon of butter, oil, or margarine
- 2 teaspoons of mayonnaise or nut butter
- 1 tablespoon of salad dressing
- 1 tablespoon of cream cheese
- 2 teaspoons of low-fat margarine or spread
- 1 tablespoon of seeds or nuts

Here are tips for serving fats and oils:

- Use your measuring spoons when you need a serving of fats. It is easy to underestimate quantities.
- Choose oils that are cold-pressed and minimally processed. Whenever you need to combine a sweet food with oil, choose cold-pressed canola oil because of its mild flavor.
- Olive and nut oils make excellent dressings and flavoring agents.
- If you must use a margarine, buy a soft tub variety, liquid, or spread. These have a lower percentage of hydrogenated oils and trans-fatty acids than stick margarines do. However, it is not wise to drench your food in any kind of fat. Mayonnaise is almost all fat, so choose a type that contains only canola oil, and use it sparingly.
- The preferred oils can usually be found in health-food stores and some supermarkets. A good oil will identify itself by its packaging. They are usually sold in small quantities to keep them fresh. Good oils should be stored in a dark, cool environment to reduce their exposure to light and oxygen. Flaxseed and other oils rich in the polyunsaturated essential fatty acids are fragile and should be packaged in dark bottles.
- Always check the label of prepared foods to avoid buying any that are high in fat.
- Never make high-fat foods a habit. Save them for occasional treats.

These oils contain a high level of monounsaturated fatty acids and are recommended:

- Nut oils such as walnut, almond, macadamia, and hazelnut, and dressings made with them
- Cold-pressed canola oil, and dressings and mayonnaise made with canola oil
- Extra-virgin olive oil (contains antioxidants too) and dressings made with olive oil
- Peanut oil
- Sesame and flaxseed oils
- Avocado oil

These oils and fats should be used in moderation:

- Tub and liquid margarines that contain liquid vegetable oil as the first ingredient (low in trans fats)
- Low-fat dressings
- Benecol. This spread contains plant stanol esters, which have been shown to lower cholesterol levels. It is like a supplement mixed with food. One tablespoon is seventy calories; a tablespoon of the light variety is fifty calories.
- Butter. It's natural, and the fatty acids in it are short-chain, so they are easily digested. Still, it is high in saturated fat, so use it sparingly.

These fats and oils should be avoided:

- Mayonnaise and dressings made with polyunsaturated-rich oils (safflower, sunflower, corn, and soybean). You get too much of these oils when you eat outside the house.
- Vegetable shortening and stick margarines (high in trans fats)
- Lard and beef tallow (saturated animal fat)

- Oils heated to high temperatures for deep-frying, especially vegetable oils (oils oxidize)
- Ghee—butter that has been heated to high temperatures (oxidized cholesterol)
- Dried butter—an ingredient in many foods. It's also heated to a high temperature (oxidized cholesterol).

Beverages

At the very tip of the top of our pyramid (on a point so small that it's almost not there) are foods you should totally avoid.

- No sweetened bottled drinks. This includes soft drinks, fruit drinks, energy drinks, and iced teas. If it is sweet and bottled, it contains high-fructose corn syrup. Read package labels, and do not eat or drink anything that lists fructose as the first ingredient. Consuming high levels of fructose promotes fat formation and abdominal obesity.
- Avoid artificially sweetened bottled drinks. More than ninety studies have found some safety concern with aspartame. The new kid on the sweetener block is sucralose, but keep in mind, though, that a small percentage of the sucralose is absorbed, and you may be sensitive to it. Our philosophy is that a whole-foods diet does not include aspartame or any other artificial sweetener. Diet sodas still contain artificial colors and preservatives and high levels of phosphate, which are linked to a decrease in bone density.

Sweets and Sugar

Also sharing space at the very top of the pyramid are sweeteners and sweets, including syrups, liquid sweeteners, jams, jellies, and fruit preserves. In a whole-foods diet, most of your sweets should come from fruits, with small amounts from natural sweeteners. Natural sweeteners bring other benefits besides carbs and calories; they are also sources of vitamins and antioxidants.

Skip syrups that are little more than corn syrup with artificial flavorings. This applies to pancake syrup and any other syrup that contains high-fructose corn syrup.

- For jam, jelly, and preserves, one teaspoon is one carbohydrate serving and fifty calories.
- For honey, molasses, pure maple syrup, and barley malt extract, one tablespoon (three teaspoons) is one carbohydrate serving and fifty calories.

Guide to Hidden Sugars

One way for a manufacturer to make a food appear to have less sugar is to hide the sugar under a different name on the ingredient label. A food is likely to be high in sugars if one of the terms found in Table 13.4 appears first or second in the ingredient list, or if several of them are listed. The term *naturally sweetened* can mean it contains sugar, too.

Some sugars (as shown in Table 13.4) are more healthful than others, but they will all increase the number of calories you consume and increase your glucose levels too.

Table 13.4 Ingredients on food labels denoting sugar

Brown sugar	Honey*
Cane sugar	Invert sugar
Corn sweetener	Lactose
Corn syrup	Maltose
Fructose	Maple syrup, pure*
Fruit juice concentrate*	Molasses*
Glucose (dextrose)	Raw sugar
High-fructose corn syrup	Sucrose

* This is a healthier choice.

Alternative Sweeteners

If using honey or sugar upsets the stability of your blood sugar levels, you should explore using one of the natural noncaloric or low-caloric sweeteners. You have choices that are not artificial. All of these sweeteners also have additional benefits beyond their sweetness. Natural low-carb sweeteners include the following:

- Lo han fruit concentrate (Slimsweet). Lo han is a sweet fruit from China, where it has been used as a sweetener for a millennium. The source of the sweetness is a group of compounds called mogrosides. The mogrosides are extracted to form a powder that is three hundred times sweeter than sugar. There is evidence that mogrosides also work as antioxidants, so they protect your cells while at the same time satisfying your sweet tooth.

- Organic yacon syrup. Yacon syrup tastes like molasses. It is fresh-pressed from the yacon root, a plant that is a native of Peru. The sugar in yacon is mainly fructo-oligosaccharide, which is a type of carbohydrate that the body cannot absorb, and a low proportion of simple sugars.
- ThermoSweet. A natural fruit sweetener made with organically grown kiwifruit, ThermoSweet has a low GI. It does not stimulate lipoprotein lipase, which are fat enzymes responsible for sending storage messages to the body's fat cells. Moreover, unlike sugar, ThermoSweet does not overelevate insulin levels. It is five times sweeter than sucrose (sugar), so a little goes a long way. It does not have a chemical aftertaste.
- Xylitol. This sugar alcohol occurs naturally in the human body and has been used in foods since the 1960s. It is a popular sweetener for the diabetic diet in some countries because the sugar alcohol is only partially absorbed. In the United States, xylitol is approved as a food additive in unlimited quantity for foods with special dietary purposes.
- Stevia. Probably the most well-known of the alternative sweeteners, stevia is a natural, carbohydrate-free, calorie-free sweetener. The active ingredient is stevioside—a white, crystalline powder extracted from the leaves of the stevia rebaudiana plant, an herbal shrub with leaves having an intensely sweet taste. Stevioside is heat stable, so it can be used in baking or in any other recipe that calls for cooking. Stevia now comes in a wide range of products and forms, from a concentrated liquid to a solid that

looks like sugar and that can be substituted in equal amounts.

If you have tried stevia and found it bitter, it's time for you to try it again. In its earlier forms, stevia was too concentrated, and consumers didn't always understand how much it had to be diluted. Today, diluted products are available. There are also a number of brands. If you don't like the taste of one brand, you can try another. You can also buy stevia plants online and grow your own! Although stevia's sweetening strength varies from one product to another, when you use a product high in steviosides, you can achieve a sweeter taste without bitterness. For information on these products, check out the "Resources" section at the back of the book.

We have included several recipes in Chapter 17 that will help get you started using natural sweeteners.

14

Counting Calories and Counting Carbs

Carbohydrate, or carb, counting is one way to structure your diet. It will help you to match your insulin dose with your meal and to distribute your carbohydrates evenly throughout the day. This technique was one of those used in the Diabetes Control and Complications Trial (DCCT) to successfully control blood-sugar levels. The DCCT, an extremely important study, found that tight blood-glucose control could decrease long-term complications of diabetic eye disease (including retinopathy), diabetic nerve damage (neuropathy), and diabetic kidney disease (nephropathy).

Before you can learn how to count carbohydrates you must first learn how to count calories. The two diets that follow in Chapters 15 and 16 are explained in terms of charts based on your caloric intake. Unlike many other diets, they are not based on your ideal body weight but on your present weight. Therefore, before you can use the diets, you have to know how many calories you burn in a typical day.

Once you have calculated how many calories you are currently eating to maintain your present weight, you can refer to the corresponding chart to determine how many carbohydrate grams you should eat each day and learn how to translate them into carbohydrate servings and food.

How to Calculate Your Caloric Intake

Your body requires a certain number of calories to maintain your current weight. How many calories you burn is influenced by many factors, including gender, exercise level, genes, environment, health, and age. When you eat more calories than you burn, you gain weight; when you eat less, you lose weight. Men burn more calories than women, in part because men have a greater percentage of muscle tissue than women, and muscle tissue burns more calories than fat. As we age, we burn fewer calories too.

While you have little influence over your gender, genes, or health, you do have control over how many calories you eat and how much you exercise. It takes approximately 3,500 calories to gain one pound. Therefore, to lose one pound you must cut 3,500 calories. This is usually done by cutting 500 calories a day, which results in a gentle weight loss of one pound a week.

Basic Formula for Calculating Calorie Intake

A bit of calculation is necessary to determine how many calories it takes for you to maintain your weight. The basic formula here will just give you an approximation. We use it because it is simple, but more accurate formulas are available on the Internet. Here's how it works:

1. From among the three categories that follow, choose the one that best matches your exercise level—little, moderate, or active—and then figure out how many calories you eat each day based on your weight and gender.
2. If you need to lose weight, subtract 500 calories from the total. This will give you a weight loss of approximately one to two pounds a week.
3. If you need to gain weight, add 500 calories from the total. Be careful not to gain weight too fast. Your goal is to gain both fat and muscle tissue.

Once you have determined your caloric intake, you can use the charts in Chapters 15 and 16 to determine the amount of fat, saturated fat, and carbohydrate grams and servings that apply.

If you get little exercise. If you do minimal exercise or have an inactive lifestyle, use this formula:

Your weight _____ (in pounds)
Daily calorie requirement (men):
    weight (lb.) × 14 = _____ calories
Daily calorie requirement (women):
    weight (lb.) × 12 = _____ calories
Do you need to lose weight?
    If yes, subtract 500 calories = _____
Total number of calories to maintain your
    weight = _____

Let's calculate how many calories it takes to maintain your present weight if you are a 180-pound woman with a sedentary lifestyle: Your base level of calories is 180 × 12, or 2,160 calories a day. To lose weight, you must subtract 500 calories; so you would calculate your total caloric intake as follows:

2,160 − 500 = 1,660 calories

If you get moderate exercise. If you have a moderately active lifestyle (three or four exercise sessions week), use this formula:

Your weight _____ (in pounds)
Daily calorie requirement (men):
    weight (lb.) × 16 = _____ calories
Daily calorie requirement (women):
    weight (lb.) × 14 = _____ calories
Do you need to lose weight?
    If yes, subtract 500 calories = _____
Total number of calories to maintain your
    weight = _____

Now, let's calculate how many calories it takes to maintain your present weight if you are a 220-pound man who gets a moderate amount of exercise: Your base level of calories is 220 × 16, or 3,520 calories a day. To lose weight, you must subtract 500 calories; so you would calculate your total caloric intake as follows:

3,520 − 500 = 3,020 calories

If you have an active lifestyle. If you are very active, with five or more exercise sessions a week, use this formula:

Your weight _____ (in pounds)
Daily calorie requirement (men):
    weight (lb.) × 18 = _____ calories
Daily calorie requirement (women):
    weight (lb.) × 16 = _____ calories
Do you need to lose weight?
    If yes, subtract 500 calories = _____
Total number of calories to maintain your
    weight = _____

How Exercise Affects Calorie Counting

What if our sample woman wanted to be able to eat more but lose the same amount of weight? Take a look what would happen if she started to live an active lifestyle—if she walked instead of drove, climbed stairs instead of taking the elevator, started lifting weights, and started to walk 10,000 steps a day. Now her equation looks like this:

$$180 × 16 = 2,880 \text{ calories} - 500 = 2,380$$

Now she could still be losing a pound a week but able to eat more (1,660 calories versus 2,380 calories!).

How often have you tried 1,200- or 1,400-calorie diets in the past? Now you understand why you were so hungry and why the results were so temporary: the amount of calories was not appropriate for a person your size. We suggest you do not cut back more than 500 calories. You don't want your body shocked into famine mode. If a whole-foods diet is going to be a big change for you, don't decrease calories for the first month. Wait and see how your body reacts to your new food choices. Many people will lose weight without decreasing calories because of the volume of food and increase in fiber.

For more information on losing weight, see the section on weight loss in Part II. Since your caloric intake is based on your present weight, you must recalculate your recommended intake as you lose weight. Every time you lose ten pounds, recalculate your diet.

Carbohydrate Counting

There are five steps to counting carbs. We suggest you only go as far as step 4 for the first week. When you have more practice, then you can tweak serving sizes.

1. Understand the definition of *carbohydrate.*
2. Understand the meaning of *carbohydrate servings.*
3. Determine how many carbohydrate servings you are allotted each day.
4. Determine how many carbohydrate servings you should eat at each meal and snack.
5. Familiarize yourself with serving sizes and carbohydrate foods.

This is a necessary skill for those using insulin and a useful skill for everyone else. For those with type 2 diabetes, gestational diabetes, or insulin resistance, carbohydrate counting helps you to follow your diet by keeping track of how many carbs you eat and when. It's easy to learn.

What Is a Carbohydrate?

To understand what a carbohydrate is, we strongly suggest you read Chapter 3 if you haven't already done so. A carbohydrate is one of the macronutrients (protein and fat are the other two), so called because they are the nutrients needed in the largest amounts. Carbohydrates provide immediate energy for the body. They are the only nutrients that directly affect blood-sugar levels.

There are three types of carbohydrates: sugars, starches, and fiber; the first two produce energy and are broken down into glucose. Regardless of the source of these carbohydrates, they all are broken down into the same unit—the glucose molecule. When the pancreas senses glucose, it releases the hormone insulin, which then unlocks the cells in the liver, fatty tissue, and muscle so glucose molecules can enter and feed the cell. When the pancreas does not produce enough insulin or when the insulin does not work the way it should, the result is diabetes.

The amount of carbohydrates you eat and the amount of insulin you take must match. In effect, insulin injections replace the pancreas. But you are no pancreas—how can you determine how much carbohydrate you have eaten? How do you know which foods contain carbohydrates? Easy! You learn how to count carbohydrates. Counting carbs teaches you which foods contain carbohydrates and how many they contain. In general, foods that contain carbs are fruit, starch, and milk—that's easy to remember.

For the purposes of carb counting, all carbohydrate-containing foods are equal. This is not true, of course; different carbohydrate-containing foods have different effects on your blood-glucose levels. Your health and long-term control of your blood glucose will be better served by confining your carbohydrate choices to whole foods that are lower GI and GL. Most of you will find they help to keep your blood sugars even. They will also protect you from other disorders. For example, people with diabetes are at greater risk to develop colon cancer. Carbo choices that are limited to whole foods will help prevent that. It will also help minimize the impact high blood sugars have on your body.

Foods that contain carbohydrates include:

- Fruits, fruit juices, and products flavored with them
- Sugar, sweeteners such as honey and molasses, and foods with sugar
- Milk and products made with milk, such as yogurt, ice cream, and sour cream
- Starches such as grains, pasta, cereals, and baked goods
- Starchy vegetables such as potatoes and yams

What Is a Carbohydrate Serving?

When you count carbs, you do not count every gram of carbohydrate you eat, although some people do. Instead, what you count are *servings* of carbohydrates. Each serving contains roughly fifteen grams of carbohydrate, so when you know how many servings you eat you also know how many grams you eat. For now you can forget about protein and fat foods; they have no effect on your blood-sugar levels. Your first goal is to normalize your blood sugar.

If you are switching over from using the Exchange Lists, carb counting is easy. Each starch, fruit, and milk exchange is equal to fifteen grams of carbohydrate and one serving. Your body has its differences and so do the foods you eat. Only you can know your body's reaction to the type of carbs in a meal. That is why it is so important to test your glucose levels frequently and keep notes about what you have eaten.

Again, each starch, fruit, and milk serving contains roughly fifteen grams of carbohydrate (Table 14.1). Pro–

Table 14.1 Serving sizes of carbohydrates

ONE 15-GRAM SERVING	AMOUNT PER SERVING
Starches	1 slice bread
	⅓ cup cooked pasta, cooked grains, hot cereals, or legumes
	¾ cup dry cereal
	3 cups popcorn or 4–6 crackers
Starchy vegetables	½ cup peas, corn, yams, sweet potatoes, or potatoes
	¾ cup winter squash or canned pumpkin
Fruit	1 small piece or ½ cup fruit juice
Milk	1 cup milk or ¾ cup plain yogurt
Desserts	2 small cookies or ½ cup ice cream

teins, fats, and most vegetables are not counted, because they do not contain carbohydrate.

Walk around the kitchen and test yourself on serving sizes. It won't be long before you have them memorized. Until then you can copy these charts and take them with you when you go out.

Use Table 14.2 for converting carbohydrates into servings. When you eat a packaged food, you must check the label for serving size and number of carbohydrates per serving. Be careful: the serving sizes of packaged foods may not be the "carbohydrate counting" serving size. For example, if the label on a small, snack-sized bag of chips says fifteen carbohydrates, don't assume the whole bag, small as it is, is one serving. It may be two servings and the whole bag then is 30 grams. Very small serving sizes is one way some manufacturers make it look like a food has fewer calories than it really does. You should also use this chart for counting the carbs in a recipe when the grams of carbohydrate are given but you are confused about the serving size. All you need to know about a food is how many grams of carbohydrate it contains and then look it up in Table 14.2.

Table 14.2 Converting carbs into servings

CARB GRAMS	NUMBER OF SERVINGS
0–5	Do not count
6–10	½
11–20	1
21–25	1½
26–35	2

You must keep a record of blood sugars in response to different foods. Keep a food diary for a week and look for patterns. If you notice that your blood glucose is higher whenever you have a certain food, it may be that your serving size for that food is going to be lower.

How Do I know How Many Carbohydrates I Am Allotted?

Your nutritionist, diabetes educator, or doctor should work this out for you and give you a meal plan. But you can work it out on your own too, if it helps you to understand. If you are a type 2 diabetic who has not yet been given a meal plan, you should learn to use carb counting to get a balanced diet. Most people haven't a clue what 55 percent of calories means or how to translate it into food. Carb counting can help you to translate those percentages into food servings. The number of carbohydrates you are allotted is determined by two factors: what percent of your diet is made up of carbohydrate and how many calories you eat.

This book contains two diets: one is 55/15/30 and the other is 45/25/30. When a diet is expressed this way, the first number is the percent of carbohydrates in your diet, the second is the protein percentage, and the last is the fat percentage. One hundred percent of calories means the total of all the calories you are to eat for the day. You cannot eat more than the sum of all you have eaten that day. Therefore, the amount of calories of the three macronutrients must always equal 100 percent. When you take

5 percent, away from one nutrient you must put it in either the protein or the fat column. If you wanted more carbohydrate in your diet than 55 percent you would have to subtract that carbohydrate from either protein or fat. A diet with 65 percent of calories from carbs would have to have subtracted that 10 percent from protein or fat. We can split the difference and take 5 percent from each, so now our diet is 65/15/20. As you can see, this is a low-fat diet. We've seen clients who want to have a high-carb/high-fat diet such as 65/15/40, but it is impossible to eat more than 100 percent of all your calories.

Let's say you prefer a low-fat/high-carb diet, so your percentage of carbohydrates remains 55 percent. Now you must determine: 55 percent of what? And let's say that your calculations show that you eat 2,000 calories a day. Refer to Table 14.3, the fat grams and servings chart: find the number of calories—2,000—in the first column, and run your finger across to see how many grams and how many servings of fat you should eat. You can eat 600 calories from fat, which is 67 grams of fat and 13 fat servings. You should also eat no more than 16 grams of saturated fat.

Now look at the carb grams and servings chart, Table 14.4. It tells you to eat 275 grams of carbohydrate, which is 18 servings.

Table 14.3 Fat grams and servings by caloric intake

CALORIES	FAT CALORIES	FAT GRAMS	FAT SERVINGS	SAT. FAT CAL	SAT. FAT GRAMS
2,000	600	67	13	140	16

Table 14.4 Carb grams and servings by caloric intake

CALORIES	CARB CALORIES	CARB GRAMS	CARB SERVINGS
2,000	1,100	275	18

Not all people have the same metabolism, so the number of calories you need to maintain your weight may not be the same for someone else. While it seems as if one person can eat piles of food and never gain weight, others just look at a carb and pile on weight.

Determine How Many Carb Servings You Should Eat at Each Meal and Snack

In order to keep your blood glucose levels even, it is best if you eat frequently throughout the day. Refer to the carbohydrate distribution listings in Table 14.5, and again look up your calorie level in the first column. The rest of the columns explain how to distribute your carbohydrate servings.

The plan calls for three meals and three snacks each day. Your work schedule will probably dictate when you eat your three large meals; then distribute the snacks so that

Table 14.5 Carbohydrate distribution by caloric intake

CALORIES	BREAKFAST	SNACK	LUNCH	SNACK	DINNER	SNACK	TOTAL
2,000	4	1	5	1	5	2	18

you don't go more than four hours without eating. Your longest fast should be overnight. It is important that you eat your nighttime snack; these are the carbohydrates that will keep your body fueled during the night. You should also schedule some protein along with the carbohydrate for this snack.

Test your blood glucose two hours after each meal and make any changes your body needs. For example, you may need a smaller snack in the morning but a larger one in the afternoon. The longer the period between meals, the larger the first meal or snack should be.

Familiarize Yourself with Serving Sizes

Reread the basic serving sizes under in the section called "What Is a Carbohydrate?" In addition, take a look at the following list of combination foods. Each serving contains about fifteen grams of carbohydrate. For packaged food, check the label for carbohydrate content. A serving equals each of the following:

- ½ cup of any casserole, such as tuna-noodle or chicken-noodle, macaroni and cheese, chili with meat, or spaghetti and meat sauce
- 1 cup cream, bean, tomato, or vegetable soup
- 1 cup beef and vegetable stew
- ⅛ of a ten-inch pizza
- ½ of a store-bought single-serving potpie, such as chicken, turkey, or beef
- 1 (3-ounce) taco

Fat Counting

Carbohydrate counting will help you control your carbo-hydrate intake. After you have been on your new diet for a month and have determined your body's response to the new food, you can determine if you need to keep track of how many calories you eat too. This probably won't be necessary because the foods that you typically over-eat are not found in this diet. You will be losing four to six pounds a month just by eliminating white flour and refined foods.

Fat and oils contain no carbohydrate or protein, just fat. Look to your chart in each of the diet plans in Chapters 15 and 16 to see how many servings a day are appropriate for you. This amount includes the fats used in cooking and seasoning and those found in other foods such as meat. Most of the fats that you eat will be hidden inside of pre-pared or processed foods. High-fat bakery goods include cakes, cookies, pies, muffins, and doughnuts and those with cheese.

- 1 serving/exchange of fat and oil is 1 teaspoon, about 40 calories.
- 1 serving/exchange of dressing is 2 teaspoons, about 50 calories.
- 1 tablespoon of a fat or oil is 120 calories; 2 table-spoons of dressing is 150 calories.

If weight control does become necessary, you will need to cut back on your fat intake or learn how to count fats. Counting fats is a lot easier and less restrictive than counting calories. You will find the appropriate amount of fat for your caloric intake in your diet prescription. These grams do not have to be as evenly distributed as your carbohydrate grams. What counts is the total amount.

Most people find they need to eat fat with carbs or protein with carbs. You do not need to have servings of all three nutrients at each meal, no matter who claims you must. There is nothing magic about eating the same macronutrient percentages at each meal. For mixed foods, add up the amount of oil you use in a recipe; for packaged mixed foods, read the label for fat content.

15

Higher-Carbohydrate Diet

This diet is an alternative to diets that are very low in fat and very high in carbohydrates. It is best described as "higher-carbohydrate." This is not just a high-carbohydrate diet: it is a whole-foods diet that has a low glycemic load and is rich in monounsaturated fats. The research on the effectiveness of high-carb diets for diabetic patients has been as mixed as the research on low-carbohydrate diets. Let your body make the choice for you. Both this diet and the one in Chapter 16 will be successful; it is just a matter of which one will cause you less hunger. This diet avoids the refined and processed foods that we think stimulate carbohydrate cravings in some people, so give it a try even if you have had problems sticking to a high-carb diet. If after six months, you have a problem with appetite or glucose control, then switch to the lower-carb diet.

Calculating Your Higher-Carbohydrate/Lower-Fat Diet (55/25/20)

First, take a look at the following macronutrient guidelines:

- 55 percent carbohydrates (stressing whole, unprocessed foods)
- 25 percent fat (10 percent from monounsaturated fat)
- 20 percent protein (stressing legumes, nuts, and seeds)
- Also note: 7 percent or less from saturated fat, less than 300 milligrams cholesterol

Most Americans eat only fifteen grams or less of fiber each day. This diet is naturally fiber-rich, with all the fibers and accompanying micronutrients that decrease your chance of developing cancer. In addition, use the information you gained in Chapter 14 to determine how many calories, carbohydrates, and fats you need. Refer to

Table 15.1 Fat grams and servings by caloric intake: higher-carb diet

CALORIES	FAT CALORIES	FAT GRAMS	FAT SERVINGS	SAT. FAT CAL.	SAT. FAT GRAMS
1,200	300	33	7	84	9
1,400	350	39	8	98	11
1,600	400	44	9	112	12
1,800	450	50	10	126	14
2,000	500	56	11	140	16

2,200	550	61	12	154	17
2,400	600	67	13	168	19
2,600	650	72	14.5	182	20
2,800	700	78	16	196	22
3,000	750	83	17	210	23
3,200	800	89	18	224	25
3,400	850	94	19	238	26
3,600	900	100	20	252	28
3,800	950	106	21	266	30
4,000	1,000	111	22	280	31
4,200	1,050	117	23	294	33
4,400	1,100	122	34	308	34

the listings of fat grams and servings by caloric intake in Table 15.1.

Then, Table 15.2 tells you how many carbohydrate grams and the number of carbohydrate servings you need to eat each day for each calorie level. If your caloric intake is in between calorie levels, move up or down toward the number to which you are closer. If you do not lose weight

Table 15.2 Carbohydrate grams and servings by caloric intake: higher-carb diet

CALORIES	CARB CALORIES	CARB GRAMS	CARB SERVINGS
1,200	660	165	11
1,400	770	193	13
1,600	880	220	15
1,800	990	248	17
2,000	1,100	275	18
2,200	1,210	303	20
2,400	1,320	330	22

Table 15.2 Carbohydrate grams and servings by caloric intake: higher-carb diet *(continued)*

CALORIES	CARB CALORIES	CARB GRAMS	CARB SERVINGS
2,600	1,430	358	24
2,800	1,540	385	26
3,000	1,650	413	28
3,200	1,760	440	29
3,400	1,870	468	31
3,600	1,980	495	33
3,800	2,090	523	35
4,000	2,200	550	37
4,200	2,310	578	39
4,400	2,420	605	40

or if you lose weight slowly, move downward to the lower number.

Once you have determined your caloric intake, use Table 15.3 to find the appropriate distribution of carbohydrates. This plan is based on three meals and three snacks a day. Remember that these are planned snacks. You must eat both your snacks and your meals at the same times each day. Don't skip any of them. You can swap morning and afternoon snack servings or take one carbohydrate serving from a meal to make a larger snack later. Let your blood sugar guide you. The largest of the three snacks is scheduled for nighttime to help keep your glucose levels up during the night and prevent low blood sugar. Low blood sugar during the night can show itself as either high or low blood glucose the next morning.

Table 15.3 Carbohydrate distribution by caloric intake: higher-carb diet

CALORIES	BREAKFAST	SNACK	LUNCH	SNACK	DINNER	SNACK	TOTAL
1,200	3	0	3	1	3	1	11
1,400	3	1	3	1	4	1	13
1,600	3	1	4	1	5	1	15
1,800	4	1	4	1	5	2	17
2,000	4	1	5	1	5	2	18
2,200	4	2	5	2	5	2	20
2,400	5	2	5	2	6	2	22
2,600	5	2	6	2	7	2	24
2,800	6	2	6	2	7	3	26
3,000	6	2	7	2	8	3	28
3,200	7	2	7	2	8	3	29
3,400	7	2	8	2	9	3	31
3,600	8	3	8	2	9	3	33
3,800	8	3	8	3	10	3	35
4,000	9	3	9	3	10	3	37
4,200	9	3	9	3	11	4	39
4,400	9	3	10	3	11	4	40

Meal Plan for 2,000 Calories

Here's a sample meal plan for 2,000 calories to get you started. Meals marked with an asterisk (*) are recipes included in Chapter 17.

Total Calories: 1,992
Carbohydrate/Protein/Fat Ratio: 54/20/26

Breakfast

| Stevia Peanut Butter Smoothie★ | 1 serving |

Morning Snack

| Banana | 1 medium |

Lunch

Lena's Vegetable Curry★	1 serving
Mixed greens	2 cups
Stevia Citrus Salad Dressing★	2 tablespoons
Nectarine	1 medium

Afternoon Snack

Raisins	3 tablespoons
Walnuts	14 whole nuts
Apple with skin	1 medium

Dinner

Halibut steak	5 ounces
Grilled tomato slices	3 slices
Brown rice	⅔ cup
Brussels sprouts	⅔ cup
Green-leaf lettuce	2 cups
Olive oil and vinegar	2 tablespoons
Sliced almonds	1 tablespoon
Honey-Whipped Parfait★	1 serving

Evening Snack

Celery sticks	2 celery stalks
Black bean dip	¼ cup
Flavored nonfat yogurt	¾ cup

Basic nutritional summary: Calories: 1,992; protein: 102 grams; carbs: 278 grams; fat: 60 grams; saturated fat: 11 grams; cholesterol: 74 milligrams

16

Lower-Carbohydrate Diet

This diet is lower in carbohydrates, higher in protein, and lower in fat. It avoids the extremes of the high-carbohydrate (50 versus 40 percent), high-protein (20 versus 30 percent), and high-fat (30 versus 40 percent) diets. If you need to lose weight, the higher level of protein can protect against muscle-tissue loss. The lower level of fat helps some people control their blood-sugar levels. Because carbohydrate is the only macronutrient to directly affect blood-sugar levels, this diet can make it difficult for a tumor to steal the body's blood glucose.

Low-carb diets have different effects on different people. For many, eating carbohydrates just increases their hunger for more. They find a low-carb diet is the only way to control their appetite and avoid strong carbohydrate cravings that result in carb binges and weight gain. For these people, this diet is the best choice. For others, it is *not* having carbs that causes carbohydrate cravings. Carbs make them feel better and help them to control their appetite. A diet this low in carbohydrates can be impossible for them to follow even though it is not as restrictive as most diets of this type. Listen to your body and let it be your guide.

· · · · ·

If you have cut calories, in the first few weeks of this diet you may lose more than one or two pounds. This is caused by water loss, not fat loss. While this is a good morale booster, after a few months your body will adapt to the lower calorie level, and you'll regain the water weight. For a few weeks, this can offset your fat loss and make it appear that your diet has stalled when it actually hasn't.

Keep in mind that all weight loss is not due to fat loss. Too often we think we have lost fat when we have really lost a combination of fat, water, and muscle. To protect your lean muscle tissue during weight loss, you must also exercise. It's a good idea not to cut calories during the first month of this diet. Many people find that they will lose weight because they are no longer eating empty calories and refined and processed foods. Allow your body to adapt gently to this diet. Diabetes puts a lot of stress on the body, and it does not need the additional stress caused by losing weight too quickly.

Be suspicious of any large, abrupt weight loss and report it to your doctor. Likewise, report any large unexpected weight gain. Your body cannot lose or gain five pounds of tissue overnight; such abrupt changes are due to water gain (edema) or loss, a side effect of some diabetes drugs.

Macronutrient Guidelines

Use the following macronutrient guidelines:

- 45 percent carbohydrate (whole, unprocessed foods)
- 25 percent protein (stressing beans, nuts, seeds, and fish)

- 30 percent fat (stressing monounsaturated and poly-unsaturated fats and oils)
- *Also note:* 7 percent or less from saturated fat

Use the information you gathered in Chapter 14 to determine how many calories, carbohydrates, and fats you need, and refer to the fat grams listings in Table 16.1.

Then, Table 16.2 tells you how many carbohydrate grams and the number of carbohydrate servings you need

Table 16.1 Fat grams and servings by caloric intake: lower-carb diet

CALORIES	FAT CALORIES	FAT GRAMS	FAT SERVINGS	CHOLESTEROL CALORIES
1,200	420	33	6	84
1,400	490	39	8	98
1,600	560	44	9	112
1,800	630	50	10	126
2,000	700	56	11	140
2,200	770	61	12	154
2,400	840	67	13	168
2,600	910	72	15	182
2,800	980	78	16	196
3,000	1,050	83	17	210
3,200	1,120	89	18	224
3,400	1,190	94	19	238
3,600	1,260	100	20	252
3,800	1,330	106	21	266
4,000	1,400	111	22	280
4,200	1,470	117	23	294
4,400	1,540	122	24	308

Table 16.2 Carbohydrate grams and servings by caloric intake: lower-carb diet

CALORIES	CARB CALORIES	CARB GRAMS	CARB SERVINGS
1,200	540	135	9
1,400	630	158	11
1,600	720	180	12
1,800	810	203	14
2,000	900	225	15
2,200	990	248	17
2,400	1,080	270	18
2,600	1,170	293	20
2,800	1,260	315	21
3,000	1,350	338	23
3,200	1,440	360	24
3,400	1,530	383	26
3,600	1,620	405	27
3,800	1,710	428	29
4,000	1,800	450	30
4,200	1,890	473	32
4,400	1,980	495	33

to eat each day for each calorie level. If your caloric intake is in between calorie levels, move up or down toward the number to which you are closer.

Once you have determined your caloric intake, use Table 16.3 to find the appropriate distribution of carbohydrates. This plan is based on three meals and three snacks each day. Remember that these are planned snacks. You must eat both your snacks and your meals at the same times each day. Don't skip any of them. You can swap morning and afternoon snack servings or take one carbohydrate serving from a meal to make a larger snack later. Let your blood sugar guide you. The largest of the three snacks is scheduled for nighttime to help keep your glucose levels up during the night and prevent low blood sugar. Low blood sugar during the night can show itself as either high or low blood glucose the next morning.

Table 16.3 Carbohydrate distribution by caloric intake: lower-carb diet

CALORIES	BREAKFAST	SNACK	LUNCH	SNACK	DINNER	SNACK	TOTAL
1,200	2	0	2	1	3	1	9
1,400	2	1	3	1	3	1	11
1,600	2	1	3	1	4	1	12
1,800	3	1	4	1	4	1	14
2,000	3	1	4	1	5	1	15
2,200	4	1	4	1	5	2	17
2,400	4	1	4	1	6	2	18
2,600	5	1	5	1	6	2	20
2,800	5	1	5	2	6	2	21
3,000	6	1	6	2	6	2	23
3,200	6	2	6	2	6	2	24
3,400	6	2	7	2	7	2	26
3,600	6	2	7	2	7	3	27
3,800	7	2	7	2	8	3	29
4,000	7	2	8	2	8	3	30
4,200	7	3	8	2	9	3	32
4,400	8	3	8	2	9	3	33

Meal Plan for 1,800 Calories

Here's a sample meal plan for 1,800 calories to get you started. Meals marked with an asterisk (★) are recipes included in Chapter 17.

Total Calories: 1,835
Carbohydrate/Protein/Fat Ratio: 46/20/34

Breakfast
Oatmeal	¾ cup
Chopped walnuts	1 tablespoon
Low-fat milk	½ cup

Morning Snack
Flavored nonfat yogurt	¾ cup
Almonds	½ ounce

Lunch
Beef and barley soup	1½ cups
Chilled Stevia Cashew Cookies★	3 cookies
Barley–Carrot Salad★	1 cup

Afternoon Snack
Apple with skin	1 medium

Dinner
Pasta with Tempeh "Sausage" and Peppers★	2 cups
Broccoli	⅔ cup
Avocado	¼

Field greens (or other packaged lettuce)	2 cups
Olive oil and vinegar dressing	1 tablespoon

Evening Snack

Carrot sticks	1½ medium carrots
Celery sticks	1 celery stalk
Cottage cheese	1 cup

Basic nutritional summary: Calories: 1,834; protein: 96 grams; carbs: 222 grams; fat: 72 grams; saturated fat: 13 grams; cholesterol: 21 grams

17

Recipes

Salads

Eating salads is a great way for you to get the fruits and vegetables you need. Even if you are a vegetable hater, chances are that you will find a few salads you like. For too long, people's idea of a salad was a wedge of iceberg lettuce drowned in French dressing. The iceberg lettuce had little nutritive value and even less flavor—hence the need for all the dressing. These days, we expect more of our salads.

Salad Assembly

The base of a salad is some kind of leafy green, usually lettuce. Romaine has replaced iceberg lettuce for many people, but you shouldn't stop there. Other popular types of salad greens include loose-leaf and butter lettuce, Chinese cabbage, arugula, and spinach. The darker the leaf, the greater the nutrition. Packed salad mixes might seem expensive, but when you factor in the waste from whole salad greens, the price difference is not as great as it first seems, particularly when you are preparing meals for only one or two. The convenience and the ability to have a wide mix of greens are worth the extra cost.

- The best salads are combinations of varied textures and tastes. The salad greens do not contain carbohydrates, but the beans and fruit do.
- Mix strong and mild, crisp and soft, sweet and savory.
- To give the salad more structure, crisp ingredients should be mixed with delicate ingredients—for example, spinach and apple slices.

Pick one or more base greens: green and red romaine, green and red oak-leaf lettuce, green- and red-leaf lettuce, butter lettuce (Boston and bib), buttercrunch, Belgian endive, red and green cabbage, and pea greens.

- **Crisp textures:** Oriental pea pods; fresh peas; cauliflower and broccoli florets; thinly cut fresh apple or pear slices; carrot curls and thinly sliced carrot discs; sliced celery; sliced cucumbers; sliced and diced bell peppers; sliced water chestnuts; sliced radish.
- **Soft textures:** raspberries; sliced and whole fresh strawberries; sliced and whole mushrooms; sliced and chopped sweet onions; chickpeas (garbanzo beans); halved, sliced, and cubed canned peaches or pears; avocado.

- **Strong or intense flavors:** leaf vegetables including arugula (rocket lettuce), beet tops, bok choy (Chinese cabbage), cilantro, chervil, green curly kale, dill, fennel, frisée, lemon balm, mizuna, mâche, parsley, pea greens, red mustard, red cabbage, radicchio, ruby chard, sorrel, and tat soi; fresh, frozen and canned artichoke hearts; sliced, chopped and curled green onions; crushed and chopped garlic; sliced, chopped, and grated yellow and white onions; whole and sliced hot peppers; sliced radishes; olives, anchovies; balsamic and flavored vinegars; sliced and juiced lemons and limes; crumbled feta; and blue-mold cheeses such as Roquefort, Gorgonzola, and Stilton; sliced and crumbled sharp cheddar; grated, shaved, and shredded hard cheese including parmesan, Romano, Asiago, and Grana Padano.
- **Mild flavors:** red kidney beans, chickpeas, and other beans; whole cherry tomatoes and sliced and diced tomatoes; sliced mushrooms and whole button mushrooms; sliced and chopped sweet onion; whole baby carrots, carrot curls and sticks; sliced and diced yellow, green, and red bell peppers; sliced, crumbled and shredded mild and medium cheddar; shredded mozzarella; sliced Colby, Monterey Jack, and Swiss cheeses.
- **Sweet flavors:** raisins; dried cranberries; dried cherries; dried and fresh berries; dried apple rings; fresh and canned halved, sliced, and chopped apples, pears, or peaches; canned mandarin orange sections; fresh orange and grapefruit sections; fresh and canned sliced and chopped pineapple rings; honey-sweetened dressings.

Toppings are a crowning touch. With the exception of blueberries and strawberries, most berries are too delicate to be tossed, so sprinkle them on top of the finished salad as an alternative to a crunchy topping—especially with a salad based on delicate greens.

- **Crunchy toppings:** croutons; crushed baked corn chips; sliced, slivered, and toasted almonds; poppy seeds; sunflower seeds; pine nuts; crushed walnuts; sliced peanuts; wheat germ; candied walnuts.
- **Sweet toppings:** berries; pomegranate seeds—both add a striking touch.

To make an entree salad, add a serving or two of protein foods such as skinless chicken or turkey breast (cook with skin on and then remove), fresh or canned salmon, canned tuna, or boiled eggs.

Simple Salad

This salad is easy to prepare, and the contrast in flavors makes it our favorite. We like to dry-roast the almond slivers, which adds a few minutes to preparation time, but the result is worth the modest extra effort.

3 cups butter lettuce
1 medium apple, thinly sliced
2 tablespoons almond slivers, dry-roasted
Spinach
Carrot curls
Tiny cauliflower florets

Quick Dressing
2 garlic cloves, minced
⅔ cup olive oil
⅓ cup balsamic vinegar

Barley-Carrot Salad

Barley should be your friend because it helps to reduce high blood sugar levels. We like to cook the barley in chicken broth, but it can also be cooked as usual in plain water. The almonds can be toasted in a dry skillet if you have the time.

3 cups cooked barley
1 cup raisins
2 cups grated carrots
1 cup finely chopped celery
½ cup green onions
½ cup finely chopped parsley
½ cup sliced almonds
¼ cup fresh or frozen lemon juice
¼ to ½ cup sesame oil
3 tablespoons tamari

Toss all ingredients together. Refrigerate for an hour to let flavors mingle. Serve on a bed of greens.

Makes about 9 1-cup servings

Nutrition information: 271 calories, 4 grams protein, 33 grams carbohydrate, 2 carbohydrate servings, 15.5 grams fat

Salad Dressings

The base of the salad determines the weight of the dressing. If your salad is all delicate greens, then you must use a delicate dressing, or the salad will wilt under the weight. Heavy dressings can weigh down a light base. For example, blue cheese dressing on baby green lettuce is going to look more like a vegetable in a sauce than a salad. But toss those delicate greens with a light vinaigrette, and you have a salad that complements a mild-tasting entree such as salmon. A savory dressing will enhance a salad with sweet ingredients. A salad of strong-tasting vegetables needs an equally robust dressing.

- Heavy dressings: blue cheese; ranch; French; Caesar; other creamy dressings based on yogurt, canola mayonnaise, sour cream, or cottage cheese.
- Light dressings: poppy seed; vinaigrette made with olive oil, canola oil, or nut oils such as walnut; flavored and unflavored vinegars.

Stevia Citrus Salad Dressing

For a light dinner, toss two cups of mixed baby greens with this dressing, and lay a poached and chilled salmon steak on the bed of lettuce. For a less-sweet dressing, do not add Stevia.

1 garlic clove, minced
¼ cup balsamic vinegar
½ cup orange juice
¼ teaspoon paprika

2 teaspoons Sweet 'n Natural Super Stevia Powder, or
  to taste
½ teaspoon salt
⅛ teaspoon pepper

1. Add the garlic to the vinegar, and let the mixture
   stand for 1 hour. Add the remaining ingredients to
   the garlic vinegar, and shake well to mix.
2. Chill until you are ready to use. Shake before using.

Makes 6 2-tablespoon servings

Nutrition information: 17 calories, 0.22 gram protein, 4
grams carbohydrate, 0 carbohydrate servings, 0 grams fat

Quick Grain/Vegetable Combos

Once a week, steam a large quantity of rice, and store it in
the refrigerator or freezer. The cooked rice quickly reheats
in the steamer as the other ingredients cook. These recipes
will give you ideas to create your own combinations using
your family's favorite veggies.

Raspberry Grain with Feta Cheese and Broccoli

This recipe adds an acid—vinegar—which decreases the
glycemic load of the dish.

1 cup chopped fresh or frozen broccoli
2 cups cooked brown rice
½ cup raspberry vinegar
¼ cup crumbled feta cheese

1. Before turning on your steamer, fill the reservoir with the recommended amount of water.
2. Place the broccoli, rice, and vinegar in the rice bowl, and steam for 15 minutes. Just before serving, sprinkle with feta.

Makes about 6 ½-cup servings

Nutrition information: 103 calories, 3 grams protein, 17 grams carbohydrate, 1 carbohydrate serving, 2 grams fat

Barley and Berries

For a contrast in taste, combine sweet with savory. Cook the grains in chicken or vegetable broth, and mix in dried fruit such as raisins, cranberries, or apples. Combine grains, too, for a contrast in texture.

1 cup cooked brown rice made with nonfat chicken broth
1 cup cooked pearled barley made with nonfat chicken broth
½ cup dried cranberries (sweetened)

1. Before turning on your steamer, fill the reservoir with the recommended amount of water.
2. Combine all ingredients in the rice bowl, and steam for 15 minutes.

Makes about 4 ½-cup servings

Nutrition information: 187 calories, 5 grams protein, 40 grams carbohydrate, 3 carbohydrate servings, 1 gram fat

Steamed Edamame Pods

We include this recipe because it is our favorite way to introduce soy foods into the diet of clients. Eating soybeans this way with your hands causes you to slow down and give your stomach a chance to communicate with your head. This recipe features immature green soybeans, called edamame, which taste more like a vegetable than the other traditional soy foods. You can substitute frozen green soybeans without pods, but the pods are more fun to open and eat. Serve these as an appetizer, or have them for a snack yourself.

1 pound fresh or thawed frozen soybean pods
1 teaspoon sea salt (you can substitute regular salt, but sea salt has a better texture)

1. Before turning on your steamer, fill the reservoir with the recommended amount of water.
2. Place the pods in the steamer basket or steam machine, and steam for 15 minutes.
3. Sprinkle with salt and serve immediately.
4. To eat, pinch the pod, and the beans will pop out, or pull the pod between your teeth to remove beans.

Makes about 4 ¼-pound servings

Nutrition information: 160 calories, 13 grams protein, 12 grams carbohydrate, 1 carbohydrate serving, 7 grams fat

Lunch and Dinner Ideas
The Never-Ending Casserole

Casseroles have been a mainstay of potlucks and community suppers, but now they are regaining their popularity with busy families. Moms and Dads can make several casseroles over the weekend to freeze for use later in the week. Casseroles are easy to cook and serve. They are also perfect for people with diabetes. Because any high-glycemic-load foods are combined with low-glycemic-load foods, you can be assured of a low-glycemic meal. Just add a green salad with a low-fat dressing to round out your dinner. Casseroles are also a good place to hide leftovers and fresh vegetables that are past their peak.

Casseroles can be dressed up or dressed down. They can be elegant, festive, or casual, depending on the ingredients you use. What follows is one very long recipe—long in its selection of possible ingredients but short in its complexity. We call it the "Never-Ending Casserole" because we never manage to make exactly the same casserole twice. Measuring is not terribly important here: just throw in what looks good to you at the moment. We have been known to make a casserole just as a vehicle for garlic.

Preparation Tips for Great Casseroles

- First choose the protein base for your creation. This usually consists of one cup of cooked legumes for every two cups of cooked grains. Well-rinsed canned beans can be substituted for fresh beans if time is a problem. Soy foods such as tofu and tem-

Ingredient Options for the Never-Ending Casserole

PROTEIN SOURCE		RAW VEGETABLES	SAUCE	SEASONINGS	TOPPINGS
1 cup cooked	2 cups cooked	1½ cups	1 cup	¼–½ cup	To Taste
Bean sprouts, raw	Amaranth	Carrots	White sauce	Miso	Sliced nuts
Black-eyed peas	Barley	Eggplant	Cheese sauce	Sherry/wine	Pumpkin seeds
Broad beans	Brown rice	Corn	Tofu sauce	Hot peppers	Raisins/cranberries
Chickpeas	Buckwheat/kasha	Peas	Yogurt sauce	Vegetable juice	Pine nuts
Kidney beans	Oat grouts	Greens	Onion sauce	Sautéed onions, garlic	Poppy/sesame seeds
Lima beans	Millet	Parsnips	Horseradish sauce	Sautéed leeks	Sunflower seeds
Navy beans	Quinoa	Rutabagas	Curry sauce	Sautéed green onions	Croutons
Pinto beans	Potatoes, cubed	Turnips	Tomato sauce	Roasted bell peppers	Bread crumbs
Soybeans	Sweet potatoes	Tomatoes	Cottage cheese	Sautéed celery	Crushed corn chips
Lentils	Yams, cubed	Cauliflower	Creamy dill sauce	Sun-dried tomatoes	Wheat germ
Tempeh	Bulgur wheat	Broccoli	Vegetable bouillon	Herbs, dried/fresh	Grated hard cheese
Tofu	Wheat/rye berries	Cabbage		Tamari/soy sauce	Shredded cheese
Split peas	Rolled grains	Squash		Dried mushrooms	Crushed peanuts
Cannellini beans	Dry bread cubes	Zucchini			Nutritional yeast

peh can be substituted for legumes. Instead of grains, occasionally substitute tuber vegetables such as potatoes, sweet potatoes, and yams.

- Limit the number of ingredients you use in each category. For example, do not use three kinds of beans, two types of grains, and a half dozen different vegetables seasoned with two types of sauces. Too many ingredients will muddle the flavors.

- Design your casseroles with a variety of textures and complementary flavors. Keep eye appeal in mind as well, and use colorful vegetables.

- Mellow out strong vegetables with mild-tasting grains.

- For a high note, add lemon juice, lime juice, fresh grated lemon peel/zest, or vinegar.

- For a sweet note, add raisins, dried cranberries, dried cherries, or dried apple rings.

- For crunch, add sliced water chestnuts, peanuts, or poppy seeds.

- Mix one or two beaten eggs or egg whites into the casserole for extra firmness.

- Brown garlic, onions, fresh mushrooms, carrots, leeks, and scallions before adding them to the casserole. Use the open pressure cooker, to reduce the amount of cookware to clean.

- For a change, try dry-roasting sesame seeds, quinoa, buckwheat, millet, teff, and amaranth before cooking.

- It is the job of the seasonings to breathe life into your creation. Hot peppers, garlic, chili powder, and curry powder all define the food they are in.

- Melding the varying textures and flavors together is the sauce. As the casserole cooks, the sauce sets, firming up the loose ingredients. (See "Ideas for Sauces" in this chapter.)
- Make your casserole more than a one-nighter. Put the leftovers into a clean casserole dish, add more vegetables, dress it up with different seasonings, reheat it in the pressure cooker for 5 minutes, and then put on another layer of topping.

Cooking Instructions

1. Preheat the oven to 325° F.
2. Coat the inside of a casserole dish with canola or olive oil.
3. Layer ingredients in the dish, being careful not to fill it more than two-thirds full, to allow room for expansion.
4. Bake until toppings are golden brown, about 30 minutes.
5. Let the casserole sit for 5 minutes before serving.

Pasta with Tempeh "Sausage" and Peppers

This was Maureen's introduction to tempeh, a soy product. If you do not have access to tempeh, you can substitute an equal amount of defatted hamburger (see instructions in Chapter 13). The fermentation process greatly reduces the oligosaccharides that make beans hard to digest for some people. Studies have shown tempeh to be essentially non-flatulent, producing no more gas than nonlegume foods.

3 tablespoons olive oil
1 pound tempeh
2 cloves garlic, minced
1 cup chopped onion
1¼ teaspoons oregano
1 teaspoon crushed dried peppers
1 teaspoon fennel
½ teaspoon thyme
¼ teaspoon paprika
1 red pepper, seeded and sliced into strips
1 green pepper, seeded and sliced into strips
1 16-ounce can tomatoes with juice, pureed slightly
2 tablespoons tomato paste
½ cup water
½ cup red wine
¼ cup minced parsley

Crumble the tempeh. Heat the olive oil in a large pan, and sauté the tempeh, garlic, onion, oregano, dried peppers, fennel, thyme, and paprika. Add the red and green peppers, and cook until softened. Add tomatoes, tomato paste, water, and wine. Bring the mixture to a boil; then lower the heat and simmer for an hour. Add the parsley, and cook for another 5 minutes. Serve over hot al dente pasta.

Makes about 10 1-cup servings

Nutritional information: *With pasta*—338 calories, 17 grams protein, 49 grams carbohydrate, 3 carbohydrate servings, 2 grams fat

Without pasta—164 calories, 9.5 grams protein, 12 grams carbohydrate, 1 carbohydrate serving, 2 grams fat

Lena's Vegetable Curry

If you think vegetables have to be boring, try this recipe. Maureen picked up this recipe from her Irish sister-in-law, Lena. It's a perfect example of how you can liven dinner up with spices.

> 2 teaspoons mustard seeds
> 2 teaspoons coriander seeds
> 2 teaspoons cumin seeds
> 2 tablespoons olive oil
> 1 large onion, thinly sliced
> 3 cloves garlic, minced
> 2 teaspoons fresh minced ginger
> 1½ teaspoons turmeric
> 1/2 teaspoon chili powder
> 1 16-ounce can chopped tomatoes with juice
> ¾ cup vegetable broth
> 2 tablespoons tomato paste
> 2 medium potatoes, cut into 1-inch cubes
> 1 medium-large sweet potato, cut into 1-inch cubes
> 4 medium carrots, cut into 1-inch slices
> 2 medium zucchini, cut into cubes
> 1 cup chopped fresh spinach
> 2 tablespoons low-fat coconut milk
> Salt

1. In a large, heavy saucepan, gently toast the mustard, coriander, and cumin seeds for 2 minutes. Transfer the seeds to a bowl, crush them with the back of a wooden spoon, and set them aside.

2. Heat the olive oil in the pan, and sauté the onion and garlic until softened. Add the crushed seeds, ginger, turmeric, and chili powder, and continue to cook for 2 to 3 minutes. Mix in the tomatoes, tomato puree, potatoes, sweet potato, and carrots, and cook until the potatoes and carrots are almost tender. Add the zucchini and spinach, and continue to cook until the zucchini and potatoes are tender. With a slotted spoon, transfer the vegetables to a warm plate.

3. To make the sauce, boil the remaining liquid to reduce it. Stir in the coconut milk, add salt to taste, and simmer for 1 minute. Pour the sauce over the vegetables.

Makes about 4 3-cup servings

Nutrition information: 251 calories, 8 grams protein, 50 grams carbohydrate, 3 carbohydrate servings, 3 grams fat

Ideas for Sauces

The following three recipes can be flavored with almost any seasonings to produce distinct sauces. We've include a grain-based sauce, a yogurt-based sauce, and a vegetable-based sauce. When time is a problem, check the bottled sauces available in your health-food store or the health-food section of your local supermarket. Avoid sauces with high levels of salt.

These sauces can be made dairy free by substituting soy milk, soy yogurt, and soy cheese for the cow's milk.

Basic White Sauce

For a basic Tofu Sauce, substitute 8 ounces of silken tofu for the milk.

> 1 tablespoon canola oil, high-oleic safflower oil, or butter
> 3 tablespoons whole wheat pastry flour (or 1 teaspoon arrowroot powder)
> 1 cup low-fat milk
> 2 teaspoons mirin or sherry
> 3 cloves garlic, minced (about 1½ teaspoons)
> Salt and pepper

1. In a saucepan, heat the oil over a low flame, and mix in the flour. Using a whisk, stir constantly while gradually adding the milk, mirin, and garlic.
2. Stir until the sauce is smooth and thick. Season.

Makes about 1 cup, or 4 ¼-cup servings

Nutrition information: *1 cup*—351 calories, 12.5 grams protein, 38 grams carbohydrate, 2 carbohydrate servings, 3 grams fat

¼ cup—88 calories, 3 grams protein, 9.5 grams carbohydrate, ½ carbohydrate serving, 0.7 gram fat

Variations: For a Cheese Sauce, add ½ cup grated strong cheddar cheese and a pinch of ground mustard. For a Horseradish Sauce, add 1 tablespoon prepared horseradish.

Basic Yogurt Sauce

1 cup unflavored low-fat yogurt
1 teaspoon honey
¼ teaspoon salt
1 to 2 cloves garlic, crushed

Combine ingredients.

Makes about 1 cup, or 4 ¼-cup servings

Nutrition information: *1 cup*—130 calories, 9.5 grams protein, 23 grams carbohydrate, 2 carbohydrate servings, 0.03 gram fat

¼ cup—33 calories, 2 grams protein, 6 grams carbohydrate, 2 carbohydrate servings, 0.03 gram fat

Variation: For a Curry Yogurt Sauce, add 2 teaspoons curry powder and 1 teaspoon lemon juice.

Creamy Dill Dressing or Sauce

You can serve this recipe hot as a sauce or chilled as a dressing. Toss 2 tablespoons of the chilled sauce with a can of rinsed and drained beans. Serve on a bed of baby greens.

1 cup nonfat yogurt
1 tablespoon snipped fresh dill
2 tablespoons fresh or frozen lemon juice
1 tablespoon finely chopped onion

1. Combine ingredients.
2. If you are going to use this as a dressing, chill it in the refrigerator for several hours to allow the flavors to mingle.
3. Store in the refrigerator.

Makes about 1¼ cups, or 5 ¼-cup servings

Nutrition information: *1¼ cups*—112 calories, 9 grams protein, 19 grams carbohydrate, 1 carbohydrate serving, 0 grams fat

¼ cup—22 calories, 2 grams protein, 4 grams carbohydrate, 0 carbohydrate servings, 0 grams fat

Desserts

Poached Pears in Raspberry Sauce

Many people have become so used to overly sweet, gooey desserts that they've forgotten what a wonderful dessert fruit can be. Poached pears are a favorite of ours. They look elegant enough for a dinner party and can be dressed up with a choice of sauces. For an added treat, drizzle a teaspoon of bittersweet chocolate sauce on top of the pears.

2 tablespoons honey
2 tablespoons pure vanilla extract
4 ripe pears, peeled, with stem left on

Raspberry Sauce
½ *cup nonfat yogurt*
¼ *cup raspberries*
2 *teaspoons honey*

1. To cook the pears, half-fill a 5-quart saucepan with water and bring it to boil. Stir in the honey and vanilla, and then place the pears in the pan. When the water returns to a boil, reduce the heat, and simmer until the pears are barely soft, about 10 minutes.
2. To make the sauce, combine all ingredients in a blender.
3. Pour 3 tablespoons of the raspberry sauce into each of four serving dishes, and place a pear on top of the sauce.

Makes about 4 servings

Nutrition information: 170 calories, 2 grams protein, 40 grams carbohydrate, 3 carbohydrate servings, 0.25 gram fat

Honey-Whipped Parfait

This is a creamy, low-fat, low-calorie dessert that is high in volume. You will need an immersion hand blender with a whipping blade to make this dessert. If you don't have one of these small appliances, they are well worth the investment just to make whipped milk like this. You must use skim milk in this recipe. Even 1 percent milk will not form a stiff whipped foam; just a trace amount of fat will cause the foam to collapse.

2 cups cold skim milk (place in freezer for an hour)
Few drops lemon juice
1 teaspoon pure vanilla extract
2 teaspoons honey
1 cup blueberries
1 cup raspberries

1. Pour the milk into a tall cylindrical container, and add the lemon juice. The volume will increase, so don't fill the container more than two-thirds full.
2. Place the wand in the bottom of the container, and turn the blender on high. Using a slow, up-and-down movement that does not break the surface, beat the mixture until it forms soft peaks. Add the vanilla and honey, and continue to beat a few more seconds until all ingredients are uniformly distributed.
3. Put a layer of the whipped milk into the bottom of each of four tall dessert glasses. Follow with a layer of blueberries, another layer of whipped milk, and a layer of raspberries. Top with a final dollop of whipped milk. Serve immediately.

Makes 4 servings

Nutrition information: 91 calories, 5 grams protein, 18 grams carbohydrate, 1 carbohydrate serving, 0.4 gram fat

Variations: An alternate way is to add the raspberries to the milk before beating and make a raspberry cream; in the serving glasses, alternate layers of raspberry cream with blueberries. Or alternate layers of sliced strawberries, small cubes of angel food cake, and whipped topping.

No-Bake Stevia Cheesecake with Blueberry Sauce

This recipe is from cookingwithstevia.com.

> 1 package unflavored gelatin
> 16 ounces cream cheese, softened to room temperature
> 1 teaspoon pure vanilla extract
> 5 teaspoons Stevia Blend, or ⅝ teaspoon stevioside
>
> **Blueberry Sauce (makes 10 ¼-cup servings)**
> 1 tablespoon Stevia Blend, or 6 packets, or ⅜ teaspoon
>   stevioside
> 1½ tablespoons cornstarch
> ⅛ teaspoon salt
> ½ cup water
> 2 cups blueberries
> 1 tablespoon lemon juice
> ½ tablespoon butter

1. To make the cheesecake, in a mixing bowl, dissolve the gelatin in 1 cup boiling water.
2. Add the cream cheese and vanilla, and begin to beat until fluffy. Add the stevia, and continue beating until the mixture is very fluffy.
3. Divide the mixture evenly among four dessert dishes, and refrigerate for about 1 hour, until set.
4. To make the sauce, combine the stevia, cornstarch, and salt in a saucepan. Add the water, and stir over medium heat until the sauce begins to thicken. Add the blueberries, lemon juice, and butter, and continue to stir until thick. Remove the sauce from the heat and allow it to cool.

5. Spoon ¼ cup of the sauce over each cheesecake, and serve cold.

Cake makes 4 servings.

Nutrition information: Cheesecake—306 calories, 18 grams protein, 0.08 gram carbohydrate, 0 carbohydrate servings, 24 grams fat

Sauce—26.5 calories, 0.23 gram protein, 5.4 grams carbohydrate, 0 carbohydrate servings, 0.7 gram fat

Chilled Stevia Cashew Cookies

From *Stevia Sweet Recipes*, an easy-to-make, high-protein cookie serves as an energizing snack.

¼ cup unsweetened coconut meal
½ cup unsweetened cashew butter
1 teaspoon pure vanilla extract
¼ teaspoon Stevia Extract Powder, or ¾ teaspoon Green
* Stevia Powder*
½ cup well-chopped raw sunflower seeds
2 tablespoons soy beverage powder
1 tablespoon powdered cocoa

1. Place the coconut meal in a shallow bowl.
2. Stir the remaining ingredients together in a mixing bowl in the order given.
3. Chill the mixture briefly if it is too soft to form balls.
4. For each cookie, roll 2 teaspoons of the cookie mixture into a ball, and coat it with coconut meal.

5. Flatten the balls to 1½-inch disks. Place the cookies in a flat storage container, and chill them in the refrigerator.

Makes 8 3-cookie servings

Nutrition information: 167 calories, 6 grams protein, 8 grams carbohydrate, ½ carbohydrate serving, 13 grams fat

Stevia Peanut Butter Smoothie

During the summer, we like to keep frozen banana slices in a bag in the freezer. Cut ripe bananas into 1-inch slices, toss them with a few drops of lemon juice to prevent browning, lay them in a shallow pan, and freeze. Store the individually frozen slices in a plastic bag. For a quick breakfast, throw a few frozen slices into a blender with some other fruit and yogurt, and you have a thick frozen treat.

> *1 cup low-fat milk*
> *½ cup plain nonfat yogurt*
> *½ large banana, cut into 4 slices and frozen*
> *1 tablespoon smooth-style natural peanut butter*
> *1 tablespoon whey protein powder*
> *½ teaspoon Stevia Blend*

Put all ingredients in a blender, and process until smooth.

Makes 1 serving

Nutrition information: 411 calories, 33 grams protein, 45 grams carbohydrate, 3 carbohydrate servings, 13 grams fat

Resources

General Resources for More Information

National Diabetes Information Clearinghouse
diabetes.niddk.nih.gov
1 Information Way, Bethesda, MD 20892-3560
Phone: (800) 860-8747
E-mail: ndic@info.niddk.nih.gov

A service of the National Institute of Diabetes and Digestive and Kidney Diseases, National Institutes of Health. For Internet information on diabetes, this should be your first stop. You will find the latest in diabetes research, treatments, statistics, and clinical trials, as well as other diabetes resources. You can call, write, or e-mail for information.

American Diabetes Association
diabetes.org
1701 N. Beauregard St., Alexandria, VA 22311
Phone: (800) DIABETES (342-2383), M–F, 8:30 a.m.–
  8 p.m. Eastern time

The ADA (not to be confused with the American Dietetic Association) is the nation's leading nonprofit health organization, providing diabetes research, information, and advocacy. Founded in 1940, the American Diabetes Association conducts programs in all fifty states and the District of Columbia, reaching hundreds of communities. For answers to diabetes-related questions or to request a diabetes information packet, call or write the ADA, or e-mail at askada@diabetes.org.

The Official Website of the Glycemic Index and GI Database

glycemicindex.com

This is the University of Sydney's website for the glycemic index. It offers a treasure trove of information on the GI and glycemic load, including a free searchable GI database that will allow you to look up the GI of any food. You can also subscribe to *The Glycemic Index Newsletter* for free and read back issues online.

Product Information

This section is provided for your information only and should not be viewed as the authors' endorsement of any product or company.

Beano®

beanogas.com

Beano prevents flatulence from legumes and vegetables. You can find it in grocery stores and pharmacies.

Stevia Smart
steviasmart.com

Stevia is a noncaloric, natural sweetener that does not affect glucose or insulin levels. At Stevia Smart, you will find information on ordering stevia, as well as tips and recipes.

Stevia Inc.
stevia.com
818 S.W. Third Ave., Suite 1340, Portland, OR 97204
Phone: (800) 851-6314

At stevia.com, you will find information on ordering stevia, news articles about stevia, and the newsletter *Low Carb Living.*

You can find related information at stevia-extract-sweetener.com.

The Xylitol Store
xylitolstore.com
273 Winged Foot Pl., Eagle, ID 83616
Phone: (877) 239-8910, 11 a.m.–7 p.m. Mountain time

An online source for xylitol, a sugar alcohol. The Xylitol Store sells XyloSweet packets as well as xylitol-sweetened syrup, ketchup, candy, mints, toothpaste, mouthwash, and gum.

You can also find information on xylitol at xylitol.org; you can find information on ThermoSweet at thermo sweet.com.

Wheylow

wheylow.com

Phone: (888) 639-8480 (toll-free, U.S. only);
   (301) 774-2433 (Maryland and outside U.S.)

Wheylow is a natural sugar substitute made with sugar alcohols (polyols). It can be used in cooking and baking, with only one effective carb per serving. You can order wheylow and find recipes for the product at this website.

Essential Living Foods Inc.

essentiallivingfoods.com

12304 Santa Monica Blvd., #218, Los Angeles, CA
   90025

Phone: (310) 571-3272

A source for two natural low-calorie sweeteners: organic yacon syrup, which owes its sweetness to fructo-oligosaccharides; and organic agave syrup, which owes its sweetness to inulin, a soluble fiber.

Arrowhead Mills

arrowheadmills.com

Phone: (800) 434-4246, 9 a.m.–7 p.m. Eastern time

A good source for whole grains, legumes, nuts, and seeds, including organic flaxseed.

Bob's Red Mill Natural Foods

bobsredmill.com

5209 S.E. International Way, Milwaukie, OR 97222

Phone: (800) 349-2173, M–F, 11 a.m.–8 p.m.
   Pacific time

Fax: (503) 653-1339

Bob's Red Mill is a source for a wide variety of common and hard-to-find grains, including organic flaxseed and other organic grains and seeds, as well as stone-ground whole grains and other whole-grain products.

Spectrum Organic Products, Inc.

spectrumorganics.com

5341 Old Redwood Hwy., Suite 400, Petaluma, CA 94954

A source for organic oils, fish oil, flaxseed, salad dressings, and canola and flaxseed mayonnaise.

Imagine Foods

imaginefoods.com

A source for organic broths, stocks, and soups.

Supplements

Vitamin Research Products

vrp.com

Phone: (800) 877-2447

An excellent source for several well-balanced vitamin and mineral products, MCT oil (medium-chain triglycerides), fish oil, and whey protein supplements.

The Vitamin Shop

vitaminshoppe.com

This site offers a wide variety of products, including Designer Whey Natural, a whey protein powder, flaxseed, and coconut oil.

Other Websites to Visit

For more about grass-fed beef, we suggest you visit the website of the University of California Cooperative Extension Service:

www.csuchico.edu/agr/grassfedbeef/

For information on buying organically raised grass-fed beef online:

www.meatshopoftacoma.com
www.nfrnaturalbeef.com
www.diamondorganics.com

For further information about the risks of mercury in fish and shellfish, call the U.S. Food and Drug Administration's food information line toll-free at 1-888-SAFEFOOD or visit FDA's Food Safety website: www.cfsan.fda.gov/seafood1.html

For more information on whole foods and weight loss for diabetes patients, visit Maureen Keane's website at keane nutrition.com.

References

Chapter 1

Lihn AS, Pedersen SB, Richelsen B. Adiponectin: action, regulation, and association to insulin sensitivity. *Obes Rev.* 2005;6(1):13–22.

Ohtsubo K, Takamatsu S, Minowa MT, et al. Dietary and genetic control of glucose transporter 2 glycosylation promotes insulin secretion in suppressing diabetes. *Cell.* 2005;123:1,307–21.

Shetty GK, Economides PA, Horton ES, et al. Circulating adiponectin and resistin level in relation to metabolic factors, inflammatory markers, and vascular reactivity in diabetic patients and subjects at risk for diabetes. *Diabetes Care.* 2004;27(10):2,450–8.

Steffes MW, Gross MD, Schreiner PJ, et al. Serum adiponectin in young adults: interactions with central adiposity, circulating levels of glucose, and insulin resistance: the CARDIA study. *Ann Epidemiolog.* 2004;14(7): 492–9.

Chapter 2

Davis WA, Knuiman M, et al. Glycemic exposure is associated with reduced pulmonary function in type 2 diabetes: the Fremantle Diabetes Study. *Diabetes Care.* 2004; 27(3):752–7.

Frezza EE, Wachtel MS, Chiriva-Internati M. Influence of obesity on the risk of developing colon cancer. *Gut.* 2006 Feb;55(2):285–91.

Goldman M. Lung dysfunction in diabetes. *Diabetes Care.* 2003 26:1,915–8.

Jelinek JE. Cutaneous manifestations of diabetes mellitus. *Int J Dermatol.*1994;33:605–17.

Krakauer JC, McKenna MJ, et al. Bone loss and bone turnover in diabetes. *Diabetes.* 1995; 44:775–82.

Nicodemus KC, Folsom AR. Type 1 and type 2 diabetes and incidence of hip fractures in postmenopausal women. *Diabetes Care.* 2001;24:1,192–7.

Reusch J. Diabetes, microvascular complications, and cardiovascular complications: what is it about glucose? *J Clin Invest.* 2003 Oct 1;112(7):986–8.

Sbarbati A, Osculati F, et al. Obesity and inflammation: evidence for an elementary lesion. *Pediatrics.* 2006 Jan;117(1):220–3.

van Leiden HA, Dekker JM, Moll AC, et al. Blood pressure, lipids, and obesity are associated with retinopathy. *Diabetes Care.* 2002 Aug;25(8):1,320–5.

Walter RE, Beiser A, et al. Association between glycemic state and lung function: the Framingham Heart Study. *Am J Respir Crit Care Med.* 2003;167:911–6.

Zanobetti A, Schwartz J. Are diabetics more susceptible to the health effects of airborne particles? *Am J Respir Crit Care Med.* 2001;164:831–3.

Zawydiwski R, Sprecher DL, et al. A novel test for the measurement of skin cholesterol. *Clin Chem.* 2001;47:1, 302–4.

Chapter 3

Carels RA, Darby LA, et al. Education on the glycemic index of foods fails to improve treatment outcomes in a behavioral weight loss program. *Eat Behav.* 2005 Feb; 6(2):145–50.

Holt SH, Brand-Miller JC, Stitt PA. The effects of equal-energy portions of different breads on blood glucose levels, feelings of fullness, and subsequent food intake. *J Am Diet Assoc.* 2001;01(7):767–73.

Holt SH, Miller JC, et al. A satiety index of common foods. *Eur J Clin Nutr.* 1995 Sep;49(9):675–90.

Jenkins DJA, Wolever TMS, Taylor RH, et al. Glycemic index of foods: a physiological basis for carbohydrate exchange. *Am J Clin Nutr.* 1981;34:362–6.

Palmer JP, Hampe CS, et al. Is latent autoimmune diabetes in adults distinct from type 1 diabetes or just type 1 diabetes at an older age? *Diabetes.* 2005 Dec;54 (Suppl 2): S62–7.

Pereira MA, Swain J, et al. Effects of a low-glycemic-load diet on resting energy expenditure and heart disease risk factors during weight loss. *JAMA*. 2004 Nov 24; 292(20):2,482–90.

Petersen KF, Dufour S, Shulman GI. Decreased insulin-stimulated ATP synthesis and phosphate transport in muscle of insulin-resistant offspring of type 2 diabetic parents. *PLoS Med*. 2005;2(9): e233.

Raatz SK, Torkelson CJ, et al. Reduced glycemic index and glycemic load diets do not increase the effects of energy restriction on weight loss and insulin sensitivity in obese men and women. *J Nutr*. 2005 Oct;135(10):2,387–91.

Schulze MB, Liu S, et al. Glycemic index, glycemic load, and dietary fiber and incidence of type 2 diabetes in younger and middle-aged women. *Am J Clin Nutr*. 80: 348–56.

Chapter 4

Kris-Etherton PM, Harris WS, Appel LJ; American Heart Association, Nutrition Committee. AHA Scientific Statement: Fish consumption, fish oil, omega-3 fatty acids, and cardiovascular disease. *Circulation*. 2002 Nov 19;106(21):2,747–57.

Rapp JH, Connor WE, Lin DS, Porter JM. Dietary eicosapentaenoic acid (EPA) and docosahexaenoic acid (DHA) from fish oil: their incorporation into advanced human atherosclerotic plaques. *Arterioscler Thromb*. 1991;11:903–11.

Chapter 5

American Diabetes Association. Patient information: guidelines for using vitamin, mineral, and herbal supplements. *Diabetes Spectrum* 2001 14:160.

Abbas ZG, Swai AB. Evaluation of the efficacy of thiamine and pyridoxine in the treatment of symptomatic diabetic peripheral neuropathy. *East Afr Med J.* 1997 Dec;74(12):803–8.

Barnard RJ, Youngren JF. Regulation of glucose transport in skeletal muscle. *FASEB J.* 1992 Nov;6(14):3, 238–44.

Basu TK, Basualdo C. Vitamin A homeostasis and diabetes mellitus. *Nutrition.* 1997 Sep;13(9):804–6.

Booth SL, Madabushi HT, Davidson KW, Sadowski JA. Tea and coffee brews are not dietary sources of vitamin K-1 (phylloquinone). *J Am Dietetic Ass.* 1995 Jan;95(1):82–3.

Borissova AM, Tankova T, et al. The effect of vitamin D3 on insulin secretion and peripheral insulin sensitivity in type 2 diabetic patients. *Int J Clin Practice.* 2003 May;57(4):258–61.

Bursell SE, Clermont AC, et al. High-dose vitamin E supplementation normalizes retinal blood flow and creatinine clearance in patients with type 1 diabetes. *Diabetes Care.* 1999;22:1,245–51.

Chan NN, Vallance P. Hyperhomocysteinaemia and neuropathy in type 2 diabetes. *Diabetic Medicine._*2001 Dec;18(12):1,008–9.

Crino A, Schiaffini R, et al. IMDIAB Group. A two-year observational study of nicotinamide and intensive insulin therapy in patients with recent-onset type 1 diabetes mellitus. *J Pediatr Endocrinol Metab.* 2005 Aug;18(8):749–54.

Cunningham JJ, Mearkle PL, Brown RG. Vitamin C: an aldose reductase inhibitor that normalizes erythrocyte sorbitol in insulin-dependent diabetes mellitus. *J Am Coll Nutr.* 1994 Aug;13(4):344–50.

Davis SJ, Gould BJ, Yudkin JS. The effect of vitamin C on glycosylation of protein. *Diabetes.* 1992;41:167–73.

Farvid MS, Jalali M, et al. Comparison of the effects of vitamins and/or mineral supplementation on glomerular and tubular dysfunction in type 2 diabetes. *Diabetes Care.* 2005 Oct;28(10):2,458–64.

Furukawa Y. Enhancement of glucose-induced insulin secretion and modification of glucose metabolism by biotin. *Nippon Rinsho.* 1999 Oct;57(10):2,261–9.

Gale EA, Bingley PJ, et al. European Nicotinamide Diabetes Intervention Trial (ENDIT): a randomised controlled trial of intervention before the onset of type 1 diabetes. *Lancet.* 2004 Mar 20; 363(9413):925–31.

Hammes HP, Du X, et al. Benfotiamine blocks three major pathways of hyperglycemic damage and prevents experimental diabetic retinopathy. *Nat Med.* 2003 Mar; 9(3):294–9.

Hypponen E, Laara E, et al. Intake of vitamin D and risk of type 1 diabetes: a birth-cohort study. *Lancet.* 2001; 358(9292):1,500–3.

Isaia G, Giorgino R, Adami S. High prevalence of hypovitaminosis D in female type 2 diabetic population. *Diabetes Care*. 2001 Aug;24(8):1,496.

Jain SK, McVie R, et al. Effect of modest vitamin E supplementation on glycated hemoglobin and triglyceride levels and red cell indices in type I diabetic patients. *J Am Coll Nutr*. 1996;15:458–61.

Knip M, Akerblom HK. Early nutrition and later diabetes risk. *Adv Exp Med Biol*. 2005;569:142–50.

Koutsikos D, Agroyannis B, Tzanatos-Exarchou H. Biotin for diabetic peripheral neuropathy. *Biomed Pharmacother*. 1990;44(10):511–4.

Koutsikos D, Fourtounas C, et al. Oral glucose tolerance test after high-dose I.V. biotin administration in normoglucemic hemodialysis patients. *Ren Fail*. 1996;18: 131–7.

Lonn E, Yusuf S, et al. Effects of vitamin E on cardiovascular and microvascular outcomes in high-risk patients with diabetes: results of the HOPE study and MICRO-HOPE substudy. *Diabetes Care*. 2002;25:1,919–27.

Maebashi Y, et al. Therapeutic evaluation of the effect of biotin on hyperglycemia in patients with non-insulin-dependent diabetes mellitus. *J Clin Biochem Nutr*. 1993 May;14(3):211–8.

Manzella D, Barbieri M, et al. Chronic administration of pharmacologic doses of vitamin E improves the cardiac autonomic nervous system in patients with type 2 diabetes. *Am J Clin Nutr*. 2001;73:1,052–7.

Moat SJ, Ashfield-Watt PAL, et al. The effect of riboflavin status on the homocysteine-lowering effect of folate in relation to MTHFR genotype. *Clin Chem.* 2003; 49:295–302.

Paolisso G, Balbi V, et al. Metabolic benefits deriving from chronic vitamin C supplementation in aged non-insulin-dependent diabetics. *J Am Coll Nutr.* 1995 Aug;14(4):387–92.

Shepherd J, Betteridge J, Van Gaal L; European Consensus Panel. Nicotinic acid in the management of dyslipidaemia associated with diabetes and metabolic syndrome: a position paper developed by a European consensus panel. *Curr Med Res Opin.* 2005 May;21(5):665–82.

Ting HH, Timimi FK, et al. Vitamin C improves endothelium-dependent vasodilation in patients with non-insulin-dependent diabetes mellitus. *J Clin Invest.* 1996;97:22–8.

Tom WL, Peng DH, et al. The effect of short-contact topical tretinoin therapy for foot ulcers in patients with diabetes. *Arch Dermatol.* 2005 Nov;141(11):1,373–7.

Ttutuncu NB, Baraktar M, Varli K. Reversal of defective nerve conduction with vitamin E supplementation in type 2 diabetes. *Diabetes Care.* 1998;21:1,915–8.

Villareal DT, Holloszy J. Effect of DHEA on abdominal fat and insulin action in elderly women and men. *JAMA.* 2004;292:2,243–8.

Vincent TE, Mendiratta S, May JM. Inhibition of aldose reductase in human erythrocytes by vitamin C. *Diabetes Res Clin Pract.* 1999 Jan;43(1):1–8.

Zhang H, Osada K, et al. A high-biotin diet improves the impaired glucose tolerance of long-term spontaneously hyperglycemic rats with non-insulin-dependent diabetes mellitus. *J Nutr Sci Vitaminol* (Tokyo). 1996 Dec;42(6):517–26.

Chapter 6

Abahusain MA, Dickerson WJ, et al. Retinol, alpha-tocopherol, and carotenoids in diabetes. *EB. Eur J Clin Nutr.* 1999 Aug;53(8):630–5.

Ametov AS, et al. The sensory symptoms of diabetic polyneuropathy are improved with alpha-lipoic acid: the SYDNEY trial. *Diabetes Care.* 2003;26:770–6.

Anderson JW, Gowri MS, et al. Antioxidant supplementation effects on low-density lipoprotein oxidation for individuals with type 2 diabetes mellitus. *J Am Coll Nutr.* 1999;18:451–61.

Anderson JW, Gowri MS, et al. Antioxidant supplementation effects on low-density lipoprotein oxidation for individuals with type 2 diabetes mellitus. *J Am Coll Nutr.* 1999;18:451–61.

Anderson RA. Chromium in the prevention and control of diabetes. *Diabetes and Metabolism.* 2000;26(1)22–7.

———. Chromium, glucose intolerance, and diabetes. *J Am Coll Nutr.* 1998 vol. 17, no. 6, 548–55.

Anderson RA, Cheng N, et al. Elevated intakes of supplemental chromium improve glucose and insulin variables in individuals with type 2 diabetes. *Diabetes.* 1997;46:1,786–91.

Anderson RA, Polansky MM, et al. Effects of supplemental chromium on patients with symptoms of reactive hypoglycemia. *Metabolism.* 1987 Apr;36(4):351–5.

Anderson RA, Roussel AM, et al. Potential antioxidant effects of zinc and chromium supplementation in people with type 2 diabetes mellitus. *J Am Coll Nutr.* 2001 Jun;20(3):212–8.

Anderson RA. Chromium in the prevention and control of diabetes. *Diabetes and Metabolism.* 2000;26(1)22–7.

————. Chromium, glucose intolerance, and diabetes. *J Am Coll Nutr.* 1998; 17, 548–55.

Anderson RA, Cheng N, et al. Elevated intakes of supplemental chromium improve glucose and insulin variables in individuals with type 2 diabetes. *Diabetes.* 1997;46:1,786–91.

Anderson RA, Polansky MM, et al. Effects of supplemental chromium on patients with symptoms of reactive hypoglycemia. *Metabolism.* 1987 Apr;36(4):351–5.

Anderson RA, Roussel AM, et al. Potential antioxidant effects of zinc and chromium supplementation in people with type 2 diabetes mellitus. *J Am Coll Nutr.* 2001 Jun;20(3):212–8.

Bauman WA, Shaw S, Jayatilleke E, Spungen AM, Herbert V. Increased intake of calcium reverses vitamin B_{12} malabsorption induced by metformin. *Diabetes Care.* 2000;23:1227–1231.

Beaulieu C, Kestekian R, Havrankova J, Gascon-Barre M. Calcium is essential in normalizing intolerance to glucose that accompanies vitamin D depletion in vivo. *Diabetes.*1993;42:35–43.

Bergossi AM, Grossi G, et al. Exogenous CoQ10 supplementation prevents plasma ubiquone reduction induced by HMG-CoA reductase inhibitors. *Mol Aspects Med.* 1994;15(Suppl):187–93.

Brown SA, Sharpless JL. Osteoporosis: An Under-Appreciated Complication of Diabetes Clin. *Diabetes.* 2004;22:10–20.

Ceriello A. New insights on oxidative stress and diabetic complications may lead to a "causal" antioxidant therapy. *Diabetes Care.* 2003;26:1,589–96.

Eriksson J, Kohvakka A. Magnesium and ascorbic acid supplementation in diabetes mellitus. *Ann Nutr Metab.* 1995;39(4):217–23.

Eriksson JG, Forsen TJ, et al. The effect of coenzyme Q10 administration on metabolic control in patients with type 2 diabetes mellitus. *Biofactors.* 1999;9:315–8.

Evans JL, Goldfine ID. Alpha-lipoic acid: a multifunctional antioxidant that improves insulin sensitivity in patients with type 2 diabetes. *Diabetes Technol Ther.* 2000;2:401–13.

Food and Nutrition Board, IOM, and National Academy of Sciences. Vitamin C, vitamin E, selenium, and b-carotene and other carotenoids: overview, antioxidant definition, and relationship to chronic disease. In *Dietary Reference Intakes for Vitamin C, Vitamin E, Selenium, and Carotenoids.* Washington, DC: National Academies Press; 2000, 35–57.

Fuhr JP Jr, He H, et al. The inhibitory effects of pure flavonoids on in vitro protein glycosylation. *J Herbal Pharmocotherapy.* 2002;2(2).

Halberstam M, Cohen N, Shlimovich P, Rossetti L, Shamoon H. Oral vanadyl sulfate improves insulin sensitivity in NIDDM but not in obese nondiabetic subjects. *Diabetes.* 1996 May;45(5):659–66. Erratum in Diabetes 1996 Sep;45(9):1285.

Hodgson JM, Watts GF, et al. Coenzyme Q10 improves blood pressure and glycaemic control: a controlled trial in subjects with type 2 diabetes. *Eur J Clin Nutr.* 2002; 56:1,137–42.

Jeejeebhoy KN. The role of chromium in nutrition and therapeutics and as a potential toxin. *Nutr Rev.* 1999;57: 329–335.

Jovanovic L, Gutierrez M, Peterson CM. Chromium supplementation for women with gestational diabetes mellitus. *J Trace Elem Med Biol.* 1999;12:91–7.

Kozlovsky AS, Moser PB, et al. Effects of diets high in simple sugars on urinary chromium losses. *Metabolism.* 1986; 35:515–8.

Laight DW, Carrier MJ, Anggard EE. Antioxidants, diabetes, and endothelial dysfunction. *Cardiovasc Res.* 2000; 47:457–64.

Lund BO, Miller DM, Woods JS. Studies on Hg(II)-induced H_2O_2 formation and oxidative stress in vivo and in vitro in rat kidney mitochondria. *Biochem Pharmacol* 1993;45:2017–2024.

McNair P, Christiansen C, et al. Hypomagnesemia, a risk factor in diabetic retinopathy. *Diabetes.* 1975;27:1,075–7.

Mertz W. Chromium in human nutrition: a review. *J Nutr.* 1993;123:626–33.

Mertz W, Abernathy CO, Olin SS. *Risk Assessment of Essential Elements.* Washington, DC: ILSI Press; 1994, xix–xxxviii.

Mortensen WM, Rassing SA, et al. Bioavailability of four oral coenzyme Q10 formulations in healthy volunteers. *Mol Aspects Med.* 1994;15(Suppl):S273–80.

Olson JA. Benefits and liabilities of vitamin A and carotenoids. *J Nutr.* 1996;126:1,208S–12S.

Ruiz C, Alegria A, Barbera R, Farre R, Lagarda J. Selenium, zinc, and copper in plasma of patients with type 1 diabetes mellitus in different metabolic control states. *J Trace Elem Med Biol.* 1998 July;12(2):91–5.

Seddon JM, Ajani UA, et al. Dietary carotenoids, vitamins A, C, and E, and advanced age-related macular degeneration. *JAMA.* 1994;272:1,413–20.

Siega-Riz AM, Carson T, Popkin B. Three squares or mostly snacks—what do teens really eat? A sociodemographic study of meal patterns. *J Adolesc Health.* 1998; 22:29–36.

Singh RB, Niaz MA, et al. Effect of hydrosoluble coenzyme Q10 on blood pressures and insulin resistance in hypertensive patients with coronary artery disease. *J Human Hypertens.* 1999;13:203–8.

Stoecker BJ. Chromium. In Shils M, Olson JA, Shike M, Ross AC, eds. *Nutrition in Health and Disease*. 9th ed. Baltimore: Williams & Wilkins, 1999 (277–82).

Trow LG, Lewis J, et al. Lack of effect of dietary chromium supplementation on glucose tolerance, plasma insulin, and lipoprotein levels in patients with type 2 diabetes. *Int J Vitam Nutr Res*. 2000;70:14–8.

Ziegler D. Thioctic acid for patients with symptomatic diabetic polyneuropathy: a critical review. *Treat Endocrinol*. 2004;3(3):173–89.

Ziegler D, Schatz H, Conrad F, Gries FA, Ulrich H, Reichel G. Effects of treatment with the antioxidant alpha-lipoic acid on cardiac autonomic neuropathy in NIDDM patients. A 4-month randomized controlled multicenter trial (DEKAN Study). *Diabetes Care*. 1997 Mar;20(3):369–73.

Chapter 7

Gillman MW, Rifas-Shiman SL, et al. Family dinner and diet quality among older children and adolescents. *Arch Fam Med*. 2000 Mar;9(3):235–40.

Lee A, Morley JE. Metformin decreases food consumption and induces weight loss in subjects with obesity with type 2 non-insulin-dependent diabetes. *Obesity Research*. 1998;6:47–53.

Pongchaidecha M, Srikusalanukul V, et al. Effect of metformin on plasma homocysteine, vitamin B_{12}, and folic acid: a cross-sectional study in patients with type 2 diabetes mellitus. *J Med Assoc Thai*. 2004 Jul;87(7):780–7.

Ranganath L, Norris F, et al. Delayed gastric emptying occurs following acarbose administration and is a further mechanism for its anti-hyperglycemic effect. *Diabetes Medicine*. 1998;15:120–4.

Chapter 9

Vogel RI, Fink RA, et al. The effect of topical application of folic acid on gingival health. *J Oral Med*. 1978;33: 20–2.

Chapter 10

Major CA, Henry MJ, et al. The effects of carbohydrate restriction in patients with diet-controlled gestational diabetes. *Obstet Gynecol*. 1998 Apr;91(4):600–4.

Metzger BE, Coustan DR (Eds.). Proceedings of the Fourth International Workshop-Conference on Gestational Diabetes Mellitus. *Diabetes Care*. 1998;21(Suppl 2): B161–7.

Patrick M, Catalano J, et al. Gestational diabetes and insulin resistance: role in short- and long-term implications for mother and fetus. *J Nutr*. 2003 May;133(5 Suppl 2): 1,674S–83S.

Chapter 11

Arauz-Pacheco C, Parrott MA, Raskin P. Treatment of diabetes in adult patients with hypertension. *Diabetes Care*. 2002 Jan;25(1):134–47.

Sowers JR. Recommendations for special populations: diabetes mellitus and the metabolic syndrome. *Am J Hypertens.* 2003;16:41S–5S.

Chapter 12

Nicklas TA, Baranowski T, et al. Eating patterns, dietary quality, and obesity. *J Am Coll Nutr.* 2001 Dec;20(6): 599–608.

Schwartz MW, Niswender KD. Adiposity signaling and biological defense against weight gain: absence of protection or central hormone resistance? *J Clin Endocrinol Metab.* 2004 Dec;89(12):5,889–97.

Chapter 13

Anderson AD, Jain PK, et al. Evaluation of a triple sugar test of colonic permeability in humans. *Acta Physiol Scand.* 2004 Oct;182(2):171–7.

Dansinger ML, Gleason JA, et al. Comparison of the Atkins, Ornish, Weight Watchers, and Zone diets for weight loss and heart disease risk reduction: a randomized trial. *JAMA.* 2005;293:43–53.

Harbis A, Perdreau S, et al. Glycemic and insulinemic meal responses modulate postprandial hepatic and intestinal lipoprotein accumulation in obese, insulin-resistant subjects. *Am J Clin Nutr.* 2004;80:896–902.

Kabir M, Oppert J-M, et al. Four-week low-glycemic-index breakfast with a modest amount of soluble fibers in type 2 diabetic men. *Metabolism.* 2002;51:819–26.

Lavin JH, et al. The effect of sucrose- and aspartame-sweetened drinks on energy intake, hunger, and food choice of female, moderately restrained eaters. *Int J Obes*. 1997;21:37–42.

Lean MEJ, Hankey CR. Aspartame and its effects on health. *BMJ*. 2004;329:755–6.

Lexchin J, et al. Pharmaceutical industry sponsorship and research outcome and quality: systematic review. *BMJ*. 2003;326(7400):1,167–70.

Ludwig DS, Jenkins DJ. Carbohydrates and the postprandial state: have our cake and eat it too? *Am J Clin Nutr*. 2004;80:797–8.

Shikany JM, Thomas SE, et al. Glycemic index and glycemic load of popular weight-loss diets. *Medscape General Medicine*. 2006;8(1):22.

Tordoff MG, Alleva AM. Oral stimulation with aspartame increases hunger. *Physiol Behav*. 1990;47:555–9.

Wylie-Rosett J, Segal-Isaacson CJ, Segal-Isaacson A. Carbohydrates and increases in obesity: does the type of carbohydrate make a difference? *Obes Res*. 2004 Nov;12(Suppl 2):124S–9S.

Index